EXPERIENCING THE ADVENTURE

RICHARD "GUS" GUSTAFSON

iUniverse, Inc.
Bloomington

Experiencing The Adventure

iUniverse books may be ordered through booksellers or by contacting:

iUniverse
1663 Liberty Drive
Bloomington, IN 47403
www.iuniverse.com
1-800-Authors (1-800-288-4677)

ISBN: 978-1-4502-8169-0 (pbk)
ISBN: 978-1-4502-8170-6 (ebk)

Printed in the United States of America

iUniverse rev. date: 12/22/2010

TABLE OF CONTENTS

Forward

This book was written from my day-to-day diary, along with my memory of twenty-four years of working with the wild animals. I am so thankful that I got in on the ground floor of working a roam free park, and for being the first American hired to work for Lion Country Safari. I was the third Chief Game Warden, and was able to go from park to park as Lion Country built new ones, training the men to become wardens and forming prides of lions, building hoof stock sections and more. I was also fortunate enough to go to Japan, and then on to Korea as a Zoo Advisor, and then back to the park in Japan.

Through the writing of this book, I discovered that there were at least three-hundred-six times that I walked through the heads and swamps to track down, tranquilize and return the lions and other animals to their huts. My good friend, Charles, was with me, backing me up most of the time, although sometimes, other men had to help me when Charles was not available. I always felt more comfortable with Charles watching my back as he did with me watching his. We often went through knee-deep water full of cottonmouths (water moccasins), a lot of vegetation and bushes so thick you could only see a few feet in front of you. I do not feel as though I can write this book without the mention of Bill York, who was an inspiration to me. All of our times working together for all those many years, we learned so much from each other, especially at a time when there wasn't anyone else we could turn to for information on anything to do with a roam-free park. As the first park to be roam-free, the animals acted the same as they did in the wild, just on a smaller scale. I hope that with all that we learned through all our trial and errors would be of some help to other wardens, and for just people in general, to make life better for the wild animals. I will never forget the good times, adventures, the learning and all the experience that we gained working with these wonderful animals. I am thankful that I was able to live my dream everyday for all those years. Above all, I thank God for having the uppermost hand in guiding me through it all.

Richard "Gus" Gustafson

Dedication

I dedicate this book to my wife, Nonie, for all the help and support she gave me writing my book. To my sons, Joe and Erik for all that they went through with me working long hours, missing being home with them for the holidays, birthdays and other special occasions, especially Christmas, which is an important holiday for children. We would have to open gifts in the early morning before I left for work, or late evening after I got off work. I thank them all for the sacrifices they made during their life so I could follow my dreams. I like to think that by them being with me that they enjoyed the ride as I did. I cannot think of anything I would rather have done than to work twenty-four years with the wild animals, especially with the lions. I also was very fortunate to meet and work with a lot of animal people who all hold a special place in my heart. I have a lot of great memories since I was part of the first roam-free park in the United States. The experiences with the animals and with the people were priceless to me. I like to think we made the animals' lives healthier for them and a lot more like being in the wild, instead of being in a cage or zoo. This book is also dedicated to our son, Bobby, who during the time was living with his mother.

Chapter 1

Start Up of the Park

Not long after leaving Ivan Tores Studios, where I trained animals for the movies, I saw an ad for Lion Country Park. They were just starting to build their first roam-free park in South Florida. They ran ads about all the wild African animals they were planning to have there. They were doing something new, and completely different for the animal world; the animals would roam free in their separate sections, and the people would drive through in their cars with the windows up. They could stay as long as they liked, watching and studying the animals from the safety of their vehicles.

The first park originated in England with the Chipperfield family. Jimmy Chipperfield and his brother owned a big circus in England, and for some reason, they decided to split up. Jimmy's brother kept the big top circus, while Jimmy took some of the money and some of the bigger animals. He then started letting some of the lions run loose on the grounds at the Lords of London in England, charging the people to ride through in their cars. They could watch the lions roam free, doing their natural thing as if in the wild. They had other African animals that also roamed free, and the idea was well received by the public in England.

The success of the roam-free park in England led to plans to open a park in the United States. Palm Beach

County, Florida, was chosen since the weather was somewhat similar to that in their natural habitat in Africa. While negotiations were in the works to purchase six-hundred-forty acres for the park, they started capturing the animals in Africa, and buying other animals from wild animal dealers, including the Hunt Brothers. Most of the animals came directly from Africa.

Before any of the animals were brought to Florida, a lot of construction work had to be completed. Contractors and many other employees had to be hired. Most importantly, the fence company had to build a double sixteen-foot-high fence to insure that the animals could not escape, making it safe for the surrounding area. A moat needed to surround the entire park area, with double fencing that had four gates at the entrance and four more gates at the exit.

The antelope section along with the seven lion sections, elephants, and rhinos, chimps, and giraffe areas all throughout the entire park were fenced and surrounded by moats. There were big islands used to separate different sections and to make the park look larger. This helped to block the view of where the people were going and where they had been. The visitor's vehicle route wound through the park like a maze.

The contractors and workers were building huts for all the animals inside the park, also different pens and huts for the pets' corner. Ponds with islands were constructed for the primates. A snake pit was being constructed. A large clinic-type facility was built and fully equipped for treating injured or sick animals.

Many of the pens were designed with glass fronts for the animals in the pets' corner, with a petting area, gift shop, restaurant and a conference room for the ranger meetings held to discuss information that might be of value to the care of all the animals.

A boat dock was constructed along with a lake for the public boat rides to observe the animals also in the petting area. The entrance road from the main road was called "the two mile stretch." Since it was not a good idea to take a pet through the lion section, dog kennels were built where people could leave their pets while riding through the park.

Construction of the main offices was to be done first as they needed a place to keep all records and management. There was also a rental car facility built for the people who did not want to drive their own cars through, especially those with convertibles.

There was a lot to be done before bringing any animals into the park. They had already been building on it for a while when I read about it in the paper, so I decided to go out to the park and see if I could get a job with them. I wanted to get in on the ground floor. I could tell them I had trained attack dogs and guard dogs in the army, and I had trained North American animals for a movie company.

So off I went to Lion Country to present myself as the good wild animal man that I knew I could be. It was at least twenty miles from my home in Lake Worth, Florida. When I arrived at the main entrance, there were a lot of earthmovers, big trucks and all kinds of machines to build the road. There was nothing but a straight line through the Florida sand, the palmettos and the pine trees with a couple of small swamps we called sloughs along the way. It would be two miles back into the woods to the temporary offices and the actual park entrance. I don't need to tell you that it seemed like the longest ride of my life.

At the entrance to the park, the construction crew was working on a set of two side by side gates that when they were done, would lead into an area with fencing sixteen feet high. This "safe zone" would be big enough to hold twelve to fourteen cars with another set of two gates at the other end. When the park was open, the gate people could control the flow of cars into the park without ever having both sets of gates open at the same time. This arrangement provided for the safety of both the visitors and the animals.

I asked a couple of people where I could find the person who was in charge of the animal park. They told me to drive through until I found someone who looked like he was in charge. I was driving a little Volkswagen that was great for driving in Florida sand, so away I went trying to find the man in charge.

The park was huge and it took me a while to find him, but I did finally find him beside one of the lion huts. Of course, I didn't know that it was a lion hut until I saw a lion looking out at me. I asked who was in charge, and one man spoke up, saying his name was Richard Chipperfield. The other man with him was an animal man from England who had come in the day before with two other animal men.

The men had brought in one rhino named Gus, one elephant named Donya, as well as one lion and one leopard. The lion had been injured on the boat ride from England, so they were checking him over.

I had already told them of my experience with animals. Mr. Chipperfield asked if I could go to the drug store and pick up some medication and other medical supplies. If I could do that, they said I would be the first American animal man to be hired. They had absolutely no idea where in the world to get the needed medication, so I told them I would be more than happy to do this for them. So off I went on my first job as the very first American animal man to be hired for Lion Country.

As I was on my way back out the two-mile stretch to civilization, I met another guy whose name I don't remember, but he was also looking for a job with animals. I told him I was just hired and was on my way to get medication for a lion. At that time, it really sounded strange to me, but he said his wife worked in a drug store and that he would go with me if I wanted. He was probably thinking that if he did this, maybe they would hire him, too.

We got the medical supplies from the drug store and headed back to the park. Richard Chipperfield and Norman Whitmarsh, the animal man from England, were in the temporary office at the front of the park just inside the main gate. They checked all the supplies that I brought back checking them off the list they had given me, saying, "Good job, mate! You two are now hired, so jump in the jeep with us. We're going to go in the pen with the lion and put some of this medication on his injury."

The lion was about a year and a half old, weighing about two hundred pounds. One look at the lion, and the guy that went to the drug store with me for the supplies, must have changed his mind about the job. I decided that is what happened because he said he had a meeting with someone and would be back in the morning. Well, the last we saw of him was the taillights of his car going down the two-mile stretch. That was his total experience of being an animal man.

We rode back to the pen and there was a 4 x 8 sheet of plywood beside the hut. Richard said we would use that plywood to get in the pen with the lion and push him in the corner. Then we would be able to put the medication on the cut as well as any other place that needed it.

There were no medical supplies at the park yet other than the ones I had picked up that morning. They also did not have a tranquilizer gun, or any medication to put him out, so needless to say, I'm thinking...what in the world am I doing here. I watched Richard and Norman go in the pen and they yelled to me, "Come on, and stay behind us and the plywood." They sure didn't have to worry about me, wherever they went, I was right behind them. I got between them and was holding on to the plywood for dear life, praying, "Dear Lord, what am I doing here in this pen with a mad lion and two men that at the moment seemed to be out of their minds!"

I wondered why I was doing what they told me to do, in a very strange way enjoying it while my heart was beating so rapidly I thought it would come out of my chest. We got the lion in the corner where Richard took over, getting the medication on the lion very fast. My eyes were glued to that lion, listening to Richard as to what to do; we backed out of the hut with the plywood between the lion, and us locking the door behind us. Richard turned to Norman and me, and said, "We might have to do this all over again in a couple of days if we have not hired a vet by then."

I was still in shock, not believing what we had just done, and halfway hoping that they did not get a vet. That way we could do it again in a few days. It was then that I knew I wanted to do this for the rest of my working life. I was ready to learn as much as I could about the animals and how to run the park, so that one day I could be in charge. Three years later, I did just that!

After that situation with the lion, I worked with Norman and the lion, and then I started working with Gordon with Donya, the elephant. For about two weeks, my job was to do whatever needed to be done, from checking the height of the fences, to how the construction of the lion huts was coming along. I also cleaned out the lion cages, elephant and rhino huts and yards. I learned all that I could, and paid close attention to all that was going on and why.

We started getting in some antelope, releasing them from their cages into the antelope section. Roger was in charge of the antelope. He watched over them, fed them and kept the grounds free of anything the construction crew left behind that might hurt the antelope. The Agriculture Department came out to check the area for any poisonous plants. Roger would stay with them and destroy any plants that were not healthy for the animals, which was very important for the safety of these and other animals.

When the construction of all the huts, fencing, canals and roads around and through the park were almost complete, we started to hire a few more people. There still were not a lot of animals, but a lot still had to be done before more animals could be brought into the park.

An island for the elephants and one for the rhinos was built with a four-foot metal fence in the middle of the moat. This would prevent a lion that got in the moat could not get on the island. In section six, there was an island for the chimps, without a metal fence in the moat since chimps cannot swim and the island was away from where the lions would be roaming free. To clean and feed the chimps, we would take the tractor across in five feet of water. That was a little tricky, so after a few months, we decided to get a jon boat, which was much easier to take the food and other things we needed to use onto Chimp Island.

As years went by, many changes were made to make it easier to run the park and for the safety of the public and the animals. Lion Country Safari was the first roam-free park, so there was no one to call for any information or knowledge or for any help on situations that would come up. As you must realize by now, we relied on a whole lot of trial and error and even more praying for the best to come out of it. I felt honored to be the first American to work in this first roam-free park with wild animals that were living in a habitat as natural as they were living in the wilds in Africa, only on a smaller scale.

Jane Goodall was there for a time watching and studying the chimps after we had gotten them adjusted to their new environment on Chimp Island. She remarked that the chimps acted the same as they did in Africa; the only difference was their territory was smaller. Randy Eaton came to Lion Country after studying the cheetah and lions in Africa. He came and studied the lions in my section for many months. He said the same thing, that what you see in the lion section is the same that you would see in Africa. Since then, he has written many books on animals.

Once we got all of the lions in all their sections, we learned that our collection of lions was the largest in captivity in the world. We had close to one hundred lions roaming free as they would in the wild, except that they enjoyed better health, and lived longer. Whatever they needed, they got, as did all the other animals in the park.

During the startup of the park, we were all going through a learning process. Most days, there was more work than could be done in a regular eight hour day so most days I would be up before dawn and home way after dark. I worked many fourteen-hour days, seven days a week, which didn't leave much time for family life.

I spent several weeks working with Gordon who worked with Donya, the elephant. One morning as we were in the jeep going to Donya's island, I told Gordon I thought I could work Donya alone and for him to stay outside and not let her see him. I would go in the barn by myself to give her water and take her shackles off. The shackles were put on at night when we fed and watered her in the barn to keep her safe in the barn overnight. Each morning we would let her out on the island to wander about as elephants would do in Africa. We would clean the barn and the outside of the island while Donya was outside.

Gordon was on the boat with Donya from England to America. The journey over was pretty rough, traveling through stormy seas; the boat pitched and rolled a lot. During the worst of the storm, Gordon took some blankets to the deck where she was, trying to comfort her with soft words and petting. He slept there all night, of course, out of her reach. He felt he had established a bond with her, being with her all that time on the boat ride to the states. Gordon proceeded to tell me that if I thought I could get in there with her and do all that needed to be done, "Just give it a try, mate, but keep in mind that we do not have an elephant hook." An elephant hook is something to control the elephant; it's like an upside down cane with a dull hook or point on it so you can touch her inside her leg or push with the dull point to control her, to let her know which way you want her to go.

When we got to the edge of the barn door, I went inside with no hook. We would normally fill a fifty-five gallon drum with water, and while she was getting a drink of water, we would put hay and vegetables outside for her to eat. Then we would go back in the barn, unshackle Donya, and take her to her food. We would start cleaning the barn and the outside area on the island, trying to spend as much time with her as we could.

Gordon forgot to tell me to watch out for Donya's trunk. If she started to tighten up the end of it, like making a fist, I should get out of the way, as she was going to sling it at me. If the trunk is up, she will come down on you with it, knock you to the ground, and then try to do a headstand on you to crush you. If her trunk was swinging between her legs, she would knock you away.

I don't need to tell you she had some powerful punches. While I was talking to her, she was drinking from the fifty-five gallon drum and I was feeling pretty good about how well we are getting along. I saw that Donya's trunk was swinging between her legs, but unaware of the danger, I proceeded to stand in front of her, patting her on

16

her trunk. The next thing I knew, I was flying through the air backwards about six feet off the ground, landing outside the barn in the dirt, rolling about another five feet. My pride was hurt much worse than my body. I looked up at Gordon, and he said, "Now don't let her do that to you, mate." I thought, okay, I'll show you who is boss, ole gal! I got up, ran back in the barn. Well, as soon as I hit her, she returned the same, hitting me with her trunk again and I was flying backwards as before, with my pride hurt once again. This time I don't even take the time to dust myself off before I run back in, and of course, she was standing there waiting for me, as I hadn't unshackled her yet. Now keep in mind that this is the third time I have tried this, so I hit her again on the trunk with my fist and away I go flying out the barn again. I looked up at Gordon and said, "You know, I think maybe I need more training on elephants, so what should I do?"

He looked at me and said, "Well, mate, I think it is best to leave her alone."

We both started laughing. That day, I let Gordon do most of the work and I watched him closely. By closing time, I had a lot more hurting than my pride; my whole body was sore, and the next morning I was so stiff, I could hardly move.

Through time, trial and error Donya and I got along okay as long as I understood her and she learned to respect me, too. There was one other time she tried as we were putting her in for the night. She was rocking back and forth the way all elephants do because of their weight. I went behind her to put on her shackles; first, she hit me with her tail and about knocked me out. I don't think she meant to do that though, but as I was tightening her shackles and watching her legs and feet as she moved back and forth, she was getting closer to the wall and all of a sudden, she leaned back against the wall and tried to crush me. I went under her belly and raised cane with her before going back and putting the shackles on her. That was the last time we went round and round.

In England, when they were moving her in a boxcar, Norman was putting the shackles on her front leg; she tried to do a headstand on him. As she was coming down on him, he turned sideways and her tusk stuck in the floor of the boxcar. She had him pinned, but her tusk kept her from crushing him. He told me about how she was twisting and turning, trying to get to him, but since her tusks were stuck on both sides of him, it was impossible for her to crush him with her head.

It took the other men quite some time to get her off Norman. He was really shaken up having her big head on him. He knew that if one or both of the tusks broke, she would most likely crush him. He went to the hospital for a few days to be checked out and get a much-needed rest. After we opened the park, Donya put three or four men in the hospital. Two different times, her trunk suddenly hit men who were standing very near her while she was drinking from the canal around the island. Since her trunk was full of water, it packed a powerful punch, knocking them both down and into the water on separate occasions. She did a headstand on them while they were in the water. By this time, she had broken both tusks and when she put pressure on them, they both slid away from her powerful head because the bottom of the canal was muddy and slippery.

18

Both of the men came out with only some broken ribs and bruises. They could have lost their lives, but they were lucky and recovered. I do not remember if those men stayed on the job or if that was their last day. By this time, we had about fifteen different elephants on the island. It was nice to see all these elephants doing the normal things they would do in the wild. Donya was good most of the time, but you still needed to keep a close eye on her when you were working with her, always remembering she was a wild animal.

Another experience of mine with good ole Donya was after the park had opened. I was on the outside cleaning up and Donya was roaming free on the island. It was very hot so I took my shirt off and was unloading feed for her from the back of the pickup truck. When I finished cleaning up, a couple of hours later, I went to get my shirt to put it back on, but it was not where I had left it. I looked and looked all over the place and could not find it anywhere. I had no idea what happened to it, so that night I went home shirtless, and needless to say, my wife was quite suspicious of me coming home with no shirt. A couple of days later as I was bringing feed onto the island for the elephants, I happened to see something lying on the ground. I walked over to it and guess what? It was the shirt that I had lost. I picked it up, saw that it had holes all through it, and elephant dung all over it. It looked to be about one hundred years old. In the pocket was my note pad and pen; the note pad was destroyed, you couldn't read anything that had been written in it. I tried the pen, and unbelievably, it worked and looked fine. It looked none the worse for wear considering where it had been! Donya had eaten it along with the notebook and shirt!

I should have written the manufacturer of the pen to tell them it was like the TIMEX watch; it took a licking and kept on writing, but other things got in the way and I forgot to do it. I did keep the pen for quite some time and used it every day. It made a good conversation piece.

Another experience with our famous Donya involved a new man with no animal experience. The roam-free park still being a new concept, the only men with experience were the ones already working in the park. Everyone we hired had no experience with such a park. Since I was by then the chief game warden, the new man was to work alongside Smitty on the elephant island. Smitty was not the regular man who worked there; Smitty normally worked a pride of lions, but we were shorthanded that day so I put him on the elephant island. He had worked with Gordon there before. Most of the rangers would have the opportunity to work with all of the animals at some time or another, so that if someone didn't come to work for whatever reason, others could be placed wherever needed. We got in my jeep and drove over to the elephant island. Smitty had Donya shackled as he felt he didn't work her much and felt better with her on the chains for the day he was taking care of her. The park visitors could still see her from their cars. I told Smitty to show the new man what to do for the day, as he would be with him. Smitty agreed, but of course, he wanted to show off in front of the new man, so he walked over to Donya and started to do different things with her. Well as you can guess, Donya decided to do a headstand on Smitty! He was about six-foot-three and maybe one hundred fifty pounds soaking wet. When she knocked him down and went to do her headstand on him, he was twisting, moving, and rolling all over in the dirt.

By the time I got to Smitty to help him, he was out of her range of reach since he still had her shackled. I helped him up while he kept saying, "I'm okay," as he dusted himself off. The new man was just standing there staring wide-eyed as if in a stupor. He looked like he was thinking what in the world am I doing here. He sure didn't seem to want to be there just then.

We stood around talking about what had just happened and how funny Smitty looked twisting and rolling in the dirt with Donya trying to get to him. At the time, it sure wasn't funny but after it was all over with and we knew that Smitty was okay, we could talk about it and laugh.

I looked over at Donya, and lo and behold, there was a wallet about two feet from her. I asked Smitty, "Hey man, is that your wallet?" He looked at it for a few minutes before he said, "Yup, it sure is." He then looked at the new man and said, "Hey, how about you going over there and getting my wallet."

The new man looked at me, then at Smitty. I can't write down what he said to Smitty, but trust me, it was not a nice thing. In no uncertain terms he said, "It's not my wallet, and you can go get it yourself."

He surely wasn't going to get the wallet. I turned and went to my jeep as I told them to work it out between them. I knew in my own mind that the new man sure wasn't going after the wallet. I told Smitty I would be back at closing time to help him put Donya up for the night. As I was driving back to the office, I was laughing all the way and to this day, it still brings a smile to my face when I think of that time and situation.

DONYA AND GARY, ONE OF MY BEST FRIENDS IN LIFE FOR 35 YEARS

MY SON, ERIK, WITH LION CUB

MY SON, JOE, WITH LION CUB

Chapter 2

Gus the Rhino and the Lions

Back to the startup of the park, we were starting to get some antelope in every two days or so. If we weren't unloading antelope, Richard wanted us working on building stands, like deer stands about twelve feet off the ground on all of the islands. We also called the islands 'heads.' I teamed up with Dan, who was about six-foot-four and quite a hefty man, and Mr. Pierce, who was an older man near retirement age. We needed to build these stands so that if a lion got over on one of the heads, they would help us to locate them.

The vegetation was so thick that it was really hard to see anything beyond about fifteen feet in places. It was so thick you couldn't drive a jeep through it. In places it was knee deep in water, with lots of snakes. A canal was dug around these islands to make it harder for the lions to get over onto the heads. We built about twenty of them, by bringing the wood across the canal. We would get into the water, sometimes going underwater, but not because we wanted to. We had to push the plywood and 2 x 4's across the canal to another man on the other side. Then we took it to the tree where we planned to build the stand. All the heads we developed had previously been untouched by humans. They were built in swamps and palmetto lowlands, which were home to a lot of snakes, with which none of us cared to, come in contact.

We only had hand tools, no power tools. One day we were going out to the head to build another stand when Dan suggested that we should build a raft to float all the wood and tools across the canal. Mr. Pierce and I thought that was a great idea. We worked on building this raft for a few days, finding different types of wood from the construction crew. When we were finished building it, we proceeded to push it into the water. As soon as the whole raft was in the water, it sank without anything on it! Needless to say, Huck Finn would not have been proud of us. We reverted back to pushing the plywood and 2 x 4's across to another person on the other side.

We worked part of the time on the stands; we were also having more animals arrive such as antelope and chimps. The lions started coming in, mostly from Africa, on flatbed semi's, from five to twenty at a time. As they came in, we would put them in different huts, starting to form lion prides. Some of the lions would not mix well with the others and fights would break out. Most of them would calm down after awhile and adjust to their new surroundings; some would not, so we would have to move the ones that didn't get along to another hut and section. We would keep moving them around until they fit in with a pride.

We would push their crate tight up to the hut door. The huts had two hooks on each side. We could wrap a chain around the crate and hook the chain to both hooks on the hut. This prevented the crate from sliding back away from the hut, when the lion went from the crate to the hut once the crate and hut door was open. If the chains were not there, it would twist away letting the lion free to come outside with us. Now that was not a good feeling, knowing the lion was right there with you. For this reason, we would take all the necessary precautions. Sometimes, we would use water on them if they didn't want to leave the crate. We had a gas engine pump on a trailer being pulled by a tractor, and we would pull this to each hut. We would throw a hose in the canal once we started this engine, and we had all the water pressure we needed.

We had a cage with a door built around the tractor driver to protect him. Every day someone would drive to each lion hut to clean and disinfect it. Before the man would get out of the tractor to clean out the huts, he would radio the man in that section watching the lions and let him know he was outside of the tractor. Hopefully, the man watching the lions would let him know if a lion started running toward the hut. This warning allowed him time to jump back in the tractor. This happened several times through the years, but no one was ever hurt by the lions.

Everyone looked out for each other knowing that no one before us had worked in this environment where the lions and other animals roamed free in a park. Not always knowing exactly what would happen, we had to try many different things. As the lion prides were formed, someone was with the lions all day, others would be unloading the new lions and working on the heads, building stands and cutting trees. Richard didn't want the same man to be with the lions everyday; he wanted everyone to work on different things to gain the most experience.

Richard and I were having one of our many talks one day when I told him I would like to run a pride of lions in section five. His instant response was to say, "It's yours, mate. When all the lions have arrived and we start letting them all out you will have section five." I thanked him and went on doing different things each day for a few more weeks.

It was getting close to the opening of the park, all the fencing was done, almost everything was finished except for a few stands, as we were floating the wood across for the last stand, Mr. Pierce lost his false teeth. We looked and looked the rest of the day but could not find them.

Another time, we were building a stand and a new man was with us. We always brought our lunches and drinks as we were far away from everyone else. As we sat down and started to eat our lunches, Dan stood up suddenly, all six foot four of him, and stood in front of the new man. With one hand, Dan lifted him up off the ground looking him straight in the eyes, and proceeded to ask him if he drank the two bottles of water that he had in his lunch box. The man stuttered and said, "Yes-ss-ss, I was still thirsty after I drank my own water, so I drank yours."

Dan said, in no uncertain terms, "Little man, don't you ever touch my lunch box again if you know what is good for you." After that, he never touched Dan's lunch box and for that matter, I don't think he ever touched anyone's but his own.

Another day, it was raining and had been for at least three days, with a lot of lightning and thunder. The park had all metal fencing around it, and sixteen foot fencing around each section with a lot of metal gates, so this could be very dangerous. A whole crew of us were working in every section picking up trash that the construction crew had left laying around. We always looked for anything that would harm any of the animals, keeping in mind all the lions were still in their huts. It was lightning really bad, so we started talking and decided we really didn't want to work in these conditions. Tex called Richard on the radio and told him we would like to stop working for the day, but Richard said to stay right there since he would be right out. We all stayed put until he got there. He pulled up in his jeep and got out. The rain was still coming down really hard, still lightening a lot, too.

Richard said, "If working with animals was easy, everyone would be doing it. If you men want to go home because of the rain, lightning, and thunder, then go home. But make sure all of you are back here at five am in the morning and you can all expect to be here way after dark, too, rain or shine. We are fighting a deadline here for the opening of the park, and everyone needs to put all they have into this project from here on out. If you can't do this, then there is no need for you to come back."

So, needless to say, we were all there before five in the morning and so was Richard. He worked side by side with us all day long and into the evening, and still it was raining but not as bad as the day before. We had a lot more respect for Richard after that day. We no longer thought of him as a rich man driving fancy cars with a family doing the same; we thought more of him, than just being our boss, he also was a fellow worker and friend. Not long after the opening of the park Richard was in Africa catching animals for the park. While he was there, he died in a car accident, which was a big loss for the park and for all of us who had become his friends.

One time before the park opened, the man taking care of section six, which was the Rhino section, went to get some feed for the Rhino and left the gate open. The Rhino, Gus, decided to take a stroll. Tex saw him from his jeep so he got on the radio and called for help to get Gus back on the island. All of the men with jeeps went to help.

We had started to get behind and beside him, when Gus decided to run for the side of Tex's jeep and charge it. He hit the side of the jeep pushing it sideways, almost tipping it over. They were in a spot in the section where it was swampy, and Tex started to go faster. Gus was right behind him, charging him again when Tex's jeep started to slide. Gus was catching up to him, and the next thing I saw, Tex was jumping out of his jeep running for mine. I stopped my jeep; Tex opened the door and jumped in. Tex looked at me, saying, "That darn jeep wasn't going fast enough for me."

We finally got Gus back to the island and closed the gate. Then we all had a big laugh about Tex running and Gus right on his behind. Tex ran really fast for being ankle deep in mud. As we were laughing about it, Tex said, "You know, I didn't run as fast as I could. I only ran as fast as I had to." Later when we got more rhinos in, Gus didn't need to go any farther than his own section for company.

It wasn't long before we received fourteen jeeps, Zebra striped jeeps, with bars on the windows. There were four tractors available to pull out vehicles that would overheat or break down. Barry, the butcher, would cut up the meat from cows and horses that the ranchers would bring in with serious injuries. Barry would cut up about ten pounds of meat for each lion every day and put it in tubs. Each man in charge of each section would go to the butcher's shack, pick up their meat and bring it back to the huts to feed the lions.

Before feeding the meat to the lions, we would sprinkle mineral powder and vitamin powder on it. We had one hundred and forty lions, the largest collection of lions in captivity in the world. Before opening, we would let one pride at a time out of the huts to roam free. We used a four-foot high hog wire fencing along with a box of rags to tie onto to it so the lions could see the fencing.

We formed a V from the runabout about one hundred and fifty feet long out into the section, putting two jeeps in the runabout and leaving the gate open. We had most of the jeeps in a line from the far end of the wide opening of the V, and some jeeps were on the far side of the hog wire. When we opened the hut door to the runabout, with the jeeps working together, we started pushing, somewhat like herding the lions like cattle. We worked very slowly the first couple of times, but after awhile the lions figured out where we wanted them to go, making it much easier on us. The jeeps at the end of the V would stay where they were. The lions just looked around, and then lay down inside the V, but sometimes some would break loose and go back to the runabout and hut. We would slowly get them back in the V, and if they settled down, all the jeeps would stop pushing them.

We did this for about half an hour and then the jeeps in the line at the wide end would start slowly moving to the runabout. Most of the time, the lions would go in. If they got excited and tried to jump the four-foot hog wire fence, the outside jeep would go to the wire. Most of the time, the lions would go in the runabout. We did this every day with different prides and left them in the V longer each day.

Some would break out of the V into the section. Then most all of the jeeps would go to the lion, let him calm down and then slowly push him back to the V. After three weeks of doing this to all of the prides, we had them pretty well use to what we wanted them to do. And most days, doing this would go without too much trouble. They seemed to know that we wanted them by the road under the shade trees. They would be in these places so the people driving through would be able to have a good view of them.

We then took down the V, they would go out into the section, and the man in charge of the section would sit and watch them. We were almost all set for the opening of the park, all the lion sections had one or two prides in them. All of them were going out of the huts really well and going back in at night.

Chimp Island was ready, the antelope section had most of the antelopes, zebras, birds, and ostrich were in there along with giraffe. Pets' corner was also ready with the small animals along with the snake pit; all of these were ready for opening.

As I mentioned before, Richard and his father, Jimmy, wanted all the men to know how to work all of the animals for emergencies, to fill in for ones calling in sick, or for ones on vacation. I had worked with Norman on Chimp Island, and was told to feed and clean Chimp Island before I started working my lions. I got the tractor, along with the tools, and some feed, then off I went to Chimp Island to do my job. I went into the canal to get to the island, and there were about fifteen chimps to greet me as I came onto their island with some food. I had done this a few times before so I knew what to expect. After feeding them, I got the rake, shovel, pitchfork and garbage can from the tractor. As I was cleaning up the island, and I was talking to the chimps, I noticed that I had left the door of the tractor open.

One of the chimps was in the tractor, where he had gotten the rake. He jumped out of the tractor with the rake in hand, swinging it all around and coming toward me. I started thinking, I'm in trouble now, this can't be a good thing. The chimp came over to me, and in his own way, he started to help me clean up, making more of a mess than helping. Then a couple of chimps came over trying to take the rake from him, and it wasn't long before all of them were fighting, kicking, biting and screaming like a regular bar room brawl. The chimp dropped the rake and they kept fighting.

I was done with feeding and cleaning up so I quickly put all the tools in the tractor. When I went back for the garbage can, they stopped fighting and were looking for the rake. Luckily, I had about six bananas in my shirt, so I started talking to them, giving them the bananas. I finally got to the tractor, closed the cage door, started the tractor, and said, "See you later, guys." Before leaving, I made sure the chimps were okay and not fighting any longer. Next time I went on the island, I made sure that I closed the tractor door.

We were told someone from Africa was coming in and was to be chief game warden; his duties were to be in charge of all of us other rangers, all the outside animals along with pet's corner. The day he came in, most of us stood outside of the office, we stood in formation like in the service. He drove up in a zebra striped car with our public relations man. He got out of the car, and the manager introduced him to us. He was wearing a safari hat with a leopard skin band around it, brown shorts and shirt with rifle pads on the shoulders and arms, a lion's claw necklace on the outside of his shirt, elephant hair bracelet on his wrist, and carrying an elephant gun on his shoulder. He was very impressive to us at the time, but we didn't really know what to think of him. We had heard three different stories of what type of job he did before coming to Lion Country.

When we had most of the lions in, I had fifteen of the lions in to my section, which was section five. I was told they were my lions; they would be my second family. I was to study them, get to know them and name each of them so I would know them by their names. I was working lions most of the time now, so I started to name each of my lions. The first one I named became "David," a very strong, proud and courageous male. He reminded me of David and Goliath. He had a beautiful nice long mane and right away became king of the pride.

Next came "Abe," not a large lion but he did have a large black mane with a thick chest and a very slim belly. Abe seemed to be the wisest of the pride of lions and the oldest of the lions in my section, so therefore he reminded me of Abe Lincoln.

"Cesar" was the largest male in the park, weighing between four hundred and four hundred and fifty pounds, very proud looking, also the youngest male in my section. He was just starting to grow a mane, and he showed great prospects of being a great male lion.

Now comes "Whitey" whose mane was of a very light color and his body was also very light. Whitey was a fitting name for him. Then there was "Buck Shot" whose coat was missing hair in spots from him rubbing on his cages and crates while he was being shipped over here from Africa. It looked as if someone shot him with buckshot.

Now for the females, the first one named was "Fannie." She had very broad hindquarters and was a large female so, therefore, Fannie seemed to be a good name for her. "Smokey" had a light coat with the ends of the hairs being black making it look like a black glaze over her whole coat, making it look Smokey. Next was "Peggy" for no real reason, except she just looked like a Peggy. She was a very quiet, friendly lion, getting along with everyone.

"Elsa" was next, and I named her that from the original Elsa of the Born Free Lions. She was a large female with a great disposition and with just her presence, she made you think of a proud beautiful queen. I would have to say she was the queen of the pride.

"Sleepy" had sleepy looking eyes so that seemed a proper name for her. Then there was "Red" and, of course, her name came from her coat being reddish in color. Now in a burst of glory came "Flare Up" who would get into a fight at the drop of a hat. Or should I say, the drop of a piece of meat. She would fight with male or female, it didn't matter. She just wanted to start a riot no matter where she went. She did that many times, she always seemed a need to make her presence known right from the get go.

"Step and a Half" seemed to have a very different walk than the other lions; you could always make her out from far away just by the way she walked. Last, but not least, was "Miss Crook" because her tail was broken, and she had a crook at the end of it, but still carried herself with pride and style.

All of these lions had their own personalities and I got very close to them, calling them my babies, everyone working with these lions having their own prides also did the same, getting close to them was easy, after all we were with them for eight to ten hours a day, and sometimes more. In my experience with lions, I have seen many a big, burly man like myself cry from the loss of one of their lions for one reason or another.

WHITEY RELAXING IN THE SHADE

MY MOTHER·IN·LAW, MADDIE, IN VISITORS CENTER

DAVID, OUR KING OF LIONS

**THE LEADER OF A PRIDE OF LIONS JOINED
BY TWO FEMALES**

Chapter 3

Lions

A few weeks later on August 29, 1967, we opened the park and everything went very smoothly that very first day. It was wall-to-wall people from the opening, until five p.m. at closing time. There was traffic backed up for miles all day long. Traffic was backed up on the main highway for two to three miles in both directions, to and from the park. We had to turn people away and could not let them enter the park after five o'clock.

One day in my section "Pacer," one of my female lions, was lying by a tree that Tex had cut down. The stump of the tree was about six feet high, and with a tractor, Tex took the cut section of a pine tree, had part of the tree on the ground, and then put the other part up on the stump. I worked with "Pacer" for weeks. I got the meat cutter to cut about ten pieces of meat, each about 4x2x2 inches, when he cut up the rest of the meat for the pride. When all the lions were away from the tree, I would drive up to the tree and put the pieces of meat on the log, starting at ground level in different spots all the way to the top. I would then call "Pacer," and after a while she would watch me put the meat up on the log. When I would get back into my jeep and drive away, she would start at the bottom of the log taking all of the meat. Then she would walk up to the top of the log, lie down and watch the cars go by. Most of the cars would stop to take pictures of her laying on top of her log, she became a star for laying up there having her picture taken so many times.

Buckshot and Whitey became good buddies, most of the time wherever one was, you would see the other; they did not stray far away from each other. One day, Buckshot was lying on the side of the road with Whitey on the other side. For some reason, most of the male lions in the park started to roar. Buckshot got up and started walking across the road to where Whitey was laying, about half way across, Buckshot started huffing up and blowing out, all of a sudden he roared, he jumped and turned around and looked real quick, thinking someone was there behind him and roared. He continued across the road to where Whitey was and laid down beside him. Then he proceeded to roar, not very well, but with a lot more practice he would get better. As time went on, he learned how to roar really well and Whitey then was joining in with him. When either Whitey or Buckshot would get into fights the other of the two would always go to help. They both were getting bigger and stronger, and decided to pick fights with David, the king of the pride. David was the biggest and strongest of all the male lions. Buckshot and Whitey wanted to become king so they kept picking fights with David, trying to overpower him. David always seemed to come out on top.

We would not let the lions fight and always stopped them with the jeeps. Sometimes it would take a while before we could get it stopped and back to normal.

One day Buckshot and Whitey challenged David again, and a real serious fight broke out. They had David down; they were all over him, biting and clawing him, pulling him in different directions. I started up my jeep and went over to them, breaking up the fight any way I could. I would put my jeep right up to them getting between them, trying to make them get their minds on something else besides fighting. Buckshot stopped fighting and ran away, while David and Whitey rolled against my jeep as they were still fighting. Whitey was beside my front fender and bumper when he decided to have himself a bite of my fender. His teeth went through the metal of the fender leaving a nice sized hole. David was busy with the bumper trying to tear it off the front of the jeep. They both were pretty angry so I kept revving up my engine and moving the jeep back and forth yelling at the top of my lungs. Finally, they decided that the zebra jeep and my yelling was just too much for them, so Whitey and David retreated to their resting places. David returned to the rest of the pride, for the rest of the day the three of them would just lay around.

The next day at feeding time, I noticed David wasn't eating; I made a note of this on my daily report sheet, a sheet that the chief game warden, Carlos, would pick up each day from each of us rangers. He would look over them the next day if there wasn't an emergency. Lions in the wild would sometimes not eat for five or six days. Then they would stuff themselves the next time they ate. So at Lion Country, we would not feed them for one day a week as this was something of their nature. So for a couple of days, I wasn't too concerned about David not eating a lot. He was still mating with the females and eating a little meat, once while he was eating, he threw his head back and looked like he was grinning at me.

Then it clicked, that while David, Buckshot and Whitey were fighting, I had broke them up with my jeep. David had taken a few bites of my bumper. I got to thinking, maybe he broke some of his teeth, so I let the

Vet know what I thought happened. The next day, he called the park and said a friend of his is a dentist and he would be glad to come out to the park and take a look at David. He said he would do whatever he could, even though he was a human dentist. The following day they came out, we tranquilized David, and the dentist didn't know what to think when he opened his mouth. David had two broken teeth, broken down below the gums. The vet and the dentist pulled them out and stitched his gums, and gave him medication.

When we left the hut where we had left David, the dentist was soaking wet with sweat, but he had a big smile on his face. "I never thought I would be working on a mouth so big, with teeth so long," the dentist exclaimed. We told him he sounded like "Little Red Riding Hood" with "The Big Bad Wolf."

He said, "If someone had told me I would pull teeth from a lion's mouth after I graduated from dental school, I would have thought they had lost their mind."

We felt good about the situation; it would be an experience he would never forget, along with us not forgetting it either. David seemed to eat better now. I would go to the butcher when I could to get fresh liver he would save it for me. He knew I was trying to build David back up again, so when he would get some in, he would call me on the radio and let me know. I would then take it to David, who most of the time would eat the whole liver. There still seemed to be something wrong with David. He was having runny eyes, losing a lot of weight and losing his hair, too. He still seemed strong and wanted to be with the pride, so I talked to Carlos, the chief game warden about David.

I said, "Maybe we should let him out of the enclosure where we have kept him since his bout with the broken teeth, and put him back with the pride. I think he will start getting healthier again."

All the medication we gave him didn't seem to be doing any good, so we needed to take another course of action. The next day we put him back in the section with his pride and let them out in their section. He stepped out of his hut with his head held high, so happy to be able to return with his pride. Dot, Fanny and Flare-Up ran up to meet him, rubbing noses and brushing up against him, letting him know they were glad to see him again. The males were not so happy, especially Buckshot and Whitey, who kept a very close watch on David.

I continued to cut up the meat for David and sprinkle minerals and vitamin powder on it. I was still giving him all the medication and antibiotics, for David was not in the healthy condition he should be in. While David was in the hut, his female companion Fanny presented him with four lion cubs. David stayed most of the time with Fanny after his release, but when he would go off by himself, the other lions seemed to pick on Fanny. They seemed to know that David preferred her over the other lions. Even though he did prefer her, he still would mate with the other females. While mating with the other females on the outside of his hut, he would guard them in fear of the other males getting them.

I then decided to put David in his hut, with his female companion at the time, "Dot." While staying in the hut, he ate well. I found that with David's departure from the pride, it left him very unsure of himself with any mate he would choose. So I decided whenever he was in season with a mate I would put him in the hut with her. It was very important that he still be on a special diet.

Once again the absence of David from his pride for three or four days at a time, gave the other males a bit more courage. At that time, they were choosing their mates with no fear of David being around. One day, as I was releasing the lions from their huts, they all seemed to be under a great deal of tension, snarling, and clawing at one another.

Little did I know, I had a very trying day ahead of me. They seemed to continue this way for the most of the morning. Then in the early afternoon, I noticed Buckshot creeping towards David. Then a few minutes later, Whitey had joined in. Before I could come to David's defense, they already had him down.

I drove up to them in my jeep, pushing Buckshot and Whitey away from him. This was very important; as once they got him down, they would go in for the kill. I could see David was in great pain and that his back leg was broken. I called Carlos to come and dart him with a tranquilizer. After doing this we waited for him to go down, keeping the other lions at bay, and then we lifted him into the jeep.

We returned David to his hut. The veterinarian came immediately and examined David, knowing that his left hind leg was broken. We knew we had to apply a cast to his leg. As far as we knew, this was another first, setting a lion's broken leg.

I went to the machine shop to tell them that I would need a pipe about an inch or more around and bent in a circle with about two and a half feet inside measurement, with two pieces of pipe going down each side of the circle,

42

cut to the size I gave them for the length of David's leg. They quit what they were doing and found all of the metal to build the brace. As soon as it was completed, I took it back to where David, Carlos and the vet were waiting. We weren't sure if this was going to work or not, but we proceeded to put his leg through the circle of the pipe, bringing it up to the top of his thigh and under his belly. We wrapped gauze around the circle and pipe where his leg met his stomach so it wouldn't irritate the skin and rub all his hair off. We wrapped tape around the straight pipe to rest his leg on.

As the vet set his leg, I pulled on it to help the vet. When he said it was good, we put tape around where his ankle would be, and then when the leg was where the vet wanted it, I wrapped tape around the leg and through the pipe, wrapping it back and forth between both pipes and around the leg until we felt it was strong enough to hold David's leg. When he would come out of the tranquilizer and try to get up on it, it needed to stay in place to support the broken leg.

The cast was made long enough so that when he stood up, his foot would not touch the floor. He could drag it on the floor and it would only be the pipes that would touch. We had given him a tranquilizer twice while we were working on his leg because he started to come out from under it before we were finished with him. We really needed to hurry and clean up all the stuff and get ourselves out of the way before he decided to wake up, which wasn't too far off.

So with this task over with, we got out of David's hut. The vet and Carlos left, but I stayed to watch David's reaction when he came to. As David was coming out of the tranquilizer, he looked around as if thinking, "Back here again." I started feeding him special meat, and all my spare time was spent on David. By this time, I was beginning to feel as though he was a very special part of my life. At night when I would arrive home, I would wonder if David was all right, and each morning with my return to work, I would first go to David's hut to check on him.

I believe he knew what time I should be there, as he seemed to be watching for me. David grew to depend on me very much, although I couldn't bring myself to completely trust him. I must admit, I wanted to pet his head and tell him it would all work out for him. He seemed to know this without my showing him, for David was a great fighter and would not give up easily.

David seemed to be coming along pretty good; the vet checked him quite often to see that everything was going well. One morning as I went to David's hut to feed and check him, I noticed the cast was off his leg. The vet was notified and after checking David, he decided to leave the cast off. He continued to do well, although the healing process would take quite some time. David was kept in his hut for about four months.

For a while, David didn't seem to do well at all. He lost a lot of weight, his hair was falling out and his eyes were watering. He also was dehydrated. I did everything I could for him, but nothing seemed to work. The vet thought he was too run down and too weak to tranquilize, so we had to go another route. We discussed it and it was decided to put him in a squeeze cage, taking him back to his hut, so we started on the medication right away.

After a few weeks I noticed that David was starting to put on weight and his hair started coming back in, David was on his way to becoming his own self again, although he still had a ways to go, there was a big improvement in him. Then one day, Mary Chipperfield and her husband came through the park, checking out how everything was going. I happened to be back at the hut with David, cleaning it out and cleaning up around it. That day I had another Ranger watching the lions, so I could be free to be near David.

The Chipperfields got out of their car and walked over to where I was cleaning. They asked me what in the world was wrong with that lion. I started telling them all that David had been through, with his broken teeth and broken leg. I also went on to tell them he was now on the road to recovery. Her response was, "That lion should be put down," she said, "I am going to the office right now and tell the manager to put the lion down."

Now keep in mind, this is my lion, I have been taking care of him for a long time. He has been through a lot in the last six months, and now he is finally looking better and getting stronger. Now, you come marching in here telling me you want to put him down?

Well, owner or not, I didn't really care. I needed to express my feelings about the situation, so needless to say, I blew up, saying, "You people think you're God, and care nothing about these animals. I have been with this lion for a few years now and he has a special place in my heart. I have been through so much with him, knowing he is getting much better, and now you want to kill him. When you leave here you will go to your fancy houses with your fancy cars and friends in England, not thinking twice about these animals."

She blew up like an ole bull frog, asked me my name, and then she said, "I am going to the office and talk to the manager to have you fired."

I told her, "Do what you have to do." I believe I was the first person to ever stand up to her and tell her what they thought. Believe me when I say she sure didn't like it. As they got into their car to drive off to the office, I said, "Oh, Boy, you've done it this time," but in my mind I knew I would not apologize for what I had said. I truly believed in every word, and the look on their faces was worth it.

About fifteen minutes later, I got a call on my radio from the manager telling me to come to the office, "NOW." I was thinking I had really done it this time, so I told Terry, the one watching my lions, that I might be taking the long ride down the two-mile stretch, because of my defense of David, but knowing all the while that I would not back down.

As I entered the office there sat the manager behind the desk. Mary and her husband were sitting in chairs looking smug and proper. There was a chair left for me to sit in. Now keep in mind, I had on dirty old blue jeans and a dirty shirt, with lion urine and feces all over it, mixed with some blood from the meat I was feeding the lions. So as you can picture, I was not a pretty site or smell.

The manager said he knew the whole situation about all that David went through, and knew that he was now back on the road to recovery. He asked Mary and her husband to give David two weeks and if, in those two weeks he wasn't any better, then we would have to put him down. He told them they needed to realize that I had been caring for David every day for a long time. Sometimes I would work ten or twelve hour days. They got up out of their chairs and said, "Okay, we will agree to that, but in the future young man, you need to watch your manners." And, out the door they went.

I thanked the manager for sticking up for David and me. When I started to leave, he said, "Have a seat, mate," as he reached in his desk and brought out some whiskey. He poured us each a drink, and said that no one had ever talked to Mary and her husband like that before. He also told me that he didn't know if he would be able to get me out of it next time. He mentioned that he felt like talking to her like that at times when they were in England, but never dared to, so he said, "Mate, go home and enjoy your evening and be back here in the morning."

I was walking on cloud nine. David got better day by day, almost all of his hair had grown back in, and soon he had no more runny eyes. He put back on almost all of his weight, looking and acting like his old self again. I was beginning to think I could put him out with his pride once again.

When it was decided that David's leg was strong enough, we again let him out of his hut, although things didn't go as well as I expected. After this long departure and all the other ones, David just didn't seem to get along with this pride any longer. They continued to fight with him every day. After a long conference with the general manager at Lion Country, we decided the best thing for David would be to move him to a section of younger lions. This was a very hard decision for me to make, since David was so much a part of my life now. To move him from my section was the thing I dreaded most to do, but for David's sake, I knew it not only had to be done, but it was the only thing I could do.

I moved David from my section a few days later. The section he was moved into had all young male and female lions. You see, the younger males didn't seem to mind the older intruder, and so David was once again "King." Soon after David's departure from my section, he became ill again. He was still not built back up the way he should have been. I believe he was just getting old and his time was getting near. David died from this illness, and along with him went a small piece of my heart. Yes, I was one of those big burley men that cried from the loss of my lion.

In memory of David, he left a great many cubs, females and many male cubs, who will continue to carry on his pride and his courage. A lion like him cannot be forgotten.

It was time now for my vacation; I really hated leaving these lions as I had been working with them for quite some time. No matter how long a vacation, I didn't want to be away from them for any length of time. I was with these lions constantly and knew these lions like you would know your own children. I could tell by their actions and just by looking at each one of them if they were sick or not. I even called out to the park a couple of times to see if they were all right, although I did enjoy myself with my family, I still worried about my lions. I felt as though I could call them mine, since I had been the only one with them from the start of the park. I finally convinced myself that I could at least take a ride through the park, so my family and I took a nice ride through. When I reached my section, I called to Abe and Buckshot and was surprised to see that they recognized me in my own car, for they had only seen or heard my voice from my zebra striped jeep. They lifted up their heads and started walking toward my car. As they reached the car, they put their faces against my window and rubbed their nose against it as if to say "Welcome back, ole buddy."

After coming back from my vacation, I noticed that Pacer wasn't interested anymore in that piece of juicy meat at the end of her log. It was getting close to the time for her to give birth, and she couldn't seem to be still or even lay down to rest. The gestation period for lions was from ninety-six to a hundred and five days, so I knew her time was getting near. That night before leaving for home, I went to the hut and tied pieces of plywood to the bars, so she would be more comfortable and feel secure. I also got a couple of bales of hay, plenty of water and meat so that she would have a very comfortable place to give birth.

I can tell you I didn't do it any too soon as Pacer gave birth two days later to three beautiful white cubs. These were the first of their kind to be born in captivity, so she became a movie star with her new cubs.

There was a big write-up in the Palm Beach Post Times. It was on the news also, so Lion Country got a lot of advertisement for the park. The cubs were really white at birth, but as the days went on, they got a little darker; they were not true albinos as true albinos have blue eyes. While taking care of Pacer, everyone was to stay away from her hut, except the chief game warden and me. Pacer was a wonderful mother to her cubs, and she was very protective of them. When I would go to them every morning to feed her, she would put them directly behind her so that I couldn't see them.

When the cubs were three weeks old, one came down with a virus and died. The other two seemed to be doing fine, but they were taken away from Pacer after the death of the first cub, so they could be given vitamins and medication so they would not become ill with the same disease. The two white cubs were taken to the nursery outside of the park where they were well taken care of by the keepers in pet's corner. They were fed every two to four hours with a baby bottle.

The two cubs did not stay as white as when they were first born. After Pacer was released from her hut, she didn't seem to care about the meat at the top of her log, I continued to put the meat up there for her for a few weeks, and I thought that maybe she was grieving for her cubs. A month later she seemed to mix with the pride again and was once again her ole self. She went back to walking up on her log to get her juicy pieces of meat at the top again.

What I am about to say, I told very few people. I want to point out that this wasn't the thing to do working with these wild animals. All the rangers in charge of their sections would pick up the small pieces of meat for their lions and bring them to their sections. We had a two-gallon pail with small chunks of meat, and we would ask the people if they wanted a lion on the hood of their car. If they did, we would throw a few pieces of meat up on it and the lion would jump on the hood and eat the meat. These people would be up close and personal with the lions.

Of course, keep in mind that they were told to keep their windows rolled up at all times, even just to ride through. If we would see someone with their windows rolled down, even just a little, we would get on the loud haler and tell them to roll up their windows.

Caesar was the largest lion in the park, and he was way too big to jump up on a hood of a car. So I would drive my jeep up beside him, if he was by himself, and I would throw him some meat. He was a gentle lion, with his mane just starting to grow out and the youngest male in my section. There were bars on the windows of every jeep in the park, for the rangers' safety. After getting up next to him, he would get up and walk to my jeep. I would roll my window down and when he got close enough, I would stick my arm out of the bars and throw the meat in the air and he would catch it. After awhile I got so confident, I would open the door and give him a piece of meat, about one inch thick and about ten inches long.

As time went on, I would get out of my jeep, hold the meat out in my hand and he would come over to me, opening his mouth, and I would drop the meat in. "DUMB ME!" I didn't do this for too long as he was getting older, turning into what we called a teenager and getting interested in females. He started acting like a mature lion, so that would be the end of my feeding Caesar by hand. After all, I needed to keep in mind, that he and all the others are wild animals and that I shouldn't trust any of them. I only did this when there was no one in my section. The ones I told about this were warned, "Whatever you do, don't be as crazy as I was, and do anything like that."

As we let lions out into their sections, there was a lot of breeding going on, so many of the lions had to be put by themselves in someone else's section and in a hut that was available to have cubs. We were having cubs born every other week for a long time. As soon as we could get one female out of the hut and back with the pride, we would put another one in. We were sure kept busy for a while.

In the wild, when the lioness would have her cubs, they would go off from the pride and have them. Another female would go with her to help her with the cubs. This female was called an aunt, and she would watch them and protect them while the mother would go hunt for food. After a while, when the cubs got old enough, the mother would take them back and introduce them to the pride.

We started having a lot of trouble with quite a few lions. They were going on the heads and in places they shouldn't be. We would go on the heads to walk around them to find the lions, tranquilize them and bring them back to the hut. We would put hay on the floor for them and then the next day, we would let them back out into the section with their pride.

This sounds like it would be easy but the heads were mostly swampland, thick with growth of vegetation, in places knee deep in water with a lot of snakes. Some lions would stay ahead of us just far enough that the chief game warden couldn't get a clear shot to dart them. If this happened, as it so often did, he would get in one of the stands we had built up in the tree, or pick a place to stand where the lion couldn't see him. Then two of the rangers would start walking and pushing the lion toward the chief game warden so he could tranquilize it.

This is not like in the movies, where when they are hit with a dart, they immediately go down. Before they are tranquilized, while we were tracking and hunting them, some lions would just hide and watch us go by. Others would lay there with their ears back and their tail snapping back and forth in a quick motion. They would look straight at you and give a short hissing sound. When this happened, we would be very cautious, as this meant they were getting ready to charge, and eat your butt up! It depends on the lion, whether it is old or young.

If it was an old one, they would go down quicker. In addition, it would depend on the weather; if it was hot, their resistance would be much less and it would take effect much quicker. Also, whether they had just eaten would cause the tranquilizer to take longer to work. Normally it would take anywhere from ten to twenty minutes before it took effect, so we would keep a close watch on them and follow behind them. They would usually just go off and lay down after they were darted with the tranquilizer.

CAESAR CATCHES A MEATY TREAT FROM GUS

DAVID IN SECTION 5

FEEDING A LION FROM MY JEEP

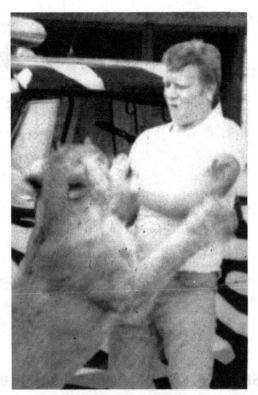

A PLAYFUL LIONESS

**LIONS RELAXING NEAR THE
PASSING TOURIST TRAFFIC**

GEMSBOK (AN ANTELOPE) AND HER BABY

Chapter 4

Feeding the Lions and First Lion to Charge

Since the opening, the way we would feed the lions, the ranger whose section we were in would position his jeep between the lions and the gate. A second man would drive up and put the meat that was in tubs in the back of his jeep, and then go back to the section. The head ranger would then get in the back of the jeep with the meat. He would have a four or five-foot long 2 x 4 with him in case one of the lions tried to get in the back of the jeep with him.

They would proceed through the section, going down the side road throwing the meat out, the ranger in the back would yell to the driver, telling him to go fast or slow. Sometimes, some of the lions would put their front paws on the jeep while walking on their back legs. When that happened, you would throw the meat in their faces so they would catch it, then get off the jeep and eat the meat. Sometimes, they wanted the man in the back of the jeep more than they wanted the meat that was being thrown in their face. When this happened, you would tell the driver to speed up, and you would use the 2 x 4 to push the lion off the back of the jeep.

The ranger would then throw out three or four pieces of meat, and they would grab that and be happy eating the meat, forgetting about that big tasty piece of meat that was still in the back of the jeep. Each piece of meat weighed about ten pounds. The rangers would throw out one or two extra. Keep in mind we always had one day that we didn't feed them at all.

One day, I was training a new man to work with the lions. I needed to show him all that was involved in caring for these beautiful animals. Before the jeep bringing the meat got to my section, I told him he would be driving the jeep while I was in the back with the meat. I told him, "Now, whatever you do, do not stop that jeep while I am feeding these lions."

During feeding time, there are many cars coming through, and on this one day, there were more cars than usual. There were many people watching us feed the lions. When the driver got to the road, instead of going down the side road, he wanted to go across the road and follow the cars. He stopped with me in the back with the meat and about fifteen lions following. They were very hungry, and all they were thinking about was the meat that was in the back of the jeep with me.

The lions were putting their front paws on the jeep, the back and the sides, really all over the back of the jeep, and I was throwing meat into their faces as fast as I could. I was praying real hard, shouting at the top of my lungs for this new man to get this jeep moving. He started moving again, and I kept throwing meat until it was all gone. I saw that all of the lions were eating on a piece of meat when the ranger got away from the pride and pulled up to where my jeep was. I got out of his jeep, and he could tell I was not a happy camper. I told him, "My friend, tomorrow is another day, and you will be the one in the back of the meat wagon. I will be the one driving."

He would get to experience the feeling of how I felt when he was so stupid to stop the jeep right in the middle of the pride of lions. He said, "Please, Gus, don't do that. I will do better tomorrow."

I told him, "Nope, I'm driving, and I'm going to stop the jeep just like you did, so you can see how it feels when the lions put their paws up on the jeep with you sitting all out in the open."

This guy was so nervous, since the wildest animals he had ever been around were his dog and cat. I don't think the poor guy slept at all that night. The next morning when we got to the section, I told him I had not changed my mind. When it came time to feed the lions, I asked, "Are you ready?"

He said, "Yes, but, Gus, please don't stop."

He got into the back of the jeep and away we went to the section. When all the lions got close to the jeep, I slowed down, almost coming to a stop. The look on his face told me that the next time he would make sure he kept that jeep going at all times.

He said, "Even if I have to drive through fire, I will not stop."

I continued at the proper speed until all the lions were fed, and when we were finished feeding, I said to him, "It doesn't feel so good does it? It's a lot different sitting in the back with all those lions out there, isn't it?"

I don't believe he was with us very long after that. Being the first roam-free park, we went through many changes and a lot of rangers. All of us told the chief game warden that someone was going to get hurt or killed, feeding that way, so he told us all to think of a better way that would be much safer and easier.

Between all of us, we did come up with a plan. We told the machine shop about it, and they built a flatbed trailer with chain link fencing eight feet high on all sides. There was a door hinged at the top, with a trap door in the back. From that trap door was a slide extending outside. It was about one and a half feet by two feet wide and two feet high. The door had a strong spring, and the meat would be thrown at the door by the ranger who remained safe inside the cage. The meat would then slide down to the lions, and the spring would close the door.

There was a shotgun in a holder just in case the ranger needed it for an emergency. The trailer was pulled by the tractor with the ranger inside the tractor's safety cage. This made it much safer for all of us.

Smitty's section was section two, and my section was section five. Between our sections was a canal. I would drive to the edge on my side, and he would drive to the edge on his side. From this vantage point, we could watch our lions and the people in their cars driving through our sections. In addition, on busy days, we would tell them to keep their cars moving on the left or right depending on which side of the road the lions were on. We were able to talk to each other if there were not a lot of cars going through our sections; all the while, we were keeping our eyes on our lions.

You could also see Giraffe Island from our sections. There was a canal between the lions and the giraffes, but the visitors coming through could not see the canal.

Smitty went to the machine shop one day to get a tire repaired that had a slow leak, When he came back to his section, he drove up to where I was watching my lions with a big smile on his face. He said, "Look what the guys at the machine shop did for me."

I stepped out of my jeep and looked through his jeep window. The passenger seat was gone, there was a big hole in the floor about twelve inches in diameter, and you could see through it to the ground.

I asked him, "Why in the world did you have that done?"

His replied, "Now, I won't have to be relieved to go to the bathroom anymore. I can just squat over the hole and do my business."

When we rangers had to go to the bathroom, we would have to call someone to come relieve us. We would go to the head between section four and five. There was a port-o-let there. You would take your radio and gun with you and park your jeep right next to the port-o-let. When you were finished, you would go back to your section.

Smitty thought that his new port-o-let on wheels was the greatest thing on the earth; I have to chuckle to this day when I think of it. The next day as the visitors were driving through the park, I noticed that Smitty was a little further from his lions than normal. I looked again and saw that Smitty was on the passenger side of his jeep. I could only see his cowboy hat, a little of his head and eyes through the windshield, and he was shouting over his loud haler, "Keep those cars moving."

I had to laugh, as I knew what he was doing, I picked up my loud haler, not the radio, with the cars driving right by him, and yelled, "What are you doing, Smitty?"

There was silence for a while, and then on his loud haler, he yelled back, "You know what I'm doing!" Then from the passenger's side of the jeep, out the window came a finger pointing up waving at me. That's when I really cracked up laughing.

At closing time, Bill Dredge, the general manager, would call the chief game warden and let him know the make of the last car to be coming through. Then the chief game warden would follow it all the way through the park, locking the gates as they went through each section, this was to make sure no one was caught inside each section. He would wait at the front gate and follow them through, staying a good distance behind them. He did not rush them; we wanted them to have plenty of time to ride through the whole park and enjoy themselves. It was a four-mile stretch of road.

As they went through section one, which was the antelope section, a guard was stationed at that gate in case the antelope got too close to the gate. About ten feet up in the air a guardhouse looked like a grass hut. The guard would come down if it looked as if an animal was getting too close and try to get the animal to go back away from the gate. If he wasn't successful, he would close the gate and call the chief game warden to come move the animal a good distance away from the gate.

He would then open the gate and let the cars go through to section two, which was the start of the lion sections. Then if a lion were to get too close to the gate going into section one, they would call on the radio and alert the game warden in the tower who would get the gate closed and then stay in the hut until the situation was under control.

Smitty would usually keep his lions a good distance away from the antelope section and closer to section three. However, sometimes we all had a situation where the lions would be fighting and running all over the section and getting close to the gate of another section.

As the chief game warden continued through the first section, he would pick up the gate man at that time. If a ranger needed some help putting his lions in, he would help him out and check that everything was okay. Before closing, the man in charge of the section would open the door to the hut after the last car went through that section. The ranger and chief game warden would push them to the hut for the night.

Once we got all of the lions into their huts, one jeep would drive to the side of the door and another would pull up in front and rev up their engine. The man at the side door in the jeep would take a hook off the door, and the other jeep would pull back quickly. The one that unhooked the door, would push the door closed. The jeep that had pulled back, would pull forward blocking the door from opening. The guy that had pushed the door would go on the other side and lock it.

We did it this way for quite some time and realized it was too dangerous. So we figured out another way to do this by rigging up a pull rope on all lion huts. Once all lions were pushed in, the ranger could go in his jeep, grab the rope, back up the jeep and the door would close. Then he would pull forward, putting his jeep bumper on the door so the lions couldn't get out and proceed to lock it.

Some of the lions would become independent and run for greener pastures. They would dart toward the heads, and of course, this would indicate we were in for a long night. We would have to hunt them down and get them darted and back to their huts. Usually, by that time, it would be nine or ten at night.

The chief game warden would lock each gate as he went through checking everything, and we would go to the next section to help the next ranger put his lions in. It went that way until we got through to the last one, making sure the last visitor's car had gone through. The exit gate was then closed and locked.

We would continue on to the office where all rangers would check in their guns that were kept under lock and key at all times when we weren't using them in the daytime. We would get in our own cars, vans, or trucks and start out the two-mile stretch. Some of us would stop at a little bar in Loxahatchee to have a few beers and talk about our day.

One evening at closing, in section seven, after getting all but one of the lions in the hut, she decided to go to the head. The chief game warden, Carlos, and rangers Tex, Charles, Dan and I, went to the head to tranquilize her and bring her back to the section. We walked all inside the head, but we didn't see any sign of her. Carlos said it was starting to get dark inside the head, so we would wait until tomorrow when we could see better in the daylight.

As we were walking on the outside of the head back to where we left our jeeps, she came out of the head. When she saw us, she ran back in the head, but just barely inside. She stopped, laid down looking at us, her tail flipping back and forth, which was not a good sign. Carlos was carrying the 375 rifle and Tex had the tranquilizer gun. The rest of us were armed with shotguns. As Tex tried to get in place with the tranquilizer gun, she was still looking dead at us. Tex shot her with the dart (tranquilizer), and he hit her in the front shoulder.

As soon as the dart hit her, she started charging toward us. We were still in the open part of the head, and she was only about thirty feet from us. Carlos then fired the 375 at her, hitting her in the head. She flipped over and didn't move; she was dead.

If she hadn't been shot, she would have gotten to some of us. We all felt sad that this had to happen, but it was a situation that was out of control, with the lion charging us. It was either her or us. As I said before, it took anywhere from fifteen or twenty minutes before the tranquilizer worked, and as soon as that dart hit her she was up and charging toward us.

This was a very sad situation, but there was no other choice for us. If Carlos hadn't shot when he did, one of us other rangers would have. This was not our first experience of hunting down lions in the head to tranquilize, but this was the first that charged us all the way. Most of our experiences of hunting these lions down were very successful, and they were all brought back to their huts safely.

CAESAR STANDING UP BESIDE DOWNED TREE

DOT IN THE BACK OF MY JEEP

**LOUD HALER DAMAGED BY ABE,
A LARGE MALE LION**

Chapter 5

Situations that Happened with Different Animals

One day in my section, most of the lions started fighting with Fanny; she swam the canal and got between Giraffe Island and Smitty's section. Smitty got to the edge of the canal because his lions had spotted her. She had also seen them coming at her.

Smitty started to rev up his engine, causing Fanny to start swimming back to her own section. I went over to her and started pushing her with the jeep until I got her back to where the pride was.

At closing one night, Peggy, one of my other lions went crazy. She started running away from the hut instead of toward it; then she went to the edge of the canal. I came up on the side of the canal with my jeep, and when she saw me coming, she started going back to the hut. Terry already had the rest of the lions in the hut, so he was on his way to help me get her pointed in the right direction toward the hut. As we both pushed her with our jeeps, she went in the hut.

The very next night at closing, she did the same exact thing, so we went through the same ritual as we did before. The next day as I was talking to Terry, I said, "You know, I think we will try to put her at the front of the pride when it comes time to put them in the hut." She would then have lions all around her, so maybe that will help her to go in. Sure enough, that is what we did, and Fanny went in without any problem. We didn't have any more trouble with her.

A secretary bird got past Mr. Gallop at the gate between the antelope and lion section, which was Smitty's section. Roger and I caught the bird while Smitty kept an eye on all his lions. We were really causing a big commotion getting that bird back to the antelope section. The lions would have liked to have that little bird for a snack, but we did get it back safely.

At closing time in pet's corner, a taper got loose so they radioed for us rangers to come in and get it back where it belonged. It somehow got out of the enclosure where it was being kept. This was so the visitors could see it, so after we got all the lions in their hut, we went to pet's corner. Dan and I were able to catch him, not without a scene though. He decided to take a bite out of Dan's leg, also to give me a few scratches. We didn't need any doctor's care; we just cleaned it with peroxide in pet's corner and then got out of there. The end of another exciting day, waiting to come back tomorrow to see what was ahead for us to tackle.

We had a situation with a mountain sheep that had given birth. The Zebras were trying to get to the baby and kill it. As many of us rangers that could went to the section to help Roger. We all got out of our jeeps and formed a V with our bodies so the mother and baby would go into the worming section. Once in there, the Zebras couldn't get to them; mother and baby were doing fine, not having to worry about those Zebras anymore.

One day, some of Dan's lions in section three were acting strangely; they were dizzy, falling down and looking up in the air sideways. One of them fell into the water but managed to get out and back on dry land. We had to tranquilize it as some of the other lions were trying to fight with her and she couldn't defend herself. We held up visitors going through the section until she went under the tranquilizer, and then we put her into the jeep to carry her back to the hut. We really had a time keeping the lions that were all right away from the dizzy ones since they were going all over the section. We finally got the ones that were dizzy back to the hut by, going back and forth getting all of the rest of the pride together again.

The next day at opening another lion in Dan's section was dizzy; two in Tex's section were also acting funny, displaying dizziness. Tex took one of the lions to the lab to see what the problem was, hoping something could be done about it. When Tex got back, two of his lions had gone on the head, so we took off to the head, going all through it looking for the two of them. It was getting really dark, plus it was raining like mad, but we finally got them both tranquilized and loaded in the jeeps. We took them back to their huts where they belonged.

The next week, they told us that they couldn't find anything wrong with the lions, so they felt it was something in the meat we had fed them. It was possibly something the cows had eaten before they were butchered.

The next day, an ostrich attacked Wayne. It kicked him hard and broke three of his ribs, and then decided to do a little dance on him. His shirt was ripped to shreds, and he had to be taken to the hospital. The doctor took him off work for a week.

The situation with those lions going into the head was getting to be a bad habit. We had already gotten six other lions off the head and tranquilized them, all of our huts were full, and so when this one went over on the head, we tracked her down through a wet swampy area. We were knee deep in water in places. It had been raining for days making it rough getting to where she was.

We finally got her tranquilized and put her in the jeep. We took her back to the hut, but we had to keep her in a crate, as it was all we had left. When we finally got her all tucked in with some hay, it was almost eight-thirty at night, time to go home.

However, as we were going out through the main gate, there were five jeeps going out. The first jeep opened the gates and drove through. By the time all of the jeeps went through, there were three Ostriches outside the gate. They started running along the two-mile stretch road heading toward the main highway where there was a lot of traffic. This is when we realized that we were in for a long night.

We had to capture these three ostriches before they caused any accidents on the main highway. Carlos yelled to Charles and me to jump in the back of his jeep. A couple of other guys jumped into the back of another jeep. Carlos yelled out the back window to us, telling us that when he drove up beside the ostrich, for us to jump out and tackle them. As we were chasing them down the road, two of them went off the road into the woods and swamp. The other one ran on the side of the road dodging back and forth. Carlos ran the jeep alongside this ostrich, and my football experience kicked into gear. Charles and I both jumped on the ostrich, pulling him down. We squeezed his legs close to his body, and managed to get him in the jeep. We kept holding on real tight as we drove back to the park and let him out back in the section where he belonged.

"Touch Down," I exclaimed as Charles and I shared a "high five" moment. The ostrich looked back to us as if to say, "Now wasn't that fun?"

We jumped back in the jeep and headed back to the two-mile stretch to help get the other two ostriches back in the park. We went to where the two went into the woods, but it was getting way too dark for us to see well enough to find them.

We went back to the office where Carlos was saying that anyone who had the day off the next day would stay all night. And anyone who wanted to volunteer could also stay.

We put a jeep on both sides of the main road in case they made it there. Then some of us in jeeps were running up and down the two-mile stretch looking for any sign of the ostriches. If the jeeps that were at the main road spotted an ostrich, they would radio us so we could warn the cars to slow down.

These ostrich weighed about three hundred pounds each, so drivers would need to slow down in case they should run in front of their cars. We all got talking and figured that the ostrich would most likely settle down for the night and lay down somewhere until daylight. In case they didn't, we would be there for the safety of everyone. Carlos asked me if I would go home and get my swamp buggy, a four-wheel vehicle with all of the body stripped off it, leaving just the frame with the floor being about six and a half feet off the ground. It had big airplane tires with chains around them to go through the swamp. A ladder in the back was used to climb up so you could get to the driver's seat and passenger's seat. In the back was a frame built about hip high with a tire around it so a man could stand inside of it, keeping his hands free to hold his gun. If the terrain got to rough, he would still be able to shoot at a deer or wild hog, but for this night, it would be the ostrich-mobile.

I went home, hooked up my buggy trailer, loaded the buggy on, and headed back to Lion Country. Carlos, Dale, Ron, and I stayed all night. About six-thirty in the morning, Carlos and I got into the buggy looking for the two ostriches. An hour later, we found them, and tried to tranquilize them but with no success.

We tried everything possible; we could see them but not get close enough to dart them. Carlos decided we had better shoot them, because if they were to get on the main highway they could cause a lot of wrecks and possibly kill someone. This was a sad end to this one experience. We took them back to the park and disposed of them. Now it was time for Carlos and the rest of us that stayed all night to go home and get some much-needed sleep for our day off.

As I was on my way to work one day, I was listening to news on the radio. I heard that someone by the name of Norman was killed last night. The report said that he lost control of his car and went into the main canal that ran along the side of the road called Southern Boulevard, which was in front of the two-mile stretch going into Lion Country.

When I heard this, I couldn't believe that he could be our Norman, the one who works with us. After all, he had just driven into my section from Elephant Island yesterday. We had sat in our jeeps talking to each other for quite some time. As I was walking to the office, Smitty came out and said, "Did you hear about Norman?"

At that time, I knew it had to be true. We lost a good, honest animal man who gave his all for the love of these animals, and he would surely be missed.

At closing time, one of Smitty's lions went on the head. All of his lions were fighting, so off to a head once again, Carlos, Smitty, Terry and I went over to track her down. It didn't take too long to find her, just a couple of hours, and we tranquilized her. We took her back to her hut, bedded her down with hay to wait while the tranquilizer wore off.

On this particular day, all of Ron's lions were getting into fights with each other, and running all over the place. Terry went to help Ron get them straightened out, then mine started going crazy. They were all fighting with my lions named Eagle, Fanny, Flare Up and Peggy started it all, but usually when a few start picking on one lion the others come to join in.

For some reason, they didn't like the way she was acting I guess. Carlos came to help me calm them down, which only took a few minutes. Once everything was under control, the lions were okay for the rest of the day.

That evening after closing down my section for the night, I went over to help Ron put his lions up. Ron was counting all of them as usual, and I was helping him count all of his lions, which were all young lions. Most of them came from pet's corner, where they were hand-raised. One of the lions started rubbing his head on the bars, so I thought, okay, buddy, I'll scratch your head for you. He quickly turned and bit me on the finger.

Seems like after you work with these wild animals for a while, you start getting a little careless, so every once in a while they will give you a wakeup call. I had to go to the doctor, and by the time I got there, the cloth I had wrapped around it was soaked in blood.

I needed to get a shot and have the bite cleaned out and bandaged up. The doctor said to just keep it clean and covered until it healed. In about a week, it had healed nicely with just a little scar. Of course, I went around for days showing everyone where the lion bit me.

A couple of days later when Ron came in and was getting ready to release his lions out in to the section, as he was checking them he found his lion, Filly, the one that bit me, dead inside the enclosure. We could only guess that they got into a fight during the night and the others had killed her. It was sad for Ron, since you do become close to these lions as if they were your children, and he had been with these lions a long time.

This one day we got in seven new zebras and three new llamas. We put them on Giraffe Island, which is right by my section. My lions tried to get over on the island, and I had a problem with them most of the day. They sure had me on my toes, but as it came close to the end of the day, they started to settle down.

At closing time, Abe did not want to go into the hut. As I tried pushing him, he attacked my jeep, putting holes in my loud haler that was on the hood of my jeep. He squashed it like a tomato. He was holding on for dear life with his teeth in there so deep, he didn't want to let go. Wayne came to help me with Abe, but when Wayne got closer; Abe turned around and attacked Wayne's jeep. He was trying to get to Wayne through the bars on the jeep's window. Smitty was there in his jeep and Abe decided to attack his jeep, too.

We had a very angry lion on our hands at this time. We had some cherry bombs with us, and we had used these before when we hunted down lions on the heads. If we were in thick underbrush and the lions were hiding, we would throw these cherry bombs, and it would flush out the lions. We threw some at Abe, but the loud noise didn't seem to faze him at all.

I shot a blank shell by him, but he still wouldn't give an inch. I had almost run into him with my jeep, and nothing seemed to make him to move, so we tranquilized him. We put him in the jeep and hauled him back to the hut.

Most lions would go down with 3 cc's of tranquilizer, and then come out after twenty-four hours, but with Abe, we had to give him only 2 cc's. It would still take about three or four days before he would be all right. Abe was the oldest lion in my section, so maybe this was why it was so hard on him, but he was still a strong lion.

In the next few days, I kept a close watch on him, then released him back out into the section. All the other lions greeted him like their long lost buddy.

Ron and I fixed a pen for Dot, a female lion who was due to have cubs soon. All the spaces in my section were full of females due for cubs. Dan had two of my females in his section in huts due to have cubs also, so I had very few out in the open now.

This one day Elsa decided to go on the head where the outhouse was, so needless to say, no one had to use that for a while. I asked Smitty if I could come sit on the passenger side of his jeep, and he said, "No way."

Carlos and I went on the head and tranquilized Dot. After hitting her with the dart, she jumped in the canal. She swam to my section and ran straight into the hut. When we saw her go in there, we ran to close the door. She went out like a light, and that was the easiest time we ever had with any lion after tranquilizing them. We didn't have to load her into the jeep or anything. We felt very proud of ourselves.

The next day, a ground rattler bit Terry while he was burying trash at the bone pit. He didn't see the snake and it bit him on the finger. Carlos took him to the hospital, and he was out for the rest of the day. When he came back two days later, he was a little weak, but doing fine. He had learned how important it is to keep a close watch when digging and always be looking down. Being so close to the swampy area, there were always many snakes around.

One day, a lion from Tex's section came into my section and then tried to get onto Elephant Island. Charles, Tex's helper, went to get some feed for the elephants with his jeep and gun. Charles was yelling at me from Elephant Island, and realizing the situation, I went over there with my jeep.

The cat was swimming beside the metal fence in the mote. She started going up on the island, so I yelled at Charles to come get in my jeep. He did not have enough time to get to my jeep.

There was an opening in the fence large enough for the lion to get through and get on the island. Tex was coming up to where I was with a gun, so I got out of my jeep and threw my shotgun to Charles. I yelled loudly to him so he would catch it, and I got back in my jeep. Tex drove up beside my jeep just as the lion tried to get through the opening.

Charles started hitting the lion with the butt of the shotgun. Tex was ready to shoot the lion, but I got on the drive over and started yelling and revving up the engine so loud that I guess the lion decided to get out of there. With all of the commotion going on, she turned back into Tex's section, greeting all the other lions by rubbing up against them, so all things turned out good.

It was really a very bad situation, just one more incident to help remind us that these animals are wild and very unpredictable. At closing, Charles needed help with the punk elephants, which were shaken up, with everything going on. They had been in the park for only about four months, and Charles had been working them since Norman died. Tex and I went over there and helped chain them up for the night.

Not long after that, Carlos decided to go over on Chimp Island by himself. He really knew better, but he hadn't been over there that much, so not having someone with him he got careless. One of the chimps bit him on his calf that required twenty-eight stitches to repair the wound. It was a very serious bite, putting Carlos in the hospital for six days.

Learning from this situation, he knew not to ever go over there alone again. I had a new man in my section, and I was training him. I told him that I was going to the meat house to get some small chunks of meat for my lions, and if he had any trouble to call me on the radio. I wasn't even out of my section when he called, and he kept calling, asking when I was coming back. He was a nervous wreck being there by himself. I was only gone for about fifteen minutes, and when I got back, we had a few words.

One day in Tex's section, his lions were out of control so I went there to help him, but we got them all straightened out with no problem. As I was going by Chimp Island, I noticed there was a lot of activity going on over there. I stopped my jeep there to investigate only to find one of the chimps was up in a large bush. He had a root that was about three feet long and was swinging the root at any of the chimps that came close enough. One chimp decided to stand up to him. He got close to him and when the other chimp took a swing at him with the stick, he took the root away from him. He then started to beat him with his own root, chasing him all over that island.

All the chimps were raising the devil. One came running up behind him, took the root from him and threw it into the water. Then every one of them calmed down, and everything went back to normal. I was really glad because I sure didn't want to have to go over there to take that root away from any of them.

When the park was under construction, an eight-foot alligator was in the pond on the outside of the park, right alongside pets' corner. We thought that with all the construction around, it would leave and find a new home, but it decided to stay there. The park's general manager decided that it being so close to pet's corner, we needed to get the alligator removed.

We called the Florida Fresh Water Fish and Game Commission about relocating the gator. We discussed with them that we would capture it. We were building an enclosure and pond in pet's corner for him and would have him in there for the visitors to observe. I told Carlos that I had experience with alligators, from having done a lot of frogging in the Everglades using airboats and jon boats.

When we got to the pond, two of us got in the jon boat and went around the pond trying to see if he would come up out of the water. It was a dark night so he should have come up a lot, but instead he only came up three times. It could have been because there were so many people on the edge of the bank watching and talking.

We went around the pond for a while hoping to see him come up again, but we had no luck. Some of the men were walking the edge of the pond, but he just wasn't showing his face at all now. We had our catchall and lariat ready in case he did show up, but by one o'clock in the morning, we decided to hang it up, going home to try another night.

My wife, Nonie, and our two sons, Joe and Erik, were there; as we were talking to the game warden, Joe, my oldest son said, "Hey, Daddy, why don't you croak him up like you did the other night when we went frogging?"

I looked at the game warden and he smiled, saying, "I didn't hear that." I thanked him and told Joe to get back in the truck and stay there; as they say, out of the mouths of babes.

We tried one more night to catch the alligator, but didn't have any luck. It was decided that he left that pond because of all the activity going on in pet's corner and around the pond. After all, there were plenty of other ponds and canals around the outside of the park that would provide a quieter home for him.

In pet's corner, we had an enclosure built with a pond that housed one alligator about eight feet long. It also had two little ones about three feet long. This was too small for the alligator we had tried to catch from the pond, so we built another one to accommodate the larger alligator.

The enclosure they were in was getting too small for them so we went in and captured the eight-foot gator. Charles, Mr. Pierce, George and I roped him, jumped on him to hold him down while we tied his mouth and legs. We then tied him to a long pipe and carried him to the larger enclosure we had just built. We went back and caught the two little guys by hand, taking them over to the new enclosure, too. Later we put the little guys back in the original enclosure, as we felt it would be better having the little ones by themselves, so in the end everyone was happy.

We were having a lot of rain almost every day during August and September, when Dan's lions were going crazy on him. Seemed like they all would go crazy when it rained and the temperature turned cooler. One of the lions went over on the head. Carlos, Ron and I started over to the head, swimming across the canal to the head. Carlos had the .357 and the tranquilizer gun; Ron and I had 12 gauge shotguns with rifle slugs. The water was hip deep in places, all throughout the head, and we could hear her in the water, but we couldn't see her. Finally, we saw her in a small opening where she stood in about six inches of water. Carlos shot the tranquilizer gun, and she charged us, but then turned away. We gave her fifteen minutes for the tranquilizer to take effect before we went looking for her. We wanted to get to her fast in case she went down in the water and could drown. After looking for a few minutes, we came across her, drug her out of the swamp, and loaded her into the jeep. It took us about three hours in all to get her out and back to the hut.

One day I was asked to take a cub to Fort Lauderdale to a police convention for a day, then come back and take it to the Palm Beach Towers for another convention the next day, this was public relations for Lion Country. I would let the people pet the cub and answer any questions they might ask. So I kept the cub at my house for the night. I got home with it around seven-thirty at night, and the boys sure enjoyed playing with the little cub. I put it in the bathroom, and in the middle of the night, my wife got up to go to the bathroom and not turning on a light, the cub attacked her, grabbing her around the legs. Her screams woke me up from a sound sleep along with all the neighbors, I think. It was nice having the little guy there for the night, but it was a lot of confusion, too. It sure let us know we didn't want one living in the house with us.

TOURIST TRAFFIC PASSING BY THE LIONS

**GUS WITH JACK PARR RELEASING
THE *BORN FREE* LIONS**

Chapter 6
The Born Free Lions

Things had been going well for quite some time when on July 28th, there was a request to take jeeps to the Miami Airport to pickup three of the descendants of the Born Free lions. Mr. Pierce, Wayne, Al and I drove four Lion Country zebra-striped jeeps to make the pickup.

Jack Parr saved these three lions after hearing that the lions were going to be killed. They had been getting out of the preserve in Africa and killing some of the livestock in nearby villages. Jack got in touch with Lion Country and asked if they could take the lions. The answer was a resounding, "Of course!"

Lion Country and Jack Parr made a deal to bring the lions from Africa to the United States where they could live within the park. It was also agreed that Jack Parr could tape a one-hour special for television called "Jack Parr and his Lions."

When we arrived at the airport, many photographers, as well as reporters from newspapers and televisions stations greeted us. We were taken to a special meeting room at the airport where we answered all kinds of questions about the lions and the arrangements made for them by Lion Country.

After the news conference, we went out on the tarmac where the cargo plane, The Flying Tiger, was parked a distance from the other planes. We used a dragline to load the lion crates into the jeeps. A lot of the news people and their photographers followed us outside and recorded the entire time we were loading the lions into the jeeps.

After securing the crates in the back of the jeeps, we began the seventy-mile trip back to Lion Country. It was nearly closing time when we reached the park. Mr. Dredge wanted to release these Born Free lions into Dan's section. It was the only one with room for more lions. All the other sections were full and Pet's Corner couldn't handle lions at the age and size of these lions.

Mr. Dredge wanted us to wait until the park closed and all the other lions were put up for the night in their huts. When we got the "all clear" sign, we transported the lions over to Dan's section. We made sure that all the photographers and news people were in place to record the momentous event. Jack Parr and his daughter, who had joined him on the trip, took their places with a good view for the release. The film crew was also in place to get footage for the Jack Parr and his Lions made-for-TV special. This was all a very big deal in terms of making the local news.

We used a tractor with a forklift to move the crates from the back of the jeeps to the ground. When we opened the crate doors to release the lions, they didn't want to come out. They just sat there looking around at all the people and vehicles. We used poles to try to push them out, but they still wouldn't move. It seemed like a good idea to give them a little time to calm down and adjust to their new surroundings. We left them alone and just watched them for about forty-five minutes. We tried again to get them to come out of their crates, but still had no success.

Carlos and Mr. Dredge decided we should leave the crate doors open and let them come out on their own during the night. We all got into our vehicles, left the section and headed home.

The next morning when we returned to work, we could not find any of the new lions anywhere. This created a bit of a problem since at the time; we had no idea where they were. We rode around the section in our jeeps, checking behind every tree and every mound, but they were nowhere to be found. We finally spotted tracks leading to the head, which was overgrown with vines, bushes and trees. Many places on the head were also covered by swamp water.

No one dreaded more than me, having to go over there to hunt these lions. Most of the head was so thick that you couldn't see more than six feet in front of you; the water was hip deep in places. We proceeded to the head with tranquilizer guns to make it possible for us to put them in the jeeps to bring them back across the head. We knew they wouldn't come back on their own, especially not back to a big pride of unfamiliar lions they weren't used to being with. Normally, we always mix new lions slowly with the pride so they will be accepted.

We were also well protected with the 375 rifle and shotguns in case a lion charged one of us. Of course, we hoped and prayed it would not be necessary to use them. We walked the head for most of the morning until we finally spotted one of the lions. At the same time, she spotted us, which sent her running away at a great speed to find a more secure hiding place. Believe me, it's no fun being on a head when you can't see the lion, but you can feel their eyes on you.

We could hear her in the water at times. We kept following her until she came out on dry land and lay down. Carlos got a good shot and tranquilized her, but it doesn't take effect immediately. She charged us, but turned away before she got halfway to us, and went back into the head. We gave her ten minutes for the tranquilizer to take effect and then went looking for her. In the process, we found the other two lions.

Carlos was able to tranquilize one lion, but when the dart hit her, they both took off and ran deeper into the head. Now we have two of the lions darted with the tranquilizer working and one not yet darted. We waited the usual ten minutes before we started going after them. Tex and I went through the head trying to flush them out toward Carlos who stayed in a good spot to dart the third one.

We found the two still together. They were only about ten feet away from us when we spotted them. The one that wasn't tranquilized was lying down by the one we had tranquilized previously. We yelled to Carlos who came over to us and was able to tranquilize the last one. She just stayed right there swishing her tail back and forth with her ears laid back and hissing at us until she went under the effect of the drug.

We dragged them back over to the jeeps and loaded them up. It took from noon until five p.m. to finally get them back to the section. We put them on one side of Dan's hut with the rest of his lions on the other side. A wire fence was stretched between the two sides so they could see each other and sniff each other, getting to know each other without actually being together. If they were allowed to be together at this point, they would fight each other.

It had rained most of the time we were on the head looking for the three lions. Carlos said they sure wouldn't hunt lions like that in Africa; it would be too dangerous with it raining so hard.

When we came into work the next morning, we realized we had only gotten two of the three Born Free lions the previous day. The third lion we tranquilized and brought off the head was actually one of Dan's original lions, which we hadn't even known she was there on the head. That was also why she was by herself and the other two lions stayed together. We now realized that the third Born Free lion was still over on the head.

Carlos, Tex and I went back to the head to hunt down the last missing lion. I don't have to tell you how dangerous it was to be over on that head looking for those lions, thinking we got them all, but not knowing there was still one in there. The good Lord sure was with us all. Now we started walking through the head and wading through the water. We finally found her after about two hours. She had laid down on a piece of ground that didn't have any water.

Carlos was able to dart her right away. She jumped and went back a little and lay down, but her tail was swinging and her ears were laid back. She was hissing at us. We just stayed put watching her for about twenty minutes while the tranquilizer took effect. When we approached her, she was totally out, so we dragged her back to the jeep and put her in a crate.

When we got back to Dan's section, we put her crate at the door to the hut. The next day we released her from the crate into the hut with the other two Born Free lions. They were all together once again and obviously happy to see each other. They kept rubbing against each other for quite a while.

Just a few days after capturing the lions, Carlos left for Germany to open a preserve over there. We all wished him well in his new adventure. The next day after closing, Mr. Dredge announced that Tex would now be the chief Game Warden and I would be second in charge. I naturally felt very good about my job and knew that there was much more in my future with the animals and with Lion Country.

It was time now to mix the Born Free lions with the pride. We started by bringing two or three lions from the pride and putting them in with the Born Free lions. We watched them closely to see that they weren't fighting much. If they started fighting too much, we would squirt them with water to stop the fight. We left them in there together for a couple of days and then moved the ones from the pride back out with the rest of the pride. Then we would bring two or three different ones in to mix with the new lions. We continued this procedure until we had mixed all members of the pride with the Born Free lions.

After this was accomplished, we opened the center door letting them all in together. All went well, so the next morning, we let them all out into the section as one big pride. The whole process took about sixteen days to complete.

Everything was going very well for about a week when one of our lions started fighting with one of the Born Free lions which went over onto the head. It was raining so hard that day that you couldn't see very well so we decided to wait until the next day to go looking for her.

In the mean time, Jack Parr had called Mr. Dredge to say that he would be there with his camera crew in a couple of days to take some pictures of the Born Free lions. Mr. Dredge told him that one of his lions was over on the head and with the weather so bad, we couldn't go hunt for her until the next day. Jack Parr asked if we could wait one more day so he could get there with his crew and get their equipment set up.

Before they got there, we set up the cherry picker on the head. We guarded the workers while they set up to be sure the lion didn't attack anyone. The next day, Jack Parr, his daughter and crew arrived. We took them out to where the cherry picker was set up, and they all loaded in it and went up into the air. Of course, we didn't know how long it would take to find the lion, direct her through the head to where they could get some good shots of us going after her.

The head was wet and thick with underbrush. Tex, Dan and I went looking for the lion and spotted her fairly quickly, but she kept staying just far enough ahead of us that we couldn't dart her. I stood up on a high stump and spotted her going through the water to a dry area where she just stopped to look around. Tex darted her and she jumped when the dart hit. Then she moved backward a few feet and then lay down. She had never even seen us so we waited about fifteen minutes for the tranquilizer to take effect.

We alerted Jack Parr that we had the lion and they could come down from the cherry picker. They came over to where we had the lion, taking loads of pictures of us and the lion while we loaded her into the jeep. We took her back to the hut and unloaded her into a crate lined with

hay. The camera crew kept taking pictures until they left.
Jack Parr and his daughter told us they would be back at a
later date to finish filming for the Jack Parr and his Lions
television special.

Within about a year after mixing the Born Free lions
with our pride, I had become the Chief Game Warden. I
was really honored to be the man in charge of the park. It
was a huge responsibility for not only the animals, but also
for the safety of the men and all the visitors who came to
the park. It was a great experience that I lived every day,
most of the time seven days a week. It was really rough
for my family though. If they wanted to see me, they
would bring out my lunch, and I would take a break so I
could spend time outside the preserve with my wife, Nonie,
and our sons, Joe and Erik.

We knew this wouldn't be like this forever so we
made the best of the situation. Of course, the boys
enjoyed coming to where their daddy worked and they
would get VIP treatment. This made them feel special like
little boys should feel. Joe was seven years old and Erik
was two at the time.

One day Mr. Dredge called me into his office to tell
me that I needed to put the three Born Free lions in the
hut by themselves, keeping them on one side of the hut as
I had done when we were first mixing them with the pride.
Joy Adams was coming to the park the next day. She
wrote the books, "Born Free" and "Elsa." Our three Born
Free lions were the grandchildren of Elsa.

Jack Parr's film crew would be there, too, to film us
releasing the three lions first and then film us releasing the
rest of the pride. Mr. Dredge told me to get ready as well
as get my men ready to do this. Smitty and Sarge would
be there to protect everyone with guns, and I would be
there with the tranquilizer gun in case anything went
wrong.

The next day, Joy Adams arrived about 4:30 p.m.
and wanted to see her Born Free lions immediately. Mr.

Dredge explained that the park was about to close, but she said, "If I don't get to see my lions tonight, by tomorrow I will be on my way back to Africa."

Mr. Dredge called me on the radio telling me to come to his office and take Joy Adams to the hut where we had put the Born Free lions by themselves in section four. As I pulled up to the hut, she saw the lions and at the same time, they saw her. She was calling and talking to them like in baby talk, and I could see that they recognized her. They all came over to the bars where she was standing and she stuck her arm in through the bars as far as she could to stroke them all over their bodies and heads. They were rubbing the bars and against her.

Joy Adams said, "I want to get in the hut with them." I told her that would not be possible. Well, she didn't like it, but I insisted that she was not going to get in there with them then. She would have to wait until the next day before she could have any more contact with the lions.

I finally convinced her to get in the jeep to go back to the office. I didn't leave the park until after eight that night. When I got home, I told my wife, Nonie, and my boys, Joe and Erik, all about the situation. I told them how I couldn't believe the difference in the lions when she put both her arms through the bars and was petting them. Their reaction to her was amazing. If someone had told me that would happen, I would never have believed them, but seeing it with my own eyes was a different story.

The next day was filled with an even bigger surprise. Jack Parr, his daughter, and his camera crew were there. Bill York and Joy Adams came in together in the first car and they were somehow tied together with cords for the TV and film crew. We released the Born Free lions first. They were about ten feet out of the hut when Joy jumped out of the car dragging Bill with her since he was hooked to her with all these cords. Mind you, this was not supposed to happen. I just knew someone was going to be attacked by a lion!

I had the tranquilizer gun ready along with Smitty and Sarge who had their guns ready. The lions were running straight to Joy as she was calling out to them. Mr. York was trying to remain calm as the lions were just walking around both of them. He was very cool and calm, having been a hunter and guide in Africa; he had been up close and personal with many animals. But remember that in Africa he had a gun and a tranquilizer gun, not a microphone that sure wouldn't give him any control over this situation.

Bill York finally talked her into getting back into the car. When they were safely back in the car, we released the rest of the pride. They all came out and went to their normal places in the section. The film crew was filming all of this. Jack Parr and his daughter were very happy as this completed his TV special, "Jack Parr and his Lions."

When we were done with the release and filming, we went over to Pet's Corner to the restaurant for breakfast and coffee. It was a very exciting time for us all, and we had lots to talk about for quite a long time afterward.

Chapter 7

Lions and Hippos

After we released the Born Free Lions for the Jack Parr Story, I went on vacation; the time off was greatly needed and greatly appreciated.

My first day back, all the lions seemed to be behaving very well with no problems. The next day, Tex took off and I was in charge of the preserve for two days. On the second day, one of Smitty's lions went on the head, so I went looking for her. When I found her, I couldn't get a clear shot so I climbed a tree to get a better aim. I got the dart off, but I think it hit a bone, as there didn't seem to be any effect on her, and by this time, it was getting dark, so I decided to try again the next day.

The next day, Dan was having trouble with the Born Free Lions. One went on the moat, but we got her out of there without having to dart her. We then went on the head to get Smitty's lion that was on there from the day before. She was almost in the same spot where we had left her. I hit her in the back leg with the dart, and she went down in fifteen minutes. We took her back to her section and all was okay.

Then suddenly, one of the Born Free Lions in Dan's section went crazy and climbed a tree. We couldn't get her to come down, and I didn't want to tranquilize her again so soon. It was a cabbage palm tree, so I got a rope to throw it around her. I tied the end of the rope to the jeep, and then pulled her down. She was stuck up in that tree for over an hour. She had not been that far off the ground, but I didn't think it would look good for people to ride by and see a lion up in a tree.

Then I went over to the hoof stock section where an Addax needed medication, so I administered the medication through a dart. Then I went to the lion section where two lions also needed medication. Then it was on to Charles' section to help him put up the elephants for the night.

Today Tex is back, so I am now back in my section taking care of my own lions. Abe decided he wanted to go back to the hut after I had already let them all out, so off I went trying to stop him with my jeep. He came charging my jeep and bashed my door in more than it already was. He took off, ran to the hut, and went inside, so I just closed him in for the rest of the day. A little later, another lion went in the head, so Tex, Dan, and I went in after him at eleven o'clock. We finally got him out of there around four in the afternoon.

There were two wildebeest engaging in battle where my lions could see them. That seemed to get my lions all fired up, wanting to get to the wildebeest across the canal. They were sure giving me a workout the whole morning, not wanting to stay where they were supposed to and trying their best to get to those wildebeest. This made for a very interesting morning, but by the afternoon, things seemed to calm down. They all seemed to go to their own special places and lay down and get quiet, but they sure did want to get to those wildebeest this morning. Tex was getting ready for his two weeks' vacation so that would mean I would be in charge.

The next day I went to Giraffe Island for about two hours checking for ticks. I gave shots to some horses and donkeys and then did some blood tests. A horse jumped the fence and went to Pet's Corner and around the restaurants and gift shops. People were running all over the place, women and men alike screaming, the children seemed to be laughing and having a good time chasing the horse. Mr. Brennan and Doc came out of the restaurant, which was by the boats. The horse went in the water so they got into the boat to try to turn the horse back to land. As they got close to the horse, the boat flipped and they both fell out of the boat, scaring the horse back on land. We caught up to the horse and took him back to the stall. I don't really know what Doc and Mr. Brennan did; they stormed off with a trail of water behind them both.

After that episode, I took the photographer around the park to take some pictures. Then at closing time, Smokey the Lion was on the fence trying to get onto Giraffe Island. I went on the island while Dan and Smitty stayed in the section, giving Smokey room. He then came back into the section where he belonged. Then he went into the hut.

I wanted to check on one of the lions that I had to tranquilize the day before. He was from my section, section five, which was being run by someone else while I was in charge. So that day, I told the one running my section that I was going to the hut to check the lion. I asked him if he had all the lions, and he said yes. I drove to the side of the hut, got out of my jeep and walked around to the back of the hut. There was Smokey, one of my lions, walking around the hut. He froze as I was coming around the corner. I was only about five feet from him, so I jumped and yelled. It really startled me, as the ranger had told me he had all the lions where he was watching them.

After working with lions, you soon learn not to close the door on your jeep when you get out, as you might need to get back in the jeep really fast. When the door is open, all you need to do is jump in and close the door behind you. So many times Nonie, our kids and I would go to town shopping or to a movie, and I would get out of the car and leave the door open from habit. Even many times coming home from work, I would go in the house leaving the car door open. Later the kids or Nonie would yell at me, "Close that darn door." So as you probably assumed, I had left the jeep door open. I went running back to my jeep, jumped in closing the door behind me, and taking a nice long deep breath and saying a little prayer.

I started up my jeep and drove around to the back of the hut. There was Smokey running back to the pride. The guy watching the lions was yelling, "Gus, there's a lion loose from the pride, and I don't know where he is." He was yelling over the radio; needless to say, I rode over to his jeep and we had a real serious talk on what to do when someone asks if he has all the lions accounted for. Not only to check them out once, but check them out twice. Believe me before I left, he knew exactly what he was supposed to do. After all of that, the photographer was back and wanted to take pictures of the elephants and rhinos so we moved on to the rest of the day.

Another day, a lion in section four swam across the moat going into section five. He was trying to get into that section's huts. I went to the hut, opened the door, and got back into my jeep. At this time, Charles was bringing the lions to the hut, so I drove around the other side and the lion proceeded to go into the hut. We closed the door, and then we went and got the rolling cage. It has a trailer hitch welded to the cage with wheels on it and the cage sits as low as possible. Instead of lifting the cage into the back of a jeep, it could be rolled up to the hut door getting the lion into the cage and then taking it in the rolling cage back to its own section or hut. All of this could be done without tranquilizing them.

The next day, three lions went from section seven to section six. George, Mr. Pierce, Charles and I started herding them back to section seven. When we start doing this, everyone watches their lions real close and keeps them real tight together as they sometimes get excited when lions start running around, especially in their own section. Between us, we all got them back where they belonged and again without tranquilizing any of them.

The next day after the lion situation, Dale, Charles and I moved three alligators from one pond to another. It was closer to the snake pit in Pet's Corner. One was eight feet; the other two were about two to three feet. We jumped on the eight foot one, taping his mouth and tying up his legs. I then called for a few more people to come help put them in the other pond, which was bigger; this whole process took us about two hours.

We will use the pond we took the alligators from to put some sea lions in. That will be a different experience for us. That day we caught three of them, but decided to wait until the next day to have some more people helping. A day or two later we tried getting the sea lions, we still didn't have the net we ordered but we were able to get two of them so now this left only one.

Charles, Dale, Clyde and I tried to get a lion in the rolling cage from section four's hut to take it to section seven. It just lay there not giving an inch, so I sent Clyde to get some pieces of meat. When he came back, I threw meat in the rolling cage and the lion went in. The door jammed though, and he ran back into the hut. I threw another piece in and he went back for it; this time we were successful closing the door. We then took him to section seven, which was his own section.

A couple of lions got into a fight, one had a big hole in its neck and a bad cut by its eye, which was bleeding really bad, I called Mr. Brennan and told him to get the vet on the phone to come to section five.

The lion really needed medical care, so I said I was going to tranquilize her and take her to the hut. She would be ready for the vet when he got there, so when he arrived the lion was in the hut. He had to clean out the wounds and put stitches in them.

Bill had trouble with Elsa in Smitty's section. We had to go to the head and we couldn't find her so we walked through the swampy section thinking she was there, but she wasn't, then we walked the edge of the head and found her tracks. She had swum to the other side of the canal in her section. Dale and Mr. Pierce had spotted her by her hut. I told them to open the door to the hut and try to put her in. She went in without any problems. They closed the door, and realized it was always nice to do this without tranquilizing them. It is easier on them and us, except we spent over five hours tromping through the head looking for her.

The next day, Mike lost a lion when he got his jeep stuck in a soft spot. It had been raining mostly every day all day long making everything soaked. We looked for her in section three, four and five, but couldn't seem to find her. Mike's section is four and in that section, it is next to the moat that the pump house is that controls the canal water. It is next to the perimeter fences that consist of two chain link fences sixteen feet high by the canal.

We looked for her for a long time. I thought maybe, just maybe, she might have gone into the pump house, so I took a look, finding tracks going into it. The door was open and there she was in all her glory.

I called to Mike to come to the pump house while I loaded the tranquilizer gun. I had a three-fifty-seven on my hip, so we were well prepared. We went to the door; saw her inside lying by one of the motors. There was a fire extinguisher by the door and I thought maybe this would get her out so I set the extinguisher off inside of the pump house. After all the smoke and dust cleared, she was still in the same place, so I just got the tranquilizer gun. With Mike ready with the gun, I stuck my head in the house, and fired the dart. She growled when it hit her, but didn't move. We gave her the usual twenty-minute waiting time, and then we dragged her out of the pump house.

She was covered with grease from all the motors and it was all over the floor, too. She looked like she had been working on cars. I told Mike to go to Pet's Corner to find some cleaner to get all that grease off her before he left for the night. I checked back with him before closing and that was the cleanest lion in all the preserve. I don't think it had ever been that clean only when it was born and its mother cleaned it.

We had three hippos arrive in one day and the fencing wasn't finished around the island, so we had to put them between the two fences at the entrance gate. There are two gates so one will be closed until we get the hippos on the island. As soon as the fencing is done around the island, we will put them in there. Until then we will leave them in the crates, then we will hook up a hose with a fine mist to keep them cool during the day. At night, we will turn the water off. We are hoping they get the fencing done very soon, since we don't want to keep them in the crates for too long. It is too much stress on them.

It took us until nine o'clock that night to get them off the truck and into the other entrance. It was a surprise to us, as they weren't supposed to be in for another week, at which time the fencing would have been completed so we would have been well prepared for them. As you will soon see, a lot of things never went as expected in the "wonderful world of animals," but I was loving it nonetheless.

A few days later, the fencing was completed so we got a boat, dragline and trailer, and we got ready to load three hippos onto the island one at a time. First, we got the dragline to the crates to hook it up and load it on the trailer. We then proceeded to the edge of the water, and then using the dragline, we took the crate from the trailer loading it in the boat at the edge of the water.

Now it was time to transport the hippo over to the island by boat. We had the construction crew put fencing around the island and in the water with a gate, to get animals on and off the island by boat. We opened the gate and drove the boat with the hippo in it to the island.

This boat was a small pontoon boat with a flat bottom. We had a couple of four-by-eight pieces of plywood for them to walk off the boat to the island after we got the boat jammed up on the shore. We had already put hay, fruit and vegetables on the island for them to see when we opened the door to the crate. They really were ready to get out of there so we didn't have any problem at all getting them out. Keep in mind we only transported one hippo at a time. We nailed three pieces of three-quarter inch plywood together so it wouldn't break as the hippos were on it going from the boat to the shore. We repeated this process with all three hippos without any problems at all. It really made for a long day, but all went well without a hitch. We all got into our jeeps heading for the office to check in and go home, at this time it was eight o'clock at night.

All was going well on Hippo Island for about a year, then one day around noon, the man that drove the boat that took people around to Chimp and Gibbon Islands to Hippo Island, called and said a hippo was off the island. He was outside the fence that surrounded the island. Bill York called me to the office; of course, this had never happened in a zoo, being we were the first roam-free park it was the first time it ever happened anywhere, we couldn't call anyone for advice. Bill had some idea of what to do and what to give the hippo to get him back on to the island, and so did I.

I would always run a situation around in my mind before it would happen anyway. It made it so much easier for me to already know what I should do. Things would go so much faster and safer by my doing this. I was usually ready for any emergency that popped up, always remembering when you are working with these animals; you always need at least two different ways to deal with a situation. Knowing what to do if one doesn't work out, "of course sometimes neither worked," and then you have to go just by instinct and any possible way to take care of the situation in a quick and safe way. As it is said, "Get-r done."

Bill asked me what I thought we should do about the situation. I told him that first we should find out where the hippo got out of the fence into the water. Bill said he thought so, too, so off we went to see if we could find out where he got out before we had two other hippos on the loose.

We proceeded to go in the boat and see how the hippo got out and try to fix it. We got there and found out where he got out. We had some wardens fix the fence, while some were watching the hippo in the water, keeping it contained. We went back to the office to figure out what kind of tranquilizer to give him and how much to give him, and also try to figure out how we were going to get him back on the island after we tranquilized him without drowning him.

Bill made a few calls to some animal people telling them the situation we had on our hands. No one seemed to be able to help us with anything. As it was, now the hippo was in the water so we had to be very careful that we didn't give him too much tranquilizer that he would drown, so we had to rely on our best judgment.

We had five wardens with us, but every time the hippo would come up and out of the water for air, we didn't have enough time to shoot the tranquilizer. Bill and I were each in a boat with a warden, waiting for the hippo to come up again and stay up long enough so we could dart him. He finally came up by Bill, and he got a dart in him. We waited for the hippo to get to the point where we could handle him in the water and that he wouldn't go down under the water so far that he would drown. If that should happen, we would all dive in the water, grab him and try to pull him to the shore. He got to acting as if the tranquilizer was starting to take effect, but not enough for us to get him back to the Island. I got a shot off at him with more of the tranquilizer that we used mostly on primates, but it worked well on cheetahs, lions and hopefully hippos.

Still after I shot him with more, he still wasn't under enough. By this time, it was eight in the evening and too late to do anything with him. We had worked from one-thirty until eight, and we still didn't get him on the island. We left vegetables, fruit and hay on the island thinking he might go back to the island by himself. We also left two wardens there for the night as the hippo didn't act like he was going anywhere, and we told them to call both of us if he started to leave the pond or got into trouble for any reason whatsoever.

The next morning, two hippos were in the parking lot walking around with the two wardens trying to get them back to the pond by the island. The one that we tranquilized the day before was back to normal, and the others broke out of the fence. We had been having a lot of rain the last month, and the water in the pond had gotten higher than normal, just enough so that the hippos could slide over the top of the fence. We first thought there was a hole in the fence. We decided to pump some of the water out of the pond to get the water level back to normal again.

The hippos were just walking around in the parking lot, not getting excited at all. Nonie, Joe and Erik were with me, so they had a ringside seat to see all that was going on. Needless to say, this was quite exciting for my sons to be able to watch what their daddy was doing and to see the hippos walking around. We used a rope from beside the meat house, and I got the rope around one hippo's neck. I didn't have time to get the dart gun and load it, so we tried the rope but he slipped it off his neck. He was just standing there not excited or anything, so I got the rope around him again.

Bill, Mac and I, along with two other wardens, were holding on to the rope when he started for the pond, running as if we weren't even holding him. He was speeding up, and as he hit the water, the rope slid off his neck. All we saw was his backside as he left us standing at the water's edge. He was somewhere out there in the pond, thinking, "I sure fooled them."

Now it was time to regroup with Bill and the two men in his boat. I had two men in my boat with me, and Bill and I each had a dart gun. We stayed a short distance from each other while searching for the two hippos that were under the water somewhere. We got six cc's of tranquilizer in one hippo, and he started to go by a bridge at Pet's Corner where the water was about four to seven feet deep. The middle of the pond was about eight or ten feet deep. He got by the bridge and bubbles started coming up a lot more, but then they all of a sudden stopped moving forward and stayed in the same place. The hippo was starting to drown.

We all six dove into the water, down to the hippo where the bubbles were coming up. We pulled his head above the water. As we were bringing it to the land by the bridge, we had a hard time holding his head up while we tried to get him to shore. This wasn't the island, but it was dry land.

A lot of people were on the bridge and all around it watching us wrestling with this hippo. We were not making a lot of headway. We all saw Willy the meat man on the bridge with all the people watching us. Bill yelled to Willy to come help us.

Well, Willy said, "Yes, sir," and dove off the bridge into the water. Then he started waving his arms and splashing around, slipping under the water and coming back up again waving his arms. We then realized Willy was drowning. A couple of us swam to Willy while the others were moving the hippo to land.

By this time, we were in about three feet of water with a hippo and could hold him up and walk to shore with him. We got Willy out of the water and stayed with him until he got his breath. Once he was okay, we had him help us with the hippo.

We were a good hour in the water with the hippo. We slid a four by eight sheet of plywood under him while he was at the edge of the shore, and then with a thick rope, we started to tie him to the plywood. As we were doing this, he started to come out of the drug, and was getting his strength back. He was trying to stand up now, so we gave him some more tranquilizer by hand. We wrapped the rope around him and the wood, and we used the tractor with a front-end loader on it to lift the hippo and the plywood onto the pontoon boat that was at the edge of the water.

We slid him safely on the board, and then transported him to the island. Once we had him to the island, we dragged him out away from the water, untied him from the plywood, and left two men to watch over him. They each had radios so they could call us if needed, keeping in mind that he was still under the tranquilizer.

Bill and I wanted to be alerted when he started coming out from under the tranquilizer. We loaded the plywood, rope, and other stuff we had used back on the pontoon boat. We headed back to the shore to tie the boat up. We all decided to sit down on the shore and talk over all that had happened while we were getting the hippo to the island. We all agreed it could have turned out a lot worse than it did.

Bill then asked Willy what in the world was wrong with him when he jumped in the water and started splashing all around. Willy said, "When Bill told me to jump in the water and help, I didn't think it was as deep as it was," but the way Bill had yelled at him, he figured he had better jump in, so he did. We all got a good laugh.

Willy was looking at us grinning, saying you all are crazy, for what we were doing with the hippo. He said we all had to be nuts diving in the water with a hippo; that to him meant we were crazy enough to do anything. He didn't want us getting mad at him, and that's why he dove in the water when Bill told him to.

We all had a long, hard day and it was time to go home. The two wardens were on the island that we left there with the hippo, and we left two wardens with the hippo in the pond.

Tomorrow was another day, we will try to get the one out of the pond and back to the island where he belonged. Hopefully, we won't have to go through what we did today again with this hippo. It took us almost ten hours, being in the water for over an hour.

You get a little on edge when you tranquilize an animal in the water to immobilize it, where you can keep it under control without anyone getting hurt. Also without hurting the animal in anyway, when everything comes out good like it did today, that's when you say, "Thank You, Lord," in the back of your mind that you hope all goes as well tomorrow.

The next morning, I had Charles, Mac, Vern, and Ron come in early so we could get with the hippo in the pond before too many people got to Pet's Corner and over by the bridge. Bill was off today so he wasn't there to help. I had told him yesterday that we would get him today and he wouldn't need to get wet, but I also said you would miss all the fun going swimming again with a confused hippo. Bill said he would live by missing all of that.

We got everything ready, Mac with me in one boat, Vern with Ron in another boat with Charles. We started looking for the hippo. It came up not too far from our boat, and I shot it with the tranquilizer gun. The hippos were all about the same size, so I knew how much tranquilizer to give this one today. The hippo started going to the same spot, right where the other one went yesterday so we didn't push him. He got about fifteen feet from shore, and then he started to sink and come back up. He turned sideways and went under the water again. We saw the bubbles, I yelled, "He's down, so let's get him."

We all dove into the water, and this time we were lucky, as he was real close to the shore. In only about three feet of water, we could stand on the bottom to walk him to land. We got the plywood under him, putting the rope around him so he wouldn't fall off the plywood, pulling the pontoon boat next to the shore and loading him on the boat as we did the other one yesterday. We pulled him to the center of the boat, and we headed toward the island. We put him on the island with the other two and all three of them were together again. We cleaned up all our mess, putting the boat where it belonged. Vern stayed with the hippo on the island until he came out from under the tranquilizer. In addition, to make sure everything was okay for the night, and then he would go to the hoof stock to feed. We finished up at three o'clock, another long day.

We started working as soon as the sun came up this morning. Mac and Ron went to their lion sections to finish the day; Charles and I went to help feed the elephants and chained them up for the night. It had been two very exciting days for us, a good learning experience, and we would surely remember. The next day I checked the hippos; all three seemed to be doing just fine on their own little island.

I don't need to tell you that we checked the water level almost daily after those two day's experiences.

ELEPHANT WITH TRUNK RAISED

Chapter 8

Exciting Days with the Animals

In the office one day, Al, the mechanic, and Mike, who worked the Lions, got into an argument. As they were arguing, Smitty decided to jump in the middle of it all, so Mike slugged Smitty in the face. Needless to say, he was fired. Mike is a good animal man, and I hated to lose him, but there was nothing I could do to stop it. After all, he had hit Smitty.

After this episode, I went on Chimp Island to finish a shelter for a new chimp coming in. All went well until five, which was closing time. "These lions know that it's time for us to go home." One of Mr. Pierce's lions decided to go to the head, after we closed the park, we went over to get her. While we were all tromping through the head, I almost stepped on a cottonmouth moccasin about three feet long. I called on the radio, saying that I was going to shoot the snake. I did this so everyone that was not on the head would know if they heard the shot what was going on. I didn't want them to think we were having trouble with the lion. Not too long after that, we found the lion. After we tranquilized her and returned to the section, we put her in the hut to sleep it off.

One morning Flar-up started fighting with Red. When I opened the hut door, Red went out of the hut running to a tree with Flar-up right behind him. Red decided to go straight up the tree with no effort whatsoever. She went about twenty feet up the darn tree, so I decided to get a BB rifle out and go after Flar-up. I took aim and shot her in the thigh. This doesn't penetrate the lion's skin; it just irritates them, making them forget what they were doing. I wanted her to forget about Red up the tree so she could come down. After hitting Flar-up a couple of times, she finally gave up, went to the rest of the pride, and laid down with them, forgetting all about Red.

Using a BB gun is so much better than having to tranquilize them. We backed up our jeeps so to give Red some room, and it wasn't long before she started to come down from the tree. When her butt hit the ground, she took off running straight to the hut. I decided to leave her in for the rest of the day.

At closing, one of Smitty's lions swam the moat and went in the head; Smitty put the rest of his lions up. He moved them to one section closing the center door between the two sections in his hut, and he then opened the outside door. At the same time this was going on, Wayne couldn't get the giraffes to go into their huts. They were running all over the island; going everywhere except into their hut. We kept trying but couldn't get them to go in, so we left them alone, considering that they might hurt themselves if we kept pushing them. We left them out for the night. Then we hurried back to Smitty's section to go in the head for his lion, but the lion decided to come back on his own and went straight into the hut. We locked the door and opened the center door, so all was back to normal once again.

The next day, Flare-up and Red were doing all right, each going to their favorite spot to lie down; thank goodness, Red's favorite spot wasn't up that tree again. Now it's approaching closing time and, of course, as many times before, trouble starts. The giraffes wouldn't go in, so

I decided to leave them alone. However, this time it was not to feed them, thinking this might make them want to go into their hut. We'd have to wait and see.

On this day, Sonny was cleaning out a lion hut in section seven, and when he was finished, he left the section, forgetting to close the door outside and open the center door. All the lions were on one side as he was cleaning the hut. When Sonny left the section to go to another one, George saw the lions that were supposed to be inside their huts. Of course, they all decided to go on the head at one time right by George's section.

We went into the head, getting them all tranquilized. I don't need to tell you it was an experience, looking for seven lions on a head at one time. It was really crowded in that head, with lions in front of us and lions behind us. As soon as I would tranquilize one, someone would take it back to the hut, and we started looking for another one. We had started looking for these lions the first thing in the morning and by two o'clock, we had walked the head and tranquilized seven lions. As soon as we finished getting all of these lions back to the huts and bedded down with hay, two more lions went on another head in section four, so off to the heads once again.

I was able to find one in about thirty minutes; the second one, when I shot her with the dart gun, she turned around and charged us. As she got about half way to us, she turned and went the other way. We tried to listen for where she had gone as it had been raining everyday for some time now, and water was all over the head. We could hear her running through the water and bushes and the tall grass, so we waited about ten minutes before going in to find her. When most of the lions go down from the drug, they lay down with their head on a bush or clump of grass, making their head above water. This head was full of water, and she had done just that. When we found her, there she was, with her head on a little bush. We took her back to the section, put her in with the other one in a separate section of the hut, and left them there for the night, and most of the next day. I couldn't believe that we had tranquilized nine lions and put them in huts until they came out of the tranquilizer. We did this all in one day's time.

Charles was getting in more elephants from Pet's Corner, and he planned to walk them from there through the back way, which went through section six and section seven. He was taking them to Elephant Island, which is in my section, and he was going to do this before we opened the park to the public. In section seven, many of the lions are left out at night, as most of them are young ones or ones that don't mix well with other lions, but they don't seem to mind the younger ones.

We tried to get all the lions in the hut, and were successful except for one, Miss Crook. I had her in my section for a long time, but every other lion wanted to fight with her for some reason. I really hated losing her but didn't want to see the other lions fight with her all the time. When they all joined in, they could really hurt her, so it was for the best. We darted her, then she started walking by the canal in the section as the tranquilizer was taking affect. She stumbled and fell into the canal, went under the water, and we could see bubbles but no Miss Crook. Tex looked in his jeep for a rope, and since I was closest to her, I took off my boots, took my wallet out of my pocket, and dove in to try to save her. She was almost out of it when she fell in the water.

I was following the bubbles and trying to feel for her with my feet, then the bubbles stopped, but I kept trying to find her. During this time Tex, Mac, George and Bill all came in and were helping to find her, too. Bill found her and started yelling, "I feel her." We all swam over to him and got her out of the water. We tried to revive her for quite some time, but it was evident that it was too late. She was gone, and every one of us felt really bad. I really was feeling bad that we didn't get her in time, but we tried our best. I shed many tears over Miss Crook. She had a special place in my heart, and many of us men shed tears for our lions if we lost them; they are like kids to us. She had been in my section for a long time. I had named her for the crook that she had in her tail. After we had taken care of Miss Crook, section six and section five were both clear of any lions being out. It was now clear for Charles to bring the elephants through to the Elephant Island. All went well, and when they were safely on the island, we opened the park about thirty minutes late.

The next day, at closing time the last car was in my section and Elsa went for a stroll along the canal bank and then ran to the head. Caesar was following her because she was in season. I put the rest of my lions in the hut, and pushed them all to one side of the hut. I called Tex to tell him I had Caesar and Elsa on the head. He said that Charles was having trouble with the new punk elephants and for me to go help him, and that he and Dan would go after the two lions in the head.

As I got to Elephant Island, Charles was having a real hard time with one of the new elephants. He had gone in the canal around the island, then broken through the fence in the middle of the canal and was in my section, which was section five. Thank goodness, I had all the lions put in the hut, except for Elsa and Caesar who were in the head. Charles and I dove in the canal and swam through the broken fence after the elephant. We finally turned her around and when she got back to Elephant Island, she got to the canal bank, which was three feet higher than the water. She jumped in the water, and all we could see was her trunk. She was on the other side on the island, but she found the other elephants so we just let her calm down before we chained her for the night.

When Charles and I got finished with the elephants, Tex and Dan had tranquilized Elsa, and then brought her back to the hut. Caesar was back in section five running to the hut so we opened the door and he went in. We pushed him to the other side with the rest of the pride, and were finally done for the day. For three days after, Elsa was not coming out of the tranquilizer too well, so we gave her some medication, but she still acted as if she was really spaced out. We found out that she took a lot longer to come out from under it then most lions did.

Today was the day that we had four goats arriving. We put them on one of the heads to see what they could do to them. We were hoping that they would eat all or most of the vegetation on the head, so when a lion got on the head it wouldn't be so hard to find them. These heads are so thick with vegetation and underbrush that you can't see more then fifteen feet in front of you in places. In addition, when a lion gets on the head, they won't really be interested in getting the goats, which will stay as far away from the lions as possible most of the time.

On the same day, one of Mr. Pierce's lions went on

Rhino Island. Gus, the Rhino, was running all over the island. The lion went in the rhino barn, but Tex was waiting for her and shot her with a dart. She ran into Gus's yard, and he started chasing her. She went into the canal and jumped through the metal fence in the middle of the canal, then back to her pride where she settled down. Then when the tranquilizer started working, we put her in the jeep and took her back to the hut until she would come out of it.

The next day when I got in the park there were two hippos, four lions, and an elephant waiting to be unloaded. Charles and I walked the elephant to Pets' Corner. We moved the lions into section two by themselves in one section of the hut, waiting until later to mix them with the others. Then on we went to Hippo Island, where the crane was, to lift the hippo over onto the island.

After that was all finished, I loaded the tranquilizer gun to go after a zebra that was all messed up from the other Zebras biting, scratching and bruising her. We needed to tranquilize her to give her medication so she wouldn't get any infections. I missed the first time I shot because she was running back and forth like crazy. I loaded the dart up again and the second shot was good, so we got her to the hut and administered medication to her and kept her away from the others for a few days. When I finished for the day, Nonie and the boys were waiting outside for me to go home and get a good night's sleep, so I could start all over in the morning.

The next day, we moved lions from Pet's Corner to section seven with the young lions. We then moved the lions we had tranquilized a few days earlier back to section six. All went well until closing until once again one of the lions of Mr. Pierce that went on Rhino Island decided to go there again. I guess she wanted to visit Gus, but she didn't stay long. She left there going into the head, so here we go again, looking for her so we could tranquilize her. We found her without too much trouble, and when we darted her, she started to charge us. She was almost at the halfway point where we were going to have to protect ourselves, when just at that time; she turned and went deeper into the head. We waited for about fifteen minutes, and as we were about to go after her, Tex almost stepped on a cottonmouth moccasin. We got a tree branch and killed the snake. Upon finding the lion, Tex pushed her with his gun and she came halfway up, and then laid back down again. We decided to give her ten more minutes, after the time period was up before we loaded her in the jeep. We took her back to section six to bed her down with the hay to sleep off the tranquilizer.

This one day when we came in, Smitty's lions were all out of the hut, some were in the head, others all over the section. Bill watched his section the day before, as Smitty was off work, and Bill didn't lock the hut door at closing. Smitty was fit to be tied about Bill not locking the door. We got all of his lions back except for the two on the head. It took about three hours, but we got them in the hut. Not long after that, I went to my section where Dot had two cubs the night before. She was still in the hut with the whole pride.

It was a real surprise, as she wasn't due for another two and a half weeks. I was careful moving the other lions and Dot to the other side of the hut and closing the door. I got some hay at the barn, put it on the floor, moved the cubs onto the hay, and made sure not to get my scent on them. Once I got them in place, I let Dot back in with them, and then proceeded to let the others out in the section. In the afternoon, I went to check on Dot and one of the cubs had died, so I pulled the other one from her, as she wasn't taking very good care of them. I took it to Pet's Corner where they would bottle feed it and take care of it.

The feed trailer slipped off the ball of the tractor again today. Bill was in it and it almost went in the canal by Chimp Island. He said it was a wild ride, all of a sudden, the tongue of the trailer bounced off the ball and was bouncing on the road and the tractor was getting on down the road. They were making small turns and he said he was just hanging on for the ride. It finally stopped about twelve feet from the canal, and we then decided we had better get the right size ball for the tractor so we wouldn't have this problem anymore.

Red has been giving us a fit for the last three weeks; she doesn't get along with anyone of the pride. They will usually start a fight with her or her with them, she won't go out of the hut, and when we finally get her out, and she will either go into a head or back to the hut. Then we have to go hunt her down and tranquilize her. We have done this at least ten times in the last four weeks. We have tried everything we could think of to straighten her out. The last time she went out of the hut, five lions were fighting with her, and she ran for the island again. Tex, Charles, Dan and I went on the head and tracked her down. It was really wet over there, as it had been raining a lot. We saw her lying over on a high spot. Tex got her with the dart and she turned to go the other way.

We found her a few days before this and decided she should go to another section, so we put her in section seven with the younger lions, hoping that they would treat her better. If she stayed in my section, we were afraid that my lions would eventually kill her, especially when they were put up for the night in the hut, with no one being there to watch. We loaded her in the jeep, taking her to the section with all the younger lions. She seemed to be very content now, and I felt really good about that as it was getting to be a big problem. Now another problem was solved. So here we go, "On to the next one."

The lions in Bates's section were fighting just before we were to open, so he got on the radio and was calling for help. They were all fighting in the hut and he had no control; he couldn't get them to stop. The tractor man that had the pump to clean huts came over and put the hose in the canal then starting the pump for water. As we were pushing two lions with a pole, using a BB gun, and also shooting blanks with the shotgun into the hut, they all stopped fighting except two male lions. Nothing we tried seemed to help, even with the water pressure shot it in their mouths and ears. One just seemed to get a tighter grip on the other's neck and roll with him trying to break his neck, and also to smother him. We finally got him to let go of the other one's neck, with spraying the water and everything else we were using. We got all of the lions in the other side of the hut except for the one he was choking. We got the center door closed so we could get to the other lion, but by the time we got to him, he was dead. We all felt bad but we sure did our best to save him.

Another lion from section seven went in the head, so Tex, Charles, Dan and I went on the head to get him back. We saw two cottonmouth mocassins, and I almost stepped on one. His mouth was open ready to strike, when Charles

118

yelled, "SNAKE!" I looked down and there he was, always when you are on a head looking for a lion you are very conscious of snakes being around, if you see one, you yell Snake so everyone will be looking down. Then if you see a lion coming towards you, you yell Lion, so everyone will look around to see where it is. I always made sure if a new man came on the island with us that he understood, what we did if someone saw a lion or a snake.

It is very dangerous if we all don't understand the situation and what the rule was for hunting on a head. We saw the lion and that Tex couldn't get a good shot, but thought he had hit her. She went to the other side of the head, and we waited fifteen minutes for the drug to take effect. Then we went looking for her. We weren't having any luck finding her, and it started pouring down rain really hard. It was getting as dark as night in the head, and it started getting very windy, too, so we decided to get off the head. All the lion men were having problems with their lions so all of us went to help them get control.

When it calmed down, we went back to the head to try to find the lion. We didn't seem to have any luck, after we looked for about three hours, the rain and wind and darkness came in on us again, so we decided to get out of there and go help the men get their lions up. They were all getting anxious to get to their huts so we got them all in. We left the door open to the hut where the lion that was on the head was supposed to go, in case she came back. We had all the others in a separate part of the hut.

The next morning we came in, went to the hut where the lion came from, and lo and behold, there she was lying down. We closed the door and opened the one between and the other lions went to her and rubbed all over each other. We decided then Tex must have missed hitting her with the dart, because if he had hit her, she would still be on the head. If she had gone down in the water, she would probably have drowned. She was all ready to go out into the section with the pride again this morning.

Later that day, an eland, which is the largest antelope, went from section one, the hoof stock section, through the gate into section two. Smitty called Tex, who brought Charles along, and they started working the eland back to section one. Smitty was working his lions away from the eland. Smitty did really well keeping his lions in line away from the eland, but seems like each time one of the antelope got through the gate, his lions were just that much closer to getting one of them.

Buck Shot, one of my lions, seemed to attack my jeep for about four days. Peggy, one of the females, was in season, so Buck Shot was fighting all the males that came around, including my jeep. When I would get close to her, he would attack my jeep, biting a hole in the hood, squashing my loud haler like a marshmallow. It still works even though he put a couple of holes in my fender and scratched my door. I was sure glad to have the bars on the windows when he would start getting really bad, attacking the jeep. I got a little rough with him, now he sees my jeep coming and he backs off from it, my jeep looks like the front and sides were shot with a shotgun where he had put so many holes in it.

About a week ago, we had two new chimps arrive in the park. Mac and I took the chimps to the island, and put them in a small hut to hold them. We went over there to release them a few days ago, and now today we went by boat to the island. As we neared the island, one of the new chimps tried to get me as I was getting out of the boat. I held a box of food in front of me and yelled at him, and then picked up a big stick going after him. He ran about ten feet away from me, and then he picked up a rock and turned around. He threw that rock right at me. It almost hit me, too! He had a really good aim and a great arm. Mac and I sure got a good laugh out of that. We put the food out and he was okay then. I know he was just testing me to see what I was going to do when he challenged me.

The next day, I got all of my lions in the hut, when Buck Shot started fighting with Caesar. I got one of the wood poles and started tapping him on the rear thigh a couple of times. He turned around and hit the pole with his paw and the pole hit me on the chin, knocking me off the cement slab and it almost knocked me out. They were still fighting, so I started hitting him and Caesar a little harder. They stopped fighting, as I was rubbing my chin, I thought I saw Buck Shot smiling at me, as if to say, "I paid you back for when you tapped me with the jeep the other day." It put a little smile on my face, but just a little one.

It has been four days now, and Buck Shot is still fighting with all the lions. Peggy is still in season, so every chance he gets, he still tries to eat my jeep up. I will have to make him respect the jeep when the time is right. This isn't good, not being able to control him when he tries to attack my jeep all the time. In a few days, he and I will have to go a few rounds, then he will calm down and respect me again...or should I say my jeep?

One of Dan's lions was bit on the paw, by a cottonmouth moccasin, and his foot swelled about twice the normal size. Tex gave him some medication and the next day it was still swollen, but it did look a little better. I gave him some more medication, checking it the next day and found it was almost back to normal.

The next morning, one lion was out in section four, but she belonged in my section five. She wouldn't go back to my section, so I tranquilized her and brought her back to the hut. We checked the rope on the door and it looked like one of them had been chewing on it. We had to think of a better way of opening and closing the door. Maybe that is what happened in Smitty's section, Zoo stayed in his section and he said he counted all the lions twice before he left for the night, and the next morning, two were out.

Mr. Dredge, the general manager, called me into the office. He introduced me to Randall Eaton. Mr. Eaton had been in Africa on a grant. Randy, as we would all be calling him, was studying cheetahs in Africa for a year or more, and he was planning to write a book all about cheetahs. He was also interested in studying all about lions, being this was the first roam-free animal park of its kind; he wanted to study them here in this environment, to compare it to the environment in Africa. After doing this, he wanted to write a book on the comparison of it all. We had been told by people from Africa that our lions and animals are all acting just the same as they do in Africa, the only difference was that their territory was on a smaller scale. So Mr. Dredge said, since I was the first American warden at the park, he wanted me to drive him around the park, also to my section, telling him all about the park. He wanted to know how the lions act in general, all the problems we've had since we opened the park. He would ride with me for a couple of days, and during this time, we would go to different lion prides in different sections. We mostly studied my lions in his own vehicle that had a sunroof. He would pull up by the pride to study them, not too close though, as he didn't want to disturb any of them. This was the purpose of studying while they were doing things naturally. For the next few days, we had some real interesting talks on his experiences in Africa and mine here at Lion Country, my hunting in the everglades in an airboat, and in a swamp buggy. I really enjoyed him riding with me; I wished him good luck on his book.

At closing time, Greg had trouble in section five. I went to give him a hand, and as we put the lions up, when counting them, he was one short. I told him to put all the lions in one side, then go look for the missing lion. I was trying to open the outside door to the empty side of the hut in case the lion came back to the hut, he just might, with any luck, go inside.

I pulled on the rope from inside my jeep, put the rope on the door, and then grabbed the door, opening it up. Much to my surprise, all of the lions were just staring at me; he had put them all in the wrong side. What a surprise I had! Standing there right in front of me was Buck Shot, who all of a sudden, decided he wanted to go after me. I slammed the door shut in his face, and I ran and jumped into my jeep. This was one of those times that you are really glad that the rule is to leave your jeep door open when you get out of it. I jumped in shutting the door real quick and starting my jeep up, pulling it up to the door so that the door couldn't open. I got out of my jeep and locked the hut door.

The lion that wasn't accounted for was over by Elephant Island and on the moat. I drove on the moat, telling Zoo, Greg and Smitty to move the lions to the other side of the hut and open the other outside door, then to pull away from the hut. As I was pushing Peggy to the hut, she jumped into the canal, swimming to the other side, getting out of the water and running right inside the hut. Smitty pulled up to the door and closed it. Peggy was finally inside the hut without having to tranquilize her, which is always a great feeling. It's better for all of us, lions included, and everyone was safe. Boy, I sure don't need to tell you what a surprise I had when I opened that door and found the whole pride of lions looking at me. I think they were as surprised to see me, as I was to see them. After this situation, I had a talk with Greg, letting him know which side of the hut we put these lions on when we have trouble with them.

The lions from Dan's section were loose this morning. They had decided to take a stroll going to one of the heads. Tex, Charles and I went to the head to find them and were able to dart the first one. As we were pursuing her, we spotted the other one. We thought we would have to shoot her as she was really watching us, growling and hissing with her ears laid back, jerking her tail back and forth. We gave her a minute to calm down, but she kept looking like a spring ready to uncoil and leap on us. Tex shot his dart gun, and when the dart hit her, she charged us, almost passing the halfway mark before turning and going the other way. We were so glad she did, as we didn't want to shoot her. Another rule is that if they come over what we consider the half way mark, we are to shoot to kill, as it will be either them or one of us. To shoot them is all we have to defend ourselves from a charging lion. We waited about ten minutes then started looking for both of them. We found one, and decided to take it back in the jeep to the hut. We looked in the hut that we were going to put her in, and there was the other one we had tranquilized earlier. She tried to get to Tex as we were bringing in the other one to put her in there, but she was out of it enough that she couldn't get up; she just watched us bringing in her partner in crime.

Later, George in section six had a lion go on Chimp Island and one on the head. Charles and Tex got them back. Then again, at closing time, Bill let five lions into section four, not knowing it, until Zoo wanted to know whose lions were in his section. We got three back to the hut okay, but two decided to go on the head so away we go, Charles and I to the head to tranquilize them and bring them back to the hut.

Donya, the elephant, decided to act up again today. She pushed a tree over, and then destroyed it. She then turned on Dale trying to get him, but he was too fast for her, so she wasn't able to get him. She did a headstand to show him how bad she really was. Sometimes an elephant will raise its trunk up in the air, wanting you to pat their tongue. When that happens, watch their trunk as it is up in the air. If it tightens the end up in a ball, look out, as they are ready to come down with their trunk to zap you with enough force to knock you down between their front legs, and then do a headstand on you. If their trunk is hanging down and they start to roll the end in a small ball, look out again. They are going to sling their trunk at you, knocking you down to the ground. When you are chaining them up for the night, or unchaining them in the mornings, you have to watch them closely, as they will try to crush you up against the wall. Donya tried all these tricks, and she had hurt six or seven people, putting them in the hospital for days. She seemed to be getting meaner as time went by. Bill York said we might have to put her down if she didn't straighten out, before she hurt, or killed someone. We had to watch her really close to see what would happen. A few days later, Dale had trouble with Donya again. There were some ducks flying around the island. Dale said they flew around her and scared the devil out of her, so she wouldn't go in the barn; Charles had to put her in and chain her for the remainder of the afternoon.

I got a call from the office that a couple had lost their dog bringing it out of the kennel. They were all upset, so I got a couple of wardens to come help. We were going everywhere, looking in the woods by Pets' Corner, looking until seven that night, and we still couldn't find the dog. We were hoping it would come back that night. I told the couple to leave a shirt or something with their scent on it so in case the dog might come back, if it did it would most likely lay down on whatever they left and stay until they came back in the morning. So they did just that, and the next morning when we came in, lo and behold, there was the dog lying on the shirt by the kennel. I went to the office, called them to tell them that their dog was there, and they came right out and picked up their dog. They couldn't thank us enough.

The next day, Dale had a problem with the ducks flying around Donya again, making her go crazy. We had to put her up and chain her, so the following day before opening, Tex shot the ducks, saying, "Now let's see if she will be okay." You know you have to be a little concerned when tons of elephant get upset, and you have to try and right the situation before someone gets hurt.

The breaking of a new day, with all the lions behaving well, some sleeping, some looking around and some playing. All of a sudden, I heard people yelling over by the Elephant Island, and I noticed there was smoke coming out of their car. I started the jeep to go over to them, and as I was driving up to them, there were five people out of the car throwing sand on it to put out the fire. I told them they needed to get back in their car. I called a tractor to come out to take them to the mechanic shop to see if they could help them or to call someone else. They sure were glad to get back on the outside of the park again. They said they didn't know what to do when the car was on fire; they didn't want to stay in the car and be burned up, but they also didn't like the other choice of getting out of the car and being eaten by lions. I told them that it was a good thing it happened by Elephant Island, away from the lions. They said that's what was scary for them, as they didn't know where the lions were.

One day when Tex was off, Mr. Pierce called me to his section. When I got to his jeep, he was grinning. He said, "Look what that lion is doing." One was by itself over by Gus, the Rhino, just looking at him. Mr. Pierce said he would do that two or three times a day, just sit there staring at Gus on the island. I told him he had better keep a close watch on him because he might want to eat him up. He was not looking at him out of love for him. Mr. Pierce said, "I really think he likes Gus, as he just lies there and looks at him, he hasn't tried to attack him." Mr. Pierce said people would stop to take some pictures of the lion gazing at the rhino.

I had some medication I needed to give to one of

the lions. I had been giving her shots for a couple of days now, so when she saw me come in my jeep, she would run from me. I would get out of my jeep and get in with Mr. Pierce and he would drive me close enough to her for me to shoot the dart at her. It went half way to her, hit the ground, bouncing up in the air, hitting her where I was aiming, and the co2 was low and had no 'ump.' We both got a real good laugh out of that. I told him I was trying to hit her the hard way, but that he dare not tell anyone that this happened.

A photographer was in today with Tex. We put some lions on the moat by Giraffe Island. AC got his lions in line with the giraffe, but I wasn't happy with putting the lions on the moat as we try to keep them off there. But this was for television or some advertising for Lion Country. I still didn't like doing this, seems like when they come in with their cameras, films and all the equipment, things started to get more complicated and dangerous. Then we would be left with a mess while they would get in their cars and go to the restaurant to talk about the great shots they had gotten. We would be staying late at night to get it all straightened out and back to normal.

Tex was off, so I checked on Sonny's lion that got in a fight yesterday. It was cut up a little, but it wasn't as bad as it looked. Her pride was hurt more than anything else.

Mac and I went to the airport to pick up some lions; we got back at eleven in the morning. An eland was having a baby, and the baby's feet were about ten inches out and the mommy was having a hard time with the baby so I called Doc Kidder, the vet. When he arrived, I took him to the eland. As we were pulling up to her, the calf was out on the ground, and the mother was starting to clean it up. Everything looked okay, so we then put the little one and mommy in an enclosed area by the antelope section. This was built for things like this. Mommy followed us in, and they both were now safe and sound. Sometimes with a newborn baby, the zebras would try to kill the baby. By doing this, it's much safer for both of them, so we will leave them in there for a month or two. It's just a chain link fence that they can see other animals through, but the others can't get to them. Roger was already bringing them food and hay so they will be just fine.

GUARDING DAN AS HE PUTS WATER INTO A TOURIST´S OVERHEATED CAR

**RELAXING WITH CHARLES AT
THE END OF A LONG DAY**

**TWO RHINOS FACE OFF AS TOURIST
TRAFFIC PASSES IN THE BACKGROUND**

RHINO ENJOYING THE WATER IN A CANAL

Chapter 9

Friends for Life
Lions, Antelope, Rhino, and Chimps

George called on the radio. A lion had gone on the head. Charles and I walked three heads, only finding tracks. Bill York called on the radio, saying he wanted to help us find her. He said, "We get to have all the fun," while he was stuck in the office all the time. I said, "Just come on over." We waited for him by the canal where we parked our jeeps. When he got there, we checked the three heads again and came up with no lions. We didn't find any clues or lions from twelve thirty to four thirty. Finally, we found her. I tranquilized her and we put her in the jeep, taking her back to the hut. Bill York was the zoology director and he spent a lot of time in the office talking to people about animals and doing public relations. He was responsible for getting in new animals and making sure everything comes together. He would call me to his office. We would then take a walk down the two-mile stretch. This seemed to help us figure out our problems with the animals, along with all the other problems of the world. We had worked together for so long that we knew what the other was doing and thinking. There was rarely a misunderstanding in the fifteen years we worked together. Sometimes, we worked in different parks. We worked all of the new parks before opening of them and sometimes after opening. We both were Airborne Paratroopers, Special Forces in the service. That was a bond between us. He was like an older brother and a super friend to me, along with being someone who I highly respected. He was someone of whom I trusted with my life, and he was someone who trusted me with his, also. That happened many times in our history of working together with all these wild animals. We had this bond throughout our lives of knowing each other, Bill moved to Oregon and the miles separated us, but we still remained friends, keeping in touch with photos and cards at holidays. Bill has since passed on, I must say I lost a special friend, and this world lost a wonderful well experienced, much loved animal man, he is in a much better place than this world now. I will forever carry the memories of us working, laughing and crying together, he was an important part of my animal history, before his passing he wrote a couple of books, of which I have both, one is called Out in the Midday Shade, the other is African Adventures and Misadventures, both are a great read. As I am talking about friends, Charles comes to mind, he became a good friend, someone I could depend on and trust. We had many talks in our time of working with each other. For many years he was my right hand man, I knew that we went into the heads, over two hundred times, walking through the water, all kinds of brush along with a lot of snakes, we weathered all of this, to tranquilize lions, we tranquilized as many as nine lions in a head all at once. We became close as Bill and I were, it was a very good feeling and a rare one, knowing that you have had two men that had your back as Bill and Charles did mine, and knowing they felt the same about me.

When I introduced myself to a ranger from Africa who came over by boat with eighteen rhino's for Lion Country, I told him my name was Gus. He said, "Yes I have heard of you, and that you were considered one of the top five men in the world that had gone in after and tranquilized as many lions as I had in the bush." This really surprised me, but at the same time made me feel good. What a rush that was, and most of the time when this went on, Charles was with me. The only time that he wasn't with me was on his days off. We couldn't make those lions stay off the heads until he got back, so sometimes I would have to go in without him, which was very uncomfortable, as we learned to trust each other knowing the other covered our backs. No matter what happened, good or bad, we were always there side by side. He was always the one I called, as he was able to leave the elephants for a while to help me.

As time went on and in our last couple of years of working together, I would call Charles, asking for help once again tracking down a lion in the head. After arriving to the place that I was waiting for him, we would load our guns, him with his shotgun, and I with my 357 pistol and tranquilizing gun, one of us would say, "Well I hope this isn't our day to be lion caught." You see, the odds were working against both of us. Many years of working with each other, chasing all kinds of animals, looking for lions on a head, the odds were indeed against us. We couldn't go on forever being so lucky, but for now, we would accept all the luck that was bestowed upon us.

The whole time working at Lion Country, all of us men had a close bond, most of them being good animal men, we learned very fast as how to run a roam free park. We were animal men and had to stick together. Bill, Charles and I were a lot closer than most. We had a great bond with each other which has lasted a lifetime, and I still keep in touch with Charles who lives in North Florida, as do

I. We are about one hundred and forty miles apart, and we call each other off and on during the year and try to meet to visit as often as we can. Of course, talking over old times, laughing about some, wondering about others, asking ourselves why are we still here. We are still as close as we were when we were working for Lion Country. If you are ever so lucky in your life as I have been, to have such a close friend that you can trust with your life, also to be as fortunate as I have, to have two great friends, you better work real hard to keep them as a friend, as true friends don't come down this road of life too often, you may have many people you meet you think are friends, but only a few true friends. I feel honored to call Charles a good friend, I only hope that he says the same about me; I shouldn't really say that, as I know he does. When we do get together, we have a great time saying, "hey do you remember when? That's the best part of the Good Ole Days.

The lion named Buck Shot was in season with the females. He was still fighting the jeep, along with fighting all the male lions. He wants to attack anything that moves. He just doesn't want anything or anyone getting near his female. He's just keeping the whole pride on pins and needles. I tapped him with my jeep, as he was starting a fight with Caesar. He turned around after I tapped him, and he attacked my loud haler, and he was on his hind legs, with his front legs on the hood of my jeep trying to get to me. He slid off the side of the jeep. When he was at my window, he tried to eat my arm up. It is a good thing there were bars on my window as it was half way down. He was really going crazy wanting to get at me. Soon he started looking for his mate. When he did this, I tapped him again a little harder this time. At that time, he found his mate and ran to her. They both decided it was a good idea to go lie down. He had enough for one day. Things got nice and quiet for a change. The rest of the pride was happy, and it made me happy not having to break up fights all the time.

One of the born free lions in Dan's section went over the fence, she almost went on the island, Dan went on the edge of the canal on his side, I went over on the island by the canal, we slowly pushed the lion from both sides, when she got closer to her hut she went back over the fence straight to the hut, Dan locked her in the hut for the rest of the day. After getting all of this over with, his lions started fighting, one got a bad cut on her neck, I checked it out, seeing it was very deep and bleeding a lot, I decided to call Dr. Kidder on this one. I tranquilized her, putting her into the hut. I had Charles close the park at five. Bill York and I stayed with Dr. Kidder while he was working on the lion; we were there until eight o'clock. The next morning when we came to work we found the lion had died during the night, we assumed she must of been bleeding internally, it was a really sad time as she was a good lion, but these things happen.

Buck Shot again started attacking my jeep, for three days he has been doing this, I don't know what he has against my jeep, but he sure wants to attack it all the time, I finally tapped him, then I ran him for about fifteen minutes, he was all worn out, sooner or later he will realize if he doesn't mess with the jeep, the jeep will leave him alone, unless he is doing something he shouldn't be doing. We let the lions do all that they naturally would be doing in the wild.

As I was watching my lions, I saw a car by elephant island, it had been there for quite some time, so I decided to start up my jeep, going over to where they were, I noticed a man and a woman in the car with their heads back on the back of their seats, I thought they were committing suicide or something, I knocked on the window, he rolled the window down, I asked if everything was okay, he said yes, except they were very tired, they had driven most of the night to get here, so they were taking a little snooze, I laughed telling them okay, I was sorry I woke them up. I told them if they were still there when I got ready to close, I would come and wake them up, they laughed saying okay thank you. So, I started my jeep up going back to my pride that was the most excitement I had for a while. By closing time I looked over there, they were nowhere to be seen, so off I went to start the closing down of the park for the night.

Today was the day that a girlfriend was arriving for Gus the Rhino. She was a beautiful white rhino from Africa. We hoped that Gus thought the same thing. We were hoping it would be love at first sight, so Gus wouldn't have to be lonely anymore. As we mixed them, she acted as if she was very interested in Gus. Of course, being a male, Gus decided to act as if it made no difference to him. I am sure there will be some arguments between them for a while, as they are just staying a little off from each other, sizing each other up.

Another day, the first thing this morning an antelope went from section one into section two, swimming the canal to section five, it then went through the gate to six and went on into section seven, then it decided to backtrack and go through all the sections again, it was a good thing no one had their lions out yet, it was good that it happened before we opened the park this morning. Everyone joined in the chase to get the antelope back to its own section, Tex finally lassoed it, and we tied it up taking it back to the hoof section. The reason we tied it up was those little antelope can beat you to death with their sharp little hoofs. All the men in their jeeps were after it, we must have looked like the rat patrol, but it was a success, we returned it back to its rightful section.

Later on in the day, two lions from Sonny's section decided to come over and visit the lions in my section, I was behind the hut, Smitty yelled, "Hey, Gus, there are two strange lions in your section." Smitty being across the canal from my section, made it possible for us to see into each other's section, we have come to look out for each other's section when the other is a way from their pride for a short time, when he yelled I was out of my jeep, checking the doors on the hut in the back, Sonny's lions was coming at me from the front, so when I heard Smitty yelled, I jumped back in to my jeep driving to the front seeing the lions coming, it is a good thing he yelled as I wouldn't have seen them until it was too late to do anything about it. Sonny drove to the side of his lions, I was pushing the lions to the gate along with Sonny, and we got them back to the section. I rode over by the canal to thank Smitty for warning me that I had company coming; we were able to make their visit a very short one.

Today was the day to let Gus and his new girlfriend, McClick-Click, out. We released them at ten thirty this morning, and they seemed to get along real well for about a half hour. Then all things got a little hairy. They started fighting. Gus, being the larger of the two, put her in the water. As they were fighting, Gus put his horn under her belly, flipping her into the air as if she weighed nothing. We had measured his horn some time ago; it measured forty-two inches long, finding out it was the longest one on any Rhino in captivity. We couldn't believe he was able to flip her up so high, she landed a good ways away from him getting up, shaking herself off, going right back at him again, just like a female. We finally got them to calm down, we decided that was enough excitement for them for one day, so we would try to put them back in the barn in separate enclosures, we checked them both over, Click Click had a cut on her hind quarters, one on her face, Gus was cut on his face, but neither was that bad. We expected some fighting for a while, so we weren't that surprised when it happened. We are hoping that they will start getting along soon.

A couple of days after all this, I had six men call in sick, if one more man was to call in, I would have to leave a pride of lions in for the day, there wouldn't be enough men to run all the prides, already there were more new men running the prides than more experienced ones.

We let Gus and Click-Click out of the barn and into the section. Right off the bat, they started their fighting again, so I decided to put them right back in. I didn't need this aggravation today of all days, with being so many men short. As bad luck would have it, Gus went in great, but Click-Click stomped her feet saying, "No, I don't want to go back in there." I tried everything and she wouldn't budge any closer to the barn. I sent one of the men to the feed barn to get some hay and fruit, some veggies along with some monkey chow. We put this down in her enclosure, then letting her settle down for a while. After fifteen minutes, we started working her again. She finally went in the enclosure. We shut the gate, and by this time, it was well past closing time. Then we went over to Elephant Island to put the Elephants up, it was dark by now, so they were ready to go into the barn to bed down for the night.

Today was the day to let the new chimp out to mix with all the others. The couple that gave the chimp to Lion Country was there to witness the occasion, and to take some pictures. All of a sudden, the older chimps started to fight with it. The new chimp turned and ran into the water that surrounded the island. It went out to where the water was too deep and started to drown. Tex and Harold jumped in, getting him in swift fashion. Then, they brought it to the side of the island. All the other chimps were just standing around looking at the new chimp. Then, they went over to him and started to groom him, instead of fighting. None of us had ever seen them turn so fast from fighting to being friendly and grooming. We explained this to the people that gave him to us that this was a sign of acceptance and friendship. They felt better knowing this. We continued to watch all of the chimps to see what was going to happen. The couple watched for a while, and then deciding they were okay, they left. A couple of wardens were left there to make sure all was going okay for the rest of the day. At closing, everything seemed to be okay on Chimp Island.

For about three months now, we have been having trouble with a new lion who seemed to mix well with all the lions in the hut, but when we would go to let her out in the morning, she would run out with the whole pride, get about a hundred feet from the hut, then she would turn around running back in to the hut. She wouldn't come back out for anything. Smitty thinks she is just a troublemaker and a mean lion. I have gotten her into the cage on wheels many times, taking her and releasing her right by the pride of lions, she would run back to the hut, if we had closed the door to the hut she would run around the hut, a couple of times, then she would lay down by the door, the warden cannot watch one lion at the hut, while watching the whole pride, sooner or later he would have a lion getting away from him, so we would go open the door and put her in. We talked with Smitty, then decided if it happens again, we would take her to section seven to try her there, as I have said before if we have trouble with any lions we seem to put them over there, as the lions are younger and don't seem to mind an intruder, and of course there are a few other troublemakers already in that section. Well I was wrong on that call, as a couple of days later George released his lions. The one from Smitty's section started fighting with all of the lions when he let her out. She fought with any lion that would come close to her. She was trying to get into the jeep. She was biting it in an attempt to get through the windows to get to the warden. Inside the jeep, George was yelling on his radio, saying the lion was trying to get inside his jeep and that he needed some help. All of his lions were fighting and running all over his section. As many jeeps and men that could get away from their sections, leaving their pride, came to help him. Finally, Tex said to close the section down, closing both gates the in one and the out one. We got all of the cars out of the section as soon as possible. Tex darted her then we put her in the hut. We would try to figure out something a little later on down the road to try to get her straightened out. However, for the rest of the day and until we decided what to do, she would stay in the hut.

Smitty was off today. The one watching his section called saying that he had a lion go on the head that we had put goats on. I called Mr. Pierce and Dale to come help me get the lion back. We went into the head right away and started looking for her. A.C. called on the radio saying he had just seen the lion by the worming section and that she had just killed a goat. She was going back inside the head, carrying the goat like a trophy she had won. That's just what I wanted to hear while I was in the middle of the head with a lion that had just made a kill. I was in water up to my knees, with a lion with her prized kill. I told Mr. Pierce and Dale to be on their toes big time now. I looked back at them and all I saw were two sets of big eyeballs darting in all directions. When they looked at me, they saw the same. We were going deeper into the head, getting to a place with a little clearing. I told them we were almost at the end of the head and for them to go to the end, swing back around, and then maybe they will drive her to me. I was in a good clearing to get a good shot at her. About twenty minutes later, I heard something coming at me through the water. I got ready, but it was Mr. Pierce and Dale coming towards me. They said they didn't see the lion, but saw her tracks on the other side of the head. We went to the other side and started following her tracks when we saw that they were going towards Rhino Island. The head we were in was the biggest in the park. It almost covered the whole length of the park and in the middle, and it was very wide. As we were getting closer to the island, we saw the goat, lying in the grass across from the Rhino Island. As we got closer, we saw the lion about ten feet from the dead goat. The lion was sitting there looking at Gus and Click. Getting closer, we had a few bushes about eight feet tall between us, so I took a shot at her to tranquilize her. When the dart hit her, she took off along canal. The bushes and growth weren't as thick as the rest about fifteen feet away, so she was running through the thin stuff with all of us right behind her. We needed to keep a distanced to avoid scaring her; yet, we also had to keep an eye on her. She lied down and we were letting the drug take effect. She was just looking around. In a couple of minutes, she got up and started walking along the canal bank. We started getting closer to her, then, she fell in the water, which was never the sign of a good thing. When she fell in the water, she started swimming down the canal, going under the water, then coming back up and swimming some more. She then went under the water and didn't come up. The bubbles started coming up, and then they started getting smaller and less frequent. I told Mr. Pierce and Dale to cover me, as I was going in after her. I took my wallet out of my pants, then took off my boots and dove into the water, hoping she was out enough that she wouldn't try to get me. I felt around the bottom with my feet and finally found her. I then dove under the water, grabbing her wherever I could, pulling her towards the canal bank. I could touch the bottom, so as I was dragging her, she was bumping against my leg. Every time she touched me, the hair would stand up on the back of my neck because I didn't have any idea which part of the lion was touching me. I was also wondering how far under the tranquilizer she was. I yelled for Mr. Pierce and Dale to come and help me. We finally got her to the bank on dry land. She was hissing at me, but didn't have full control of her faculties. I would always carry extra drugs along with a needle and an extra dart with me in its case. I gave her a little more of the drug by hand. After all that, we backed away from her, and sat in the grass, looking at her. We were talking about the crazy thing we had just done. When she was completely out, we drug her to the jeep, taking her back to the hut. This whole episode took about five hours.

***

Today was a very different day. There was a big write up on Gus and Click, the two rhinos, saying they were going to get married today, and if anyone wanted to come to the wedding, a plate supper would be provided at the cost of fifty dollars a plate. There were a multitude of cars and buses coming in to be at the wedding. All of the lions in my section were getting all excited, because this was across the canal from my section. All day long, my lions were acting up. I think their feelings were hurt because they weren't invited to the wedding. There was so much commotion going on over there with all the cameras and the photography. The environment was becoming dangerous because the commotion was making it harder to control the lions. In late afternoon, Fanny one of my lions stood, all she could stand. She left the pride, going on the head then swimming to Smitty's section. Tex darted her and brought her back to the hut. I don't like doing things that are unnatural, like a wedding for animals. (I think people come to see the animals to study them and enjoy them in their natural habitat, doing things that are natural to them. Not seeing them dressed in funny clothes and hats, but of course, that is my own personal opinion. I was so glad that little show was over, allowing things to get back to the normal way for these animals.

Farmers were crop dusting with a small plane in a vegetable field near Lion Country; the plane was flying low while it was dusting near us. One of Mr. Pierce's lions started chasing the plane to the end of the section. She jumped the canal and over to the moat that is between the perimeter fence and the canal. She started walking down the moat. When Mr. Pierce told me where she was, I went to the outside, along the perimeter fence. When she got to Elephant Island, Mr. Pierce was on the canal side inside the park. I couldn't do anything until I got inside on Elephant Island. Once I was there, I slid the gun, loaded with a dart through a little opening under the fence to Mr. Pierce with the safety on. When he got the gun, the dart fell out. He picked it up, dusted it off and put the dart right back in the gun. I told him to get to Elephant Island as fast as he could, as Dale and Gary were with the elephants. He needed to let them know that the lion was on the island with them.

He found them, and let them know the details of their mission. They got into the truck used for Elephant Island. I got back to the island, taking the tranquilizer gun again. I, with Mr. Pierce, went to the back of the elephant barn, and there she was, just laying there watching that crop duster plane. I didn't know how much drug was in the dart as it had fell out of the gun; but I didn't have time to fix another dart. Therefore, I was hoping there was enough to put her down. I shot the dart, hitting her on the first shot. I waited the proper amount of time, and after she went down, we took her back to the hut. That day turned out to be good after all.

The next day, one of Sonny's lions got into Dan's section and started fighting with Dan's lions. We got her to the gate between the sections, and I tried to rope her to bring her back to her section. Then, she tried to get in the jeep with me. There were cars all around us, so I decided to dart her. After I darted her, she went beside the canal. I was trying to get behind her with my jeep but there were too many cars blocking me. Sonny was also trying to push her away from the canal, but the cars were blocking him too. She fell into the canal, so Sonny and I dove in the canal trying to save her, but we were too late. By the time we got to her and got her out of the water on the bank, she was already gone. I feel really bad when this happens, but I try to do all I can. Sonny felt bad after losing one of his lions. I knew just what he was going through, as I had been there a few times myself. I told him if he wanted, he could put his lions up for the rest of the day and go home. He said he would rather stay with the rest of his lions, so he went back to his section for the remainder of the day.

Nonie, my wife, came in today. On my break, we went to Pets' Corner. We were walking around, looking at all the animals and at all the scenery. All of a sudden she said, "I feel like I am going to faint." Then, she fell on the sidewalk. We were close to the nursery, so I yelled to the girls to help me get her inside. They came and helped me and we dragged her inside. Later she told me we ruined her high-heeled shoes by dragging her. We got some sacks putting them under her head. While she was lying down on the floor, we put a damp cloth on her head. As she was waking up, Tex came in with the chimp called Butch. Butch was looking at her close in her face, and when she opened her eyes, she let out a scream. She didn't know where she was or what happened; she thought she had died and went to Hell. She was face to face with Butch, who was jumping up and down, grunting as chimps do. She woke up real fast, and then told me to take her home. So, I took the rest of the day off, taking her home and staying with her to make sure that she was all right. She completely recovered from that, except there is the picture still in her mind of Butch jumping up and down, grunting right in her face, and knowing that that was a dose of what was in hell. She sure didn't want to go there.

***

The next day, I had the chance to be surrounded by fifty-two beautiful college queens. I had to go to the college to have my picture taken for public relations for Lion country. It was really a tough job but somebody had to do it and of course, when they asked me, I couldn't turn them down.

Vern, one of the wardens, was over on the island feeding the chimps. One got a little too friendly with him, biting him on his arm and on his leg. He was taken to the hospital where they put some stitches in both places, bandaged them up, and sent him back. After coming back the next day, he went right back over on the island. The same chimp went after him again, biting him on the arm. It wasn't as bad as the first time though, so we cleaned it out with some peroxide and put a bandage on it. As time went on, Vern conquered the chimp, making him like him and became his friend.

While we were at home last night, one of Mr. Pierce's lions was really busy; she delivered two lion cubs while in the hut with all the other lions. Most of the time, we know when the lion will have cubs. They are usually born within ninety to one hundred five days after mating. Usually two weeks before that time, we put them in the hut that has been prepared for them by boarding up all sides of the hut. After doing this, we would put hay all over the hut floor, and then check on her every morning. Sometimes, two or three times during the day, only the chief game warden and the one who ran the section would go around her. If everything was okay with the cubs and mother, after they are born we leave them alone so she can take care of them; but, if for some reason the mother doesn't take care of them, we transport them to Pets' Corner, where qualified people are there to take care of them. If all goes well and the mother takes care of them, we leave them with her for about three month. After this time, we take them to Pets' Corner. We have been discussing for four months about letting the cubs stay with the mother, letting her raise them, then after the three months of her being in the hut with the cubs, and all the cats looking at each other, let the pride out, letting them settle down a bit. After we could see that they were settled, we would let mother and the cubs out of the hut, trying to bring to the pride, or let the mother introduce them to the pride. If this worked, it would be great for everyone concerned. Of course, it would be good for us working at the park also. I think this will happen soon.

Mr. Pierce's lion was giving birth to two cubs at night with the whole pride In the hut. That morning when we were releasing the pride, the mother went right out with them, leaving her cubs back in the hut alone. We left the door open for her to go back in. She didn't really want anything to do with them, so we closed the center door, closing her on the other side of the hut away from the cubs. I went in to the hut, getting the cubs, and taking them to Pets' Corner of where they would be taken care. We decided to leave the mother in the hunt for the rest of the day. I guess in this legal climate, one would call that child abuse and child abandonment. Some of the lions just weren't good mothers. It was up to us to check and have them pulled if necessary before something could happen to them.

Tex was off this day, so I was in charge again. We had Argosy magazine come in today. A few days ago, we had a meeting with them to find out what they wanted to do. We had somewhat of an idea of what they wanted, and they took shots of Bill York and me preparing medication for the lions. Then, they took another picture of us darting a lion that fell in the canal, with Bill and me jumping in after it, dragging her to the edge of the water, and reviving her. We gave her medication then, putting her into the hut.

We went over to the Rhino Island, with my getting on the back of Gus, the rhino, for them to take pictures. They also took pictures of Bill chasing the giraffes. Then, pictures were taken of both of us on the radio, talking to each other from our jeeps, and acting as if we were trying to rope a lion as it ran away. Bill almost fell out of the jeep while all of the lions were out. I grabbed him and pulled him back. One of the wardens said the lion was running behind us, and when Bill almost fell out of the jeep, the warden pushed the lion away from our jeep with his jeep. He said the lion was really watching, just waiting for Bill to hit the ground. We decided to do it the way we always did, having someone like Bill or me on the passenger side, with our head out the window with the tranquilizer gun aimed at a lion running in front of the jeep. The next day, they took photographs of Bill and Tex tranquilizing a zebra and giving it medication. It was two fun filled days.

Not everything we did while photos were being taken was done the same way as when we were actually running the park, but I had to keep in mind always that having the safety of the animals and people was our first concern. One of George's lions that we just put into his section from Pets' Corner went on the moat in section six. Zoo was in that section and he was holding his lions back so that they couldn't get to the little one on the moat. I drove up to the little one, as she knows me from Pets' Corner. The girls in Pets' Corner were getting a little leery of her as she was getting to be a good size lion. She was two and a half years old now, weighing around two hundred and seventy pounds, so I would take her to the pit while they would clean out her pen. She and I became friends. Pets' Corner had raised her from the time I pulled her from the mother. Her mother wasn't feeding her so she was used to being taken care of by humans, which in some ways isn't good. She was getting to be too much for the girls to handle so about a week ago we put her in George's section. She was doing really well until today. Zoo watched his lions as I drove up to the canal and got out of my jeep. Standing there, I started calling her from across the canal. She recognized my voice and began to come to me. She got In the canal, swimming over to me while I watched her like a hawk. I was hoping all the time that she was swimming to me, that she wanted to see me, and not eat me up. She got to me, rubbing up on my side just like a regular cat. I told Zoo that I was going to walk her back to her section, as it wasn't too far from the gate to section seven where her pride was. Zoo watched his lions to make sure we were able to get back there safely. When we got to the section, she knew where she was. She went right back to her pride. Zoo had followed us, so now I got into his jeep so he could take me back to mine. After getting back in my jeep, everything got back to normal, at least for now.

One day after we had opened the park, Tex saw a chimp in my section. Noticing it was Butch, my lions saw him about the same time that Tex had seen him. I blocked my lions from going to him, and then Tex went over and got Butch. He put him in his jeep, taking him back to where he belonged. He sure was in the wrong place at the wrong time, as lions aren't too friendly with chimps.

Today, I had a new man to train how to run the tractor with the water pump on it. I was showing him how to use it to clean out the lion huts, while Peggy, with her cubs, were in the hut. We opened the middle door, pushing them to the other side, and closed the door. The new man cleaned the side where they had been. After cleaning, we put the hay down. Then, we opened the door. Peggy went in but the cubs stayed on the other side. They were about three months old, so we closed the door, leaving them where they were. We worked all doors with a rope from the outside, so I told him I would go in the hut with the cubs and for him to work the door, and at the same time spray Peggy with the water and open the center door, making it possible for me to push the cubs back in with Peggy. I told him to make sure he does it fast, as she will want her cubs back. So, the first time I got two back in. Then, we did it again and I put the last cub in. When he opened the door, he dropped the door and it only went half way down, sticking. He sprayed Peggy with water, but she went for her cub with the door half open with me on the other side. She was looking at her cub and I at the same time. I kicked the door, making it close all the way. Needless to say, I felt so good when I saw that door going down. Later we fixed the door so it wouldn't stick again.

This was the beginning of Tex's two-week vacation. All went well until around two thirty. Two lions from section four went for a little stroll over on the head that the goats were. I tranquilized one, and then Dale and I went after the other one. We didn't have any problems, as we found him and tranquilized him, and took him back in the jeep with the other one. We transported them back to their section.

Later I took Butch from the island to Pets' Corner for about forty-five minutes, letting the people see a chimp walking around, holding my hand. I took him back to the island, went on into the park, and started the process of closing so we could all go home for the evening. It had been a very good day today, so I felt good at the end of the day when I headed down the two-mile stretch.

The next day was going to be a very busy day. A man brought in some chickens for us. We put worming medication into the chickens after killing them to worm the lions. We wormed them every six months. We would do that through the chickens because the lions would eat the whole chicken and get the worming medication along with the natural vitamins. This man would bring a truckload of chickens once a week, leaving the crates there and would pick them up when he delivered the next batch of chickens the following week.

After finishing the worming of all the lions in each section, we went to the hoof stock section. A baby impala was born in the section where all the hoof stock was. The zebras were getting really close to the baby, so we got out of the jeep and ran the baby down then took it to Pets' Corner.

Our next project was to move Scar Face, the lion, from section six to section four. We were going to put her in the hut, as she was due for cubs soon. The day seemed to go pretty well all day until five o'clock when Zoo said that his lions were really restless and wanting to go to the hut. He was trying to hold the lions back from going in until the people had gone through his section. When I got to his section, I started helping him to keep all his lions out and under control, I was trying to keep about eight lions from going to the hut, when all of a sudden, two broke away from the others heading for the hut. I called to Zoo to head them off, and he went for them. When he got by a bend in the road where we had put some large rocks on the corner to keep people on the road, Zoo hit a rock going about forty five miles per hour. The jeep was going that fast.

After hitting the rock his jeep flipped over on its side, sliding on the side for a short ways, then flipping on the top, still sliding. It finally stopped in front of six lions that Smitty was holding back from going to the hut. With the jeep still on its top, I drove over to where it had stopped. Not knowing what happened to him, I looked into the window; he was lying on his belly with his shotgun in front of him looking at the lions that he was holding back, not saying a word. Every one carried a shotgun with them for reasons such as this. I yelled three or four times and he never answered me, so I got out of my jeep, crawling into his and getting him out, then getting him into my jeep. By this time, we had lions all over the section. I told the wardens to put all the lions up if we could find them all. We got them all in and counted them, finding out that we had lost one in to the head. All of us went over to Zoo's jeep, flipping it over onto its tires. Smitty and Zoo pulled it to the machine shop to be fixed. Charles, Jeff, and I went to the head after the lion. We looked for a good while, finally finding her. After I darted her, we waited the usual time then took her back to section six and bed her down to sleep off the tranquilizer. We didn't get finished with all that until eight thirty that night, made for a very long day.

The following day, my lions were being very good, lying under the trees. Some were sleeping, some were just playing around with each other, and some were just lying, looking around. Not too far from the lions, a car stopped with four women inside. All of a sudden, they started screaming. The door opened up and all four women were outside of the car. I started my jeep going over to where they are, stopping my jeep between them and the lions. I told them they had to get back into the car. They proceeded to tell me, "No way are we getting in that car, there's a spider in there! Are you crazy?" they said. Then, it was my turn to tell them, "Well ladies, there are eighteen lions out here." All the lions were keeping a close watch on all of us being out in their territory. I told them there was no way all of them would fit into my jeep, and they had to get back into their car. "They said again, "No way. Not with that spider in there!" I asked them where the spider was. One said that it in the back seat, so I opened the back door, looking inside. I looked in front and back, looking under the seats. Then, I jumped back, hitting the floor with my hand. I told them, "There! I killed the spider." One asked me if I was sure. I told them "Yes, now get back into the car." During this time, some of the lions decided to stand up and get a better view of what we were doing. After they got in the car, they all yelled, "Thank you," driving off with smiles on their faces, and feeling safe now that I had killed the spider. I was only hoping that spider would stay in hiding, at least until they got through the park. That was the only way I could convince them to get back into the car. I was smiling to myself as they drove off.

AN ALMOST ADULT MALE LION TRIED TO JOIN ME IN THE JEEP

Chapter 10

Ostrich

Today, Mr. Gallop called me on the radio, saying an ostrich got to the gate from the hoof stock section. The ostrich went into Smitty's section and he called saying that he saw the ostrich, but that his lions didn't see it yet. I got there as fast as I could, and started working the ostrich back to the gate. Smitty was keeping his lions together and busy by moving his jeep back and forth. As I was pushing the ostrich, he turned and started running towards Smitty's lions. They had seen him as well as me in my jeep coming towards them. Smitty was having a time keeping his lions altogether. I finally got the ostrich turned towards the gate, but he was running faster, dodging back and forth, and throwing his head from side to side. I got him almost to the gate and we were in a patch of pine trees. As he turned to miss a tree, he leaned his head to the side to go around the tree, and his body missed the tree, but his head didn't. It hit the tree with such force that his feet flew up in the air, landing him on his back. He wasn't moving at all. I couldn't believe what I had just witnessed. I stopped my jeep, and got out to check him. He definitely wasn't moving; he was dead. Mr. Gallop closed the gate, then came and helped me load him in to the back of my jeep. I called Smitty to see if all his lions were okay. He said they were all under control now, but that he just couldn't believe what he had just seen. I took Mr. Gallop back to the gate, and the ostrich to the meat house. Willy and I unloaded the ostrich, and I told Willy to save me one of the legs, telling him I would pick it up in a couple of days. That same night, about four of us were going to stop at a place we often frequented on the way home. It had a few pool tables, and they served burgers along with some other foods, and beer. We have been stopping there for a long time. A husband and wife ran the place. I thought I should ask before bringing it in, so I asked the woman if I brought an ostrich leg in, could she cook it up for us. She agreed, saying, "Sure, that would be something different."

The following night, we all walked in the door, and I had the ostrich leg over my shoulder. As we were walking in I yelled, "I got the biggest drumstick in the world!"

She took it and said, "I am glad you didn't bring the whole chicken. I don't know if I got room in the freezer for it, but I will have it cooked for you by tomorrow night."

The next night she had it cooked. We enjoyed it and I brought some home for Nonie and the boys, who liked it too.

I told them, "I hope no one gets to really liking it so much that I would have to bring some home every night."

This all happened before people started raising them for food. This was a different experience for us, so it made it all a little more exciting working for Lion Country. Something was happening different every day.

Today, all was quiet until around three o'clock when a lion went on a head. Dan, Charles, and I went after it. There was a lot of water in the head, as it was the rainy season. This was always a bad time to go hunting lions on the heads. After about two hours, we found her. It was really thick and I couldn't get a good shot at her. We were next to a stand we had built in the tree, so I climbed the tree, getting into the stand. It was a clear shot from there. When the dart hit her, she charged us and just before getting to us, she turned and went on the other side of the head. We waited for eleven minutes, then, we found her, almost out, but not quite. We decided to wait the full fifteen minutes because of this. We then took her back to the hut.

The next day, another lion went over on a head. It took us about all day to look for him. We couldn't seem to find him, which made me think that he was staying just ahead of us, leading us all around the head. It was raining really hard and it was very dark on the inside of the head, so we decided to leave it there for the night and start again the first thing in the morning. If we were lucky, the rain would stop by then.

Bill York called when he heard that we were going in the head again to look for the lion. He said he wanted to go with us, so I said, "Sure come on, we can always use your help." So, it would be Bill, Charles, Mac and me that would be going in to look for him the next day.

***

Today, Tex came back from vacation, and an eland was back in section two again. Smitty, Harold, and I got him back. It was in there before opening and it took us until ten thirty to get him back to the hoof stock section. After getting him back, Bill, Tex, Charles, and I went on the head to tranquilize the lion that went over there yesterday. Tex and Charles each got in a tree stand. Then, Bill and I went through the head to find him or push him to Charles and Tex in the stands. It was still soaking wet, and the water was up to our knees in places. We finally found him.

He was staying ahead of us all the time and we could hear him splashing through the water. When Bill and I walked by a tree stand, I climbed on it and looked around. It was then that I finally saw some bushes moving. I could only see the lion's eyes, ear, and part of his neck. I took the shot with the dart gun, and he started charging us. He charged us until he was about ten feet from the tree, then turned and ran through the water. We started to follow him slowly. We found him in a little while and he was dead. He was on the other side of the head, and we could only figure that because the dart hit him in the jawbone, the drug went to his brain too fast killing him. He was a very large lion, about four hundred and fifty pounds. We dragged him out of the head and back to the jeep. We all were feeling bad about the way things turned out. After two days of looking for him, the shot that killed him would be the only shot I would have. I felt I used my best judgment, where this time wasn't good enough, but in the world of wild animals, sometimes one doesn't have any more choices, so one must deal with what one has. I felt bad, as I always did when something happened to an animal. We could not afford to let him run around the head any longer, with the possibility of hurting or killing someone. As we were coming off the head with the lion, someone radioed that four lions from section four had went into another head, so off we went again. The goats were on this head. Charles, Tex, and I went on to the head. We got to the head, and as we went in, we found out that it didn't have deep water like the other one we just came off. It did have some standing water, though.

When we first started, we found two goats that the lions had killed, so we knew they weren't too far away. We soon found two of the lions and tranquilized them. We waited a few minutes, and then we went looking for them, all the while, keeping our eyes open for the other two lions. Very soon, we found the two we had darted, so we took them back to the section, giving them to other wardens to put in the hut and bed them down. As we returned to the head, it was another time to be alert, as we were in a head with goats and lions. All of a sudden, we heard something coming at us through the water. It was the goats, running by us like lighting, wide-eyed and bushy tailed. We thought that the lions were after them. We had left the other two dead goats, thinking maybe the lions would go back to them, which that's what they did. When we got to where the dead goats were. Two lions were feeding on the goats. Tex and I each had a dart gun along with a three fifty seven magnum. Charles had a twelve gauge with rifle slugs. We all got in a place to get a good shot at the lions, and counted to three. We both shot the darts at the same time, both hitting our targets. Both lions jumped when the darts hit them. They went back to the goats, no longer eating them, but keeping their claws in them, having their ears back with their tail swishing back and forth in quick jerks. They had their jaws lying on the goats so nothing could take the goats away from them. We all stayed where we were until they were fully out. Then we took them back to section six, as no more rooms were available in section four. Then, Charles and I took the dead goats over to the meat house. By this time, it was already seven o'clock and time for us to get out of here and go home to our other families.

When we came in the next morning, an addax had killed an eland. The addax had blood all over its horns and on its head. There was a spot in the hoof section where they were fighting. It looked like they had been fighting a long time, noticing how the ground was all tore up as a bunch of wild hogs had been there. We loaded the eland on a truck and took it out of the preserve to be taken care of.

We were short on men today, so before we opened up, I had to get someone from Pets' Corner to work inside the preserve. Some of the men in there were trained for that reason. Overall, the day turned out to be a fairly good one with not too many things happening. We had a meeting to go to at the office. After closing the inside of the park, we were all standing, talking, and waiting for Mr. Dredge, the general manager. Smitty was talking to Wayne. When Smitty would get excited and into what he was talking about, he would start getting real close to whomever he was talking to, getting right in their face. Smitty was about six foot one, weighing only about one hundred and fifty pounds. Wayne started backing up as Smitty started getting closer to him and right up in his face again. Wayne's back was now right up against the wall with Smitty's faces about four inches from his. Wayne couldn't go any further back, so, Wayne grabbed Smitty by the back of his head, planting a big ole smacker on Smitty's face. His eyes got really big, and he took his hands and wiped his face off where Wayne kissed him, puffing up like an ole bullfrog, yelling, "What the heck is wrong with you?" Wayne looked at him and said, "Well Smitty, you got so close to me that I thought you wanted me to kiss you."

Smitty said, "Don't you ever do that again." Wayne came back with the answer, "Then don't get all up in my face when you are talking with me from now on."

After that occurrence, when anyone of us was talking with Smitty, if he started getting close to us, we would tell him that if he didn't back up, we would give him a "Wayne." He would back off and puff all up, saying not to even think of it. From then on, he would keep a normal distance from us. We always knew after that situation how to get Smitty fired up.

A week later, we were told that that it would be Tex's last day, as he had given his notice. We would all miss him, as he was a good animal man. He was also a good chief game warden. We had some really good times and many tough times hunting down lions while we were working together for the past four years. We have many good memories of all our working hours and all of our many talks of things and situations through which we had been.

***

Today was a good day for me. This morning, I was told I was now the chief game warden, and I was feeling very good after hearing that. This had been my sole reason for working here. I had told Nonie many years ago when I started working for Lion Country, that one day I would be the "MAN." This was the day that it finally happened. I was very proud of this position and I would try to do a good job at keeping everyone and all the animals safe. I also knew I would not tell someone else to do something that I wouldn't attempt to do. I knew that I had really worked hard at doing a good job in whatever task asked of me, and did it to the best of my ability, knowing all the time that my first concern would be for my men and right behind them would be all the animals. I have come to have a great feeling for each of these animals, knowing them by their actions, caring more for some than others, just like people do. I like some people better than others, so this is the same in animals as well, but my heart is really with the lions.

My first day as the "MAN" seemed to be going real well until four thirty, when a lion in section six decided he would head at full speed going to a head. So, off we went, into the head, Charles and I tracking him down, when we found tracks in the second head. We soon found him, doing the usual thing. We then transported him back to the hut. Altogether, this took us about seven hours. Now it was seven thirty, time for us to stop for the day. All of this made my first day as Chief Game Warden, and Charles as second, seemed to have gone pretty well.

Over the next two days, we crated twenty-seven lions from section seven to go to a new park that was starting up in Canada. This was no easy task; however, we got the job done getting the trucks on their way.

One morning at opening, I was just going through the front gate when Jim called me on the radio, telling me that Sarge was feeding the chimps. When the boat got to the island, two chimps got in the boat with Sarge. He was just learning the chimps. Wayne was usually with them for the most of the time, so when the chimps got in the boat with Sarge, he got nervous, and stood up in the boat. When he did this, the boat tipped over, throwing Sarge in the water and the chimp jumped onto the island. While the other chimp held on, staying in the boat, Sarge went back to shore. Jim was watching all of this happen, so he called me. As I got there, Sarge was soaking wet and dripping water. I looked out, seeing the boat in the middle of the canal that goes around Chimp Island, with the chimp jumping up and down making all kinds of noise. Before I came out to the island, I stopped at the meat house and I got a bunch of bananas. As I was talking with Sarge, I noticed that his holster was empty. I asked him where his gun was, he said, "I dropped it in the boat."

I was thinking to myself, "Boy this is really great. There is a chimp in the boat that's full of water out in the middle of the canal floating around to a section where there are lions and in this boat with this chimp is a three-fifty-seven pistol. This is not good."

This made for a very bad situation. So I took off my boots, stuffing the bananas in my jeans pockets, jumped in to the water, and swam over to the boat with the chimp in it. Knowing that before I got in the boat, I was going to throw the chimp a banana and while he was eating it, I would get in the boat. Doing just that, I jumped into the boat. I saw the gun in front of the chimp on the floor. I picked it up, and put it in my belt. Then, I got the paddle and started paddling to the shore of Chimp Island. When I got close to the island, all of the chimps were standing on the bank ready to greet me. They were standing really close to the water, but not in it, as they can't swim. Knowing this, I would get cautious when they get close to the edge of the water. They were all jumping up and down, doing their chimp thing. As I got a little closer to shore, I started throwing the bananas over their heads so they would go after them. As I was doing this, the one in the boat with me decided that he wanted to get some of the bananas too, so he jumped out of the boat onto the island. When this happened, I thought that it would be a good time for me to make my exit, so off I paddled to the other side. Once there I gave Sarge his gun, telling him to finish cleaning up the island, and to be sure not to let the chimps on the boat again, knowing that we may not be so lucky the next time. I think this was a good experience for him; it made him realize just how much these chimps could and would do.

After this episode, I went to move six lions from Pets' Corner to section seven; it was a very busy day.

The next morning when I came in, I saw that Stumpy had five cubs. This was very unusual because they would only have three for the most of the time, but every once in awhile, they would have four. However, this litter of five was the most I had seen. While watching them and their mother, I could see that she wasn't taking care of them, so I put her on the other side of the hut. When I opened the middle door, she jumped up and darted through it, going on the other side of the hut and not even looking back. I shut the door and could tell that she didn't want to be in there with her cubs. If a mother was separated from her cubs, she usually would get very aggressive while trying to get back to her cubs at any cost, but this wasn't the situation with Stumpy. She didn't want anything to do with them so I took all five of them to Pets' Corner. As I went in there, I brought one in at a time. When I brought the fourth one, they all said, "Wow that is really something." I didn't say anything and just turned around, going back to my jeep to get the fifth and final one. When I came in with that one, they all said, "No way!" They couldn't believe that she had five cubs and it was really something to see the looks on their faces. They were all in awe of the five of them.

The women in Pets' Corner talked with Bill and me about two lions that were getting too big for them to handle. They were saying that they thought they were big enough to go out in to the preserve. They now weighed two hundred pounds. They were taken away from the mother when they were only two of three days old because she didn't have enough milk to feed them, so the women in Pets' Corner raised them. Bill and I talked, deciding that we thought it would be best to put them out into section seven. I asked Charles what he thought about walking two lions from Pets' Corner to section seven. Charles agreed, so we put a chain on both of the lions and started walking them to the exit gate.

Bill was in a jeep behind us with a dart gun ready, George was waiting for us in the section, and the guard was at the gate, ready to open it. Everyone knew what their job was, so we were all covered. We looked like we were taking our dogs out for a stroll. We went on the edge of the parking lot of Pets' Corner, where there were few people, but the ones that saw us was giving us plenty of room. The lions were very young. My having been with them for two and a half years made them unafraid of people. When we got to section seven, George was watching his other lions while Charles and I took the chains off the two lions we had just walked over there. They were staying close to each other for quite awhile, but soon they started mixing with the other lions in the pride. All seemed to be going well.

We had been letting the cubs that were four months old or more out in the section now for about a week or so at this point. They were doing really well. The first couple of times we let them out, it would take us about thirty minutes to get them to where the pride was. They would stop and check out the long grass and the little rocks. Then, they decided to play around with each other and with their mother as young cubs do. After fooling around for a bit, they would follow their mother to where the rest of the pride was where they stayed most of the time, which was by the road. At first, they were afraid of the cars. Additionally, when a breeze would come through and blow the palms, they would jump, being scared of that noise, not having seen or heard them blowing before. Once they got use to it, they settled down, they looked really good out with the whole pride playing around with each other and their mother. They would run over to where Abe was and start playing with his tail. Then, they would jump on him while he was lying down. When they got tired of pestering Abe, they would go back to their mother again. At times, they would play around with all the pride, just as young ones do. The older lions didn't have a naughty chair to put them on, so they would put up with it as long as they could, then roar or hiss to let them know they had enough. All in all, the grown lions had a lot of patience with them. Having the cubs out in the pride sure put on a nice show for the people coming through.

***

The man that delivered the hundred and forty chickens each week for Lion Country decided not to do it anymore, so I told Mr. Dredge that I would buy a used truck and start delivering the chickens myself. I got in touch with a friend of mine that had an old truck that he wanted to sell without the bed, and I bought the truck.

After getting it home, I built a bed on the back for it out of wood. Then, once a week, Nonie, Joe, and Erik, along with me went to the chicken farm to get the hundred and forty chickens. We would bring them home and park them in the yard for the night.

The next morning, we took the chickens to Lion Country. I drove to the meat house where Willy would unload them, and then if I had time I would go back to the meat house and help Willy get the chickens ready to feed the lions. Willy would get in the cage and we would bring them through the park, dropping them off to the lions, with us feeding the lions the chickens. They would get most of the vitamins and minerals they needed if they ate the whole chicken.

This all worked out fine until the farmer I got the hens from moved to central Florida. When this happened, we had to go to another form of protein and minerals for the lions. Along with the powdered minerals and vitamins, we were giving them the chickens.

Later that day, it seemed like section five was having a bit of a problem. Wayne called me on the radio, telling me a couple of the lions had started fighting, so I came to help him break the fight up. When I got there, three of the lions were fighting big time. They were fighting over a female that was in season. When we finally got them calmed down and separated, Wayne counted his lions as they were all over the section, so we started closing in on them, trying to get them back under the cabbage palms where they always liked to stay. This was my section for four years, so I knew these lions really well. They were my babies.

We finally got them under the trees where the

people were able to see them up close and personal. After we got them settled down, we counted them and they were all there except for one cub. During the breaking up of the fight, one of the lions bit Wayne's tire so needless to say, it was losing air. I called for a jeep from section six to come over and help while Wayne went to the shop to fix his tire before it went completely flat. My jeep got a few more holes in the loud haler. When the jeep got there, I started looking for the cub. I checked from section four, and as I was on my way back to where the pride was, I saw this little guy running as fast as he could to the pride, then finding his mother Peggy. He was rubbing on his mother as if to say, "I'm sorry that I ran away, Mom." I think he was trying to explain to his mother that when the fighting started, he just took off running like the wind and hid until it was all over. It was something spectacular to watch these beautiful creatures and to see how they reacted to different situations; the things they did always amazed me.

***

Today was a very sad day for all of us that had been honored to work with Smitty all of these years. He was a great animal man in general, and specifically, a good lion man. Smitty had decided to retire from the wild world of animals and would be missed a lot. We had lost about four of the older men to retirement that had been here for some time; however, we had also been able to hire some new ones that were very good animal men. Every time we lost, someone that has been here for a long time it is sad, as we were comfortable with each other and trusted one another. Now it would take trial and error and time to learn to trust the new man, but that all comes with time and experience.

George, in section seven, had gotten an overabundance of lions now. He had two prides, roughly about eighteen in each pride. There is also another man in there with him. The other man called me on the radio saying that he had a lion missing. Many of them were turning into adults and starting to give him a lot of problems. When I got there, I went behind the lion hut and lo and behold, there was his lion, on the head side. I was on section seven's side; I shot the dart gun and missed. The lion charged me, but stopped at the edge of the water in the mote, then turned, going back into the head. I called Charles on the radio along with Dale and George. When they got there, we all went to the head to find the lion. It only took about thirty minutes to find him. I darted him, thanked Goodness that he didn't charge this time, and he just went back about twenty feet and lied down, watching us.

Fifteen minutes later, he was out; so we took him back to the hut, everything seemed to be settled down in George's section.

We were letting the cubs out in section five by this time. They had continued to do really well. I knew that in time, they would start getting into trouble every now and then, but for that point in time, they put on a good show. They were getting more playful around all the other lions and around their mother, so now when we let the lions out in the morning, they go running right along with the rest of the pride. They would start out really well in the morning playing, and then they get a little rough with each other, and just like kids, one would get mad, and get rough right back. Then, the mother would step in and showed them who ruled and they would lie down and go to sleep, just like children.

Today, a woman in section three got out of her car and started walking out of the preserve. Dan called to tell me she had said she wasn't going to be in the same car as her husband. So, off I went to try to solve a domestic problem. Therefore, I proceeded to tell her that she needed to either get back in the car, or get in my jeep, and then I would take her outside of the preserve. I told her that she wouldn't make it walking through the preserve. I also told her that she could go outside to use the phone to call a taxi to come and pick her up, so she got in my jeep and I took her to the parking lot, with her husband following us. Once we got to the parking lot, she told me her whole life history. I told them both that I hoped they could get things worked out. I left them there, and went back into the preserve.

The following day Elsa, named after the born free lions, was in my old section, section five; she decided to take a stroll. She left the pride and went over to the head. About the same time that this happened, another one in section seven went on the mote, so I decided to go after the one in section seven first. I darted her as she was on the mote and not in the head. I was on the other side, so Charles and I swam across the canal. After about fifteen minutes, the tranquilizer took effect. I tied a lariat around her, then, Charles and I swam back across the canal. Charles, George, and I pulled her across the canal to our side, then loaded her into the jeep and took her to bed her down. Now, it was time to go after Elsa. Charles, AC, Vern, and I went over on the head. We were tracking and looking for her for almost three hours, then Dan called, telling me that Elsa just swam the canal to section five, hauling buggy to the hut. It was my guess that she didn't feel like giving us a hard time; it sure didn't hurt our feelings any. It was really nice to get a break.

At closing, I got a call from section three, with them telling me that they were putting the lions up and one decided not to go to the hut. Instead, she went to the head.

I radioed Charles and when he got to me, we were off to the head. I radioed Harold and told him that the park was closed to all visitors now, and to follow the last car through, to make sure that everyone was out of the park, then, to close it down. After that, Charles and I went out through the gates, locking them behind us and thanking the good Lord for another day of not being caught by a lion. This was really a very busy day; we were sure ready to head down that two-mile stretch, en route to home and to our families.

The following day, I really thought that these lions liked trying our patience, as the next morning, section seven again had a lion go through the gate in section six, running to the canal, swimming the canal, then going on the head. She didn't seem to be too excited, as she was just looking around, as if she was out for a leisurely stroll. I loaded the dart gun, but she was too far for me to get a good shot. I swam the canal, and after I got all wet and on the other side, she decided to swim back across the canal into section six. So, of course, I jumped back into the canal, swimming across. I jumped into my jeep, put the butt of the tranquilizer gun on the floor, and leaned the gun on the front of the seat. The lion was headed back to her own section, but she was still close to the canal. I was trying to catch up with her to get between her and the canal so she wouldn't go back across again. The ground was really rough, and as I was bouncing along, I hit a small ditch that was draining into the canal. My jeep left the ground, and somehow the gun got caught on the floor shift, firing the dart. The dart went in the back of my seat; it had just missed my shoulder by a few inches. I had two cc's of tranquilizer in the dart, and if that would have had hit me, I would have been walking behind all kinds of animals and snakes. I would have even seen them coming out of the wall. It would have affected me for at least three days and it sure wouldn't have been a pretty sight to see. I stopped the jeep, and during all this time, the lion did swim back across the canal, which didn't make me worry about her. I just wanted to check myself really well, making sure that the dart didn't hit me. After checking, I thanked the man upstairs for guiding the dart away from my shoulder. After making sure I was just fine and dandy, I called Harold to come on and go on the head to get this lion.

It didn't take us long and we found her: I darted her, waited fifteen minutes and she still didn't go out, so I decided to wait another ten minutes. Even after all this time, she still wasn't out all the way. As I have said before, I always carry extra tranquilizer with me for instances like these when I lose a dart that goes into my seat. We found a limb of a tree and put it in her mouth. Then, I grabbed her by the tail and gave her a half cc of the tranquilizer by hand right into her thigh. We waited another fifteen minutes, and then she was then completely out of it. After that, we got her into the jeep and back to the hut and back in the section that she belonged.

***

Today, we had a drunk that was driving too fast through the sections one and two, and going on into three. He almost ran over a couple of antelope, as he was just flying low through the park. Dan called from section three, asking me if I wanted him to stop him or slow him down. I told him to stop the man before he killed someone or some animal. Dan stopped him, and when he did, the man wanted to fight with him, calling him all kinds of names. Dan couldn't stand it anymore, so he got out of his jeep, walked over to the car, and just as he got to the car the drunk rolled up his window, just sitting there, looking at Dan.

Now, Dan was a very large man and he can be very intimidating just by his size. He was giving the man a mean look, but truth be known...he is really just a big ole teddy bear.

When I got there, I told the man to drive out of the park slowly or if he couldn't abide by my rule, then I would have a tractor come and hook up to his car and tow him out of the park. Then, of course, he wanted to fight with me. I told him, "Fine, come on out of the park, and we will see what happens."

I followed him out of the park and when we got out of the exit gate, he stopped. I got out of my jeep and walked up to his car. As I got to the back of his car, he stepped on the gas, going through the parking lot and as I saw him leaving. He was giving me the Hawaiian good luck sign and yelling something. We were all sure glad to get rid of him, but we couldn't understand why he would even want to go through the park as he was going so fast he couldn't see anything anyway.

On my day off, Charles was in charge. There were four elephants that went from their section to a lion section. All of the lions were chasing after the elephants. Charles said one elephant went by him with three lions hanging on to him, trying to eat him up. Then, the elephant went over into the canal and swam across onto the head, followed by the three lions. They had finally gotten all the lions away from the other elephants and put the elephants back on their island and putting the lions in the hut, except for the three that were over on the head with the other elephant. Then, Charles went with two other men to the head to find them. After getting on the head and looking for a while, they found the elephant dead; the vet said it most likely died of a heart attack.

They continued looking for the three lions, but with no luck. At this time, it was getting too dark to be going through the head, so Charles decided to wait until morning to hunt for them again. The next day, when I first saw Charles, he said that I should have been there yesterday. "You missed all the fun," he said. He proceeded to tell me all about it. After he had finished, he said, "But...ole buddy, we did save a little fun for you, knowing your feelings would have been hurt if we didn't."

I fondly thanked him and said, "Okay, are you ready to go get them? Let's go!"

Well, this work turned out to be a four-hour journey. Just as we were bedding down the last of the three lions, the girl from Pets' Corner called saying that they had the chimp that was getting too big for them to be handling in a cage and wanted us to come and get him. We had talked about bringing him out to Chimp Island and letting him mix with the other chimps. Charles and I went to Pets' Corner, picked him up, and took him to the island. We let him out of the cage on to the island and we stayed there on the island to watch him. Everything seemed to be okay, so we left the island, still watching them from a distance on the other side of the canal. The chimps were fighting a little, as they always did when someone introduced a new chimp. Then, the new chimp was in the water, sinking like a rock. We jumped in the water, feeling all around for him with our feet. It took us about fifteen minutes before we found him.

We brought him to the shore, but sadly, it was too late. He was already dead. We put him in the back of the jeep and continued on our way to the head where the elephant was. We had a tractor on the head, digging a grave for the elephant. When the man operating the tractor finally got the hole big enough, we put a chain on the elephant's leg, with the tractor pulling him over the hole.

This was in July, and we didn't get started digging the hole until afternoon. It had been twenty-four hours since the elephant died and he was starting to swell up. While we were dragging him, the elephant became hung up on a sharp root. Not being able to get him off, we were trying to figure out how we could get him off the root before he blew up all over us.

We got the machete out of the tractor, and cut off the root without hitting the elephant. We finally got the elephant to the hole, and we laid the chimp on top of the elephant, knowing they both were going to the happy hunting ground. We had to hurry, as we could hear the elephant's skin stretching, making all kinds of noises as it was swelling. It was at least one hundred degrees out there, but we made time to say a few words over the two. We were very relieved when we got back off that head. It was almost closing time now, and it surely seemed like the day went by fast. We all were glad to be going home tonight. A rough day had surrendered to a tranquil night, holding hope for a better day tomorrow within its cloak of darkness.

***

All seemed to be going great the next day up until closing time. Again, I really think the animals know when we are ready to go home, and they just like to see what we are made of. A lion from section three went on the head. We looked for this lion for a long time but didn't find her until it was eight o'clock.

We had seen her twice. I got one shot at her with the dart gun, but missed, so I decided it was too dangerous to stay on the head for much longer. We would try again on the morrow.

The next morning, Charles, Harold, Ron, and I went back to the head. Going all through the head, we finally found her at around noon. I tranquilized her and we loaded her in the jeep taking her back to the hut. This is when I realized that it seemed like we spent an awful lot of time going through these heads looking for these lions. However, this made it exciting and interesting to be able to be with and take care of these wild animals, wanting all the time for them to be able to live as if they are in the wild instead of being in barred enclosures. But, to be honest, I think they enjoy the excitement as much as we do; it gives them a sense of being in control, until they wake up the next morning that is.

I know we seem to be going on a head hunting a lion all the time, but each situation is very different. One can never think that it will be just like the last one, and if we were to do this we would be letting down our guard and I don't need to say that this would be very dangerous.

OSTRICHES RAISE THEIR HEADS TO OBSERVE PASSING TRAFFIC

**A LION CUB ABOUT ONE HOUR
AFTER IT WAS BORN**

Chapter 11

Greg, the Snake Man
A Lion Charging all the Way

Greg, the snake man, is in charge of all of the snakes in Pets' Corner. In Pets' Corner, there was a big snake pit as well as a number of glassed sections where people could walk through and look at all of these snakes. There were snakes from all over the world. My son, Joe was only about seven when I started working at Lion Country. He was interested in snakes, so for Christmas, his grandmother gave him a boa constrictor measuring about three feet long. He would see snakes around the house and always try to catch them. I asked Greg if I brought Joe out to Lion Country, would he take him by the hand and teach him the poisonous ones from the non-poisonous, and to let Joe be his sidekick. Greg had some small pieces of plywood and old boards that were laid down all around the park and out in the woods. He would check the boards once or twice a week to see if there were any snakes under them. I told him that I would appreciate it if he could do that for me, but being cautious, I also told him to be sure not to let him handle any poisonous snakes. I also told Greg to teach him whatever he could, so that he would know enough about snakes to keep him from being bitten by the poisonous ones.

If we see a snake when I take him hunting or fishing, I can tell him if the snakes we see are poisonous or not. I could tell him a lot about them, but surely not as much as Greg could. Greg spent a lot of time with Joe, helping him learn about snakes.

I would take him to work with me almost every day for quite a while, where he would spend the whole day helping Greg and learning all about snakes. I thanked Greg for having Joe as his sidekick and for teaching him all that he did. Joe still remembers all the good times he had there with Greg. Greg always told me to call him if any of us see a snake there at the park and he would come and get it.

One day, as I was riding through the park away from the lions, I saw a rattle snake about four feet long he was sliding across the road, so I gave Greg a call and he said that he would be right there. Before he got to the snake and me, the snake was trying to get off the road, so I pulled my jeep close to it to move it back to the middle of the road. When Greg finally got there, he got out of his jeep with an old burlap bag and a golf putting iron. He walked to the snake, being only about two feet away from it, pushed the putting iron down on it, grabbed the snake by the back of the head, tossed it in his le burlap bag, twisted it, then threw it in his jeep, and thanked me. I told him about the snake trying to get away and that I was afraid I was going to make it mad, and it would make it hard for him when he would go to catch it. Greg said that it didn't bother him. I said, "Alright I'll do that and then we'll see." A few months went by, and I saw a rattlesnake going across the road. It wasn't close to the lions, but it was in the lion section. This one was about five and a half feet long, and was quite fat. I called Greg to tell him that I had another snake for him. He told me that if I desired to, to go ahead and get him mad, so of course I said, "Will do." I started getting stones from the side of the road, and as the snake started moving to the side of the road. I got about eight feet from the snake and threw stones at it. When I threw the stones at the snake, it would turn and go the other way. I kept throwing them, and lunging towards him, which made him coil up with his head being about a foot off the ground, sounding off his rattles. I kept throwing stones at him until it looked like a battleground. The snake raised its head two feet off the ground like a cobra. He started coming at me, then coiled up again with his rattlers singing. Greg came up in his jeep and got out with his sack and his putter. He looked at the snake, and then at the road. He finally looked at me and said, "Man, you really got him fired up, you'll need to get a tractor out here to move all these boulders, and fill in all the holes they make."

He started walking to the snake. I told Greg that I really had him upset now. I threw many rocks at him and he lifted up like a cobra, he just smiled and said that that was okay. He walked over to the snake, put the putter on its head, reached down, picked him up, and stuffed him in his old burlap bag. Then, we started talking about the mess I made in the road. I said, "Man, you're crazy to be working with those snakes," and he said, "No way, you're the crazy one working with those lions." We both had a good laugh saying different strokes for different folks. He thanked me and took off back to his snake pit and me back to my lions and other animals.

A good while after this situation, Greg was cleaning on the glass cages that had a mamba in it. I don't remember what type of mamba it was, but I do know that it was a poisonous African snake. The snake bit him and he was lucky, as it only got him with one fang. Greg was in the hospital for quite a few days. While he was in there, Mac took care of the snake pit. During this time, the snake up and died. When Greg came back to work, he still had a little green tint to his skin and was very tired for a long time afterwards. It took a while before the green went away and he was back to his old self once again.

***

The following day, the lions went wild. All of the sections were fighting, with each other running all over their section. All day long, this mess kept going on. I was running from one section to the other, helping the men keep their lions straightened out. I helped section two five times in this one day. Almost all of the females were in season, which kept all of the males fighting for their attention and trying to protect the females that they think are theirs. This made for a very trying day.

One of the cubs in section three followed a female lion over on the moat. The lions swam back to the section, but the cub was scared of the water and he wouldn't come back across it. It was almost closing time, so after we got section three's lions in and accounted for, I swam the canal and almost was bitten by a cottonmouth on the other side. I got the cub and started back across in the water, but the cub got scared and started scratching me, trying to get on me, and out of the water. I pushed it away and toward section three and she followed me to the other side. I put her in the hut with her mother and they both were glad to see each other.

We received for Pets' Corner a stuffed and mounted adult lion. It was to be situated with a backdrop of a scene from Africa, which was to be used by the visitors to have their picture taken. They could put on a safari shirt and hat, stand behind the lion holding a spear, and get their picture taken like a big game hunter in Africa. They weren't ready for it to be used yet, as the guy who came from California to paint the backdrop wasn't finished. When he first came here and started painting for the first week or so, it just looked like a big mess; not even the blue sky or the green for the grass looked right. After about two weeks, it started looking like what it was supposed to, which was a scene from Africa. When he was almost finished, it looked great. He even painted some rocks and small boulders in it. He also ordered some rocks, put them in front of the scene, and put some paint on them. I thought he did a great job, so we moved the mounted lion to the side door inside Pets' Corner.

When the people that brought it left, the women and I were checking it all out. We got talking how the meat man, Willy, was so scared of lions, that we wondered what he would do if he walked in with that lion by the door. The women said that they had just passed him walking in Pets' Corner, so I called him on the radio and told him to come to the side door in the building. We moved the lion where when he came in, he wouldn't see it right away. We were in the corner. He came in, closed the door, and looked at us. I yelled, "Look out!"

As I was looking past him at the lion, he turned and saw this full-grown lion. He yelled and ran straight to us and got behind us. Still yelling, we all started laughing. He looked at us and then at the lion, sweating like a pig. I was getting a little worried that he might have a heart attack. He was so scared of just a lion cub, much less a full-grown one with a black mane. Needless to say, he called us some well-chosen names and used a few choice words on us. He finally calmed down and started laughing with all of us, telling us he would surely get even with us. He took the joke pretty well after he knew that the lion wasn't real. I don't think I would want to try it again on anyone else, as I might not be so lucky the next time.

I had to leave as I was on my way to give some medication to some of the animals. I went to the section and started to give a lion some medication with the dart gun from my jeep. Some of these lions and antelope that I gave the medication to have to know the sound of my jeep, and they associated it with them getting a shot, so as soon as they heard me coming, they would take off. Sometime, I would get out of my jeep, and get in the jeep of the one watching that section. By doing this, I could get closer to them, but I didn't do that this time. As I aimed and shot, the lion took off. I shot a small tree in that section. We both had a good laugh, and I told him I did it on purpose because the tree looked sickly, again we laughed. With the next shot, I hit my target, medicating the lion, so all went well. About a month later, he called me to his section, telling me to check out that tree I shot with the medication dart, he said it looks a lot better, the funny thing is, it did look better.

Another day, at eight o'clock in the morning, section three lost a lion. I saw her in the high grass on the mote. The mote was along the perimeter around the whole park against the two sixteen foot high fences with five strands of barb wire on top, leaning to the inside of the park. A canal was on the other side of the mote, so I was on the mote, I could ride in a jeep or walk all around the park and swim to any of the sections. I drove on the mote with my jeep, trying to dart her. When she saw me coming at her, she jumped into the canal and swam to a head. I called Harold to meet me by the head and when he got there, we started looking for her. She was just staying ahead of us, then. She went back on the mote to another head. I got Ron and Sonny to watch for her on the mote and at the edge of the heads. She was working her way to the biggest head that we had in the park, which was also the wettest one. Ron had seen her go to the big head, so Harold and I went in. I told Sonny and Ron to come to the head where the lion went in and that we would meet them there. I told them to bring their guns with them. After they got there, I told them that I wanted them to find a place in the head just off from where we were and for them to stay there. I wanted to be sure to know where they were. I said that the lion was just staying ahead of us, and that they should call me on the radio if they saw the lion. Harold and I started walking the other way. We walked the whole head and came back to where they were waiting. It took us two or three hours. I told them to be very careful as we had been after her for six hours already and she might decide to make her stand. Harold and I went in the head. We zigzagged through the head for a couple more hours and turned up nothing. It was now closing time. I called Charles and told him to close the park. I told him that when we got the lion, we would come out. The men started talking on the radio, and I said to have radio silence, as I needed to hear Ron or Sonny on the other side of the head if they should call.

Mr. Dredge said that Nonie was there to pick me up. He told me she would be in the office waiting for me. She was hearing all that was going on over the radios, as the base set was on in the office. Harold and I kept walking the head, and we finally saw her, lying or crouching down by a small bush; we couldn't tell which. She was watching us with her ears back and the end of her tail swished back and forth in quick jerks. I told Harold that she was making her stand now, and that she was tired of us hunting her down. I picked my shot in her thigh.

I said, "Harold if she starts charging us and if she goes past a small tree that had fallen down between her and us, to shoot her," as she would be coming all the way. I then shot her in the thigh, and as soon as the dart hit her, she charged us, going past that small tree. I threw down the tranquilizer gun and as it hit the ground, I kneeled on one knee and drew my .357 pistol. As I pulled it out of the holster, Harold pulled the trigger of the 12 gauge double barrel shot gun. As I was looking at the lion, Harold was going back. Everything was going a hundred miles an hour now. I thought, "I can't believe it, he's leaving me." At the same time when Harold shot, he hit the lion in the front side and leg. She flipped over, did a headstand, and got up to come at me again. I shot the .357 and hit her. She fell back, and again, she flipped over going backwards. I shot one more time and she continued to charge me. For the third time, I shot and she just kept coming, only closer this time. By now, she was about ten feet from me and covered with blood, with an evil look in her eyes. I was hoping that she would stay down and not get up again. I shot again, but still, she kept coming. I shot really quickly, and she fell only about five feet from me. I was thinking now if she were to get up again, I would have to stick my hand and arm in her mouth and try to get a brain shot. I didn't know how many shots I had shot at her, but I thought that I had five. Thinking that I only had one left, she got up again, came within two to three feet of me, she turned around, limped to the place where I had first shot her with the tranquilizer gun, and started licking her wound, all the time looking at me with her ears back, and her tail swishing back and forth. I figured that she wasn't going anywhere, as she had been tranquilized and shot with a shotgun and not really knowing how many times I shot her with my .357 pistol, so she wasn't going anywhere. I started running back to my jeep to get the 375, which was used as an elephant gun. Harold was now running back to me. I asked him why he left me with that lion, and he said, "Gus, I didn't leave you. When I pulled the trigger on the double barrel shot gun, I pulled both triggers on the gun and it knocked me back. I tripped on a cypress tree, fell down, and I forgot to bring any more shells. So when this happened, I got up, ran to the jeep to get more shells, and was coming back to help you."

I said, "What in the world is the matter with you?" You know better than that. You know when you go in a head with a shotgun loaded with two shells in your left hand and two or three more in your pocket."

He said, "Gus I know that, man I just forgot, we've been hunting this lion for eleven hours, I just forgot." I told him that I would surely remind him next time. Harold was a good lion man. I would trust him to have my back anytime; he just messed up this time. We went back to the lion and she was at the same place that she was when I left her. She was shot too many times, and the only thing to do was to put her down. I asked Harold if he was ready, and did he have extra shells with him now, which he did. I took a head shot with the 375 rifle and shot the lion. I felt really bad about it, but there wasn't anything else we could do.

About that time, Bill York called on the radio, as he lived on the park with his wife. He said that he heard the shots, knowing we were in the head looking for the lion. He had gone to the office to call me on the radio and he said, "Gus, is everything okay?"

I told him "Yes, but with one less." He knew what I was talking about and I told him that I would be bringing her in. Bill said, "I heard all those shots, thinking that the lion must have been shooting back at you."

I said, "She just didn't want to go down and stay there and that she kept getting up and charging me." Harold and I checked the lion over to make sure she was dead. As I said, we both felt really bad even though she did charge us; she was just doing what comes natural for lions. She was a wild animal, but it still hurt that we did what we had to do. She had been shot numerous times with a .357 at close range as well as a shotgun. We dragged her back to the jeep. Then Ron, Sonny, Harold, and I took her outside where Bill checked her out. After that, we took her to the freezer, went to the office where Bill Dredge, the manager, Bill York, and Nonie were. As I walked in the door, Nonie said that I needed to get another job, as this job was killing me. I told her that I didn't know of any job I would rather do. She said, "I know, so let's go home or stop where you do to play pool after work," so out the door we went, heading down the two mile stretch. By this time, it was nine thirty.

The next day, a man and a woman were fighting in their car inside the park. She was hitting him with her purse, then, she decided to get right out in the middle of a lion section. I went over to her and told her to get in my jeep and I would escort her outside of the park to Pets' Corner. She got in my jeep and her husband or boyfriend followed us out. It seemed like a rerun of the last episode with the other two. I made the deduction that it must have been something about the lion sections that get men and women to start fighting, or so it seemed.

When I got to work the following day, I found that we had six men out, which made for a very thin crew to run the park. A chimp got off the island on the boat and drifted on the other side. Then, he went out of the park and jumped on the roof of the restaurant in Pets' Corner. I went to the restaurant with apples and bananas in my pockets, hoping that this would help get him off the roof. I asked where there was a ladder and they told me that it was in the back of the restaurant. I retrieved it, then, I told the people that worked at the restaurant to get me about eight popsicles. After they brought them to me, I climbed the ladder.

I was on the roof with the chimp. I called to him, showing him the popsicles. I took a bite out of it and smacked my lips, trying to make a lot of noise to let him know how good it was. He came over to me and sat right down in front of me, putting his hand out as if to say, "May I have one." I gave him half of a popsicle, and he liked it. I started talking to him as I was walking to the ladder. He followed me and I gave him another half of the popsicle, then I started down the ladder. As I was going down, I yelled that I needed more popsicles, so someone ran and brought me four more. After we got down to the ground, he held my hand as we walked to my jeep, eating popsicles. I opened the door to my jeep and threw one on the seat. He jumped in and sat in the seat, eating his popsicle as we went back inside of the park. I ran out of the popsicles, so I started giving him apples and bananas along with some oranges. We got to Chimp Island and to where the boat was, so I threw a banana into the front of the boat. He jumped right in and sat down to eat his banana. When I got over to the island, I only had about three left, so I threw them about five feet on to the island. The chimp jumped off and started to fight the other chimps for the bananas. I went to the other side of the canal, tied the boat up, and thanked the Lord for making it so easy to get the chimp back to the island. After all that, we had an antelope born around three o'clock. We took it to Pets' Corner because the zebras were trying to get to it and the mother wasn't trying to protect it, so I thought it best to put the little one in Pets' Corner.

Wayne lost one of his lions, Peggie, and her three cubs. We looked for them all through the section, and we finally found them in the rhino section. We worked them back to the hut, after which, I got a call telling me that a lion from section seven went to the head, so George, Vern, Charles and I went to the head to get her. She decided to go on the moat where she was walking between the fence and the canal. Vern and I went to the outside, walked along the fence, and she charged us between the fence. As she was going toward the exit gate, Vern was getting her attention as I went around by the gate standing by the post. She was watching Vern very closely, and when she got by me I darted her when she was about three feet away. She didn't even know I was there between the fences. When she went down, we took her back to section seven's hut, and bedded her down.

Gus, the rhino, took another stroll off the island and walked around in section six. I was at the food shack, checking to see what I needed to order for all the animals in the park when I got a call from section six to alert me of Gus being in his section with his lions all going crazy to get to him. Gus was walking towards the lion prides. I went out into the preserve, and as I was on my way, I radioed the man in section seven, telling him to get to section six, and to let him know he needed to tell all the people to get out of the section. He would do this over his loud haler, telling him to make sure they all got out of there, and then, he would close gates six and seven. I called Charles telling him to bring me some sweet feed so I could give some to Gus trying to pull him away from the lions. I then called section five and told the worker to close five and six gate and not to let the people through because of we had an emergency right now. I also told him to wait at the gate to let me through, and to close it behind me. I told the man in section six to open his hut door and start putting what lions he could up in the hut, letting him know I would be there to help him. When I got there, three lions were after Gus. He was headed towards section five by the canal. I told the ranger of the section to stay with the lions and to put up as many as he could.

I tried to separate the lions from Gus, then, Charles and Dale got there. Between the three of us, we got the lions to the hut. Gus was just watching the lions and us as we put them up. We got all the lions in the section in their hut even though they were all fired up with all the excitement going on. Charles, Dale, and I went to get Gus back to his island. We got to him and gave him some sweet feed. Dale and Charles sat on the back of my jeep with a pail of the sweet feed, with Gus following us to Rhino Island's gate and onward, into the barn. We closed him in the barn for the rest of the day and decided to leave the lions in the hut. I called into the office and told them to open all the gates between the sections. We found out that Gus went under the pipe fence at the canal, and the water in the canal was low. We would have to put another pipe on the fence to keep him on his island. He was getting to like these little strolls that he took from time to time.

The next day, Charles and I worked on putting another pipe under the bottom one of Gus's island until I got a call from George. He had a lion on the mote. We both went over to the section and were able to tranquilize the lion. It took twenty minutes for her to go down, but she still wasn't under enough for us to handle her, so Charles and I swam across the canal. I gave her one cc by hand and we waited another five minutes. She was then out enough so that we could drag her across the canal and take her to the hut. After all this was done, we headed back to the island where Gus was because we needed to finish putting down the pipe fence. The next day, we would let Gus out of his barn to see what he would do with the fence.

After opening the park, we let Gus out and the very first thing he did was stroll over to where the pipe fence was and try to get under it; but thank goodness, he couldn't do it. He just walked slowly away...as if to say, "Oh well, just thought I'd give it a try."

I had a lot of running around that day; we had four lion cubs born in section six. Then, we had a new lion down by the hut, away from the pride. We were able to get her back where she should be. Harold had trouble in section three, five, and six because all of the animals were going wild. We finally got them all back, except for one that was by Elephant Island. We got him back with the others on the moat. Then, at closing time, we had him darted. We then went to section four, where I darted that lion. After she went down, we swam across the canal, tied a rope to her, and dragged her back across. After getting her taken care of, a lion went on the head and killed a goat. George and I went over to that head, got her tranquilized, and brought her back to the hut. We took the dead goat to the freezer. While all of this was going on, a lion in section three got some camping equipment off a car top. He just sat there and tore it to shreds. Finally, it was time to close the place up. I couldn't wait to head down that two-mile stretch. It was a long and busy day.

***

A couple of days later, at closing time, a lion in section four went on the moat. At about the same time, a lion in section six went around the hut with one jeep coming on one side and another from the other. The lion jumped up on the roof. I couldn't believe it when they told me what happened. When I got there I darted her right on the roof and she just lay down, looking around as if she really liked being up there. It took about fifteen minutes for her to go under so we could handle her. Three other rangers and I got up on the roof. We tied a rope around her, then, put her over the edge, letting her down carefully to the other rangers on the ground. Then, the rangers took her to the hut and bed her down until the next morning.

I was called to section four to tranquilize a lion that had gone over on the moat. After darting it, we waited the allotted time, swam across the canal, put a rope around her, and brought her back across the canal. Two others helped us lift her in to the jeep, and we took her to the hut.

It wasn't long after all that happened that I was putting seralyn, an anesthetic that's used as an immobilizing agent, in a dart to tranquilize a lion. As I was filling it, I did it a little too fast and got some of the seralyn in my eye. I told Charles to take care of the lions as I was going to Pets' Corner to lie down. When I got there, I was seeing many little animals coming out of the woodwork. I told Bill what had happened; he told me to go lay down, and that he would check on me later. It took most of the day before I felt like moving around. I will tell you, it sure wasn't a good experience to go through, but it sure taught me to be a lot more careful when filling the dart.

***

Things went fairly well this day until closing time. As I said before, I think all the lions get together and say, "Okay it's time to raise a little cane." So off went three. A cub decided to climb up a tree when they were putting them up in the hut. She went up the tree and wouldn't come down. We tried everything to get her down. Then, we moved the jeeps away from the tree to give her room so as not to push her. She still wouldn't budge, sticking to her guns. I had no choice but to dart her. After the tranquilizer began to take effect, she was slowly sliding down the tree. When she got about three feet from the ground, she just flopped on the ground. She wasn't all the way under so I put the catchall on her and walked her to the hut; we put her in by herself so the other lions wouldn't mess with her.

A film crew came in the park the next day to advertise for kids' shoes, which took up most of my day. They first brought in about twelve kids. We went to Elephant Island. They wanted to put a big blanket that had a name of the kids' shoes over Donya, and then put some kids under her belly with a few kids running around her. I told them that there was no way I would allow that to happen, as she had already put two men in the hospital, and under no circumstances would that happen. I told them that, between them and me, we needed to come up with a better idea. They weren't very happy with me, but we came up with something that was okay. We let some of them stand in front of Donya with the blanket on her while some of the kids were in front of the ones standing, playing marbles and a few other low key games, so all went well. I was running around with them most of the day; just making sure, they didn't get into any trouble. After the film crew left, it was time to put the lions up for the night. That darn little cub in section three decided to go up the same tree again, so we had to go through the same ole thing. I didn't waste any time seeing if she would come down, so I just darted her and down the tree she slid. We then took her and put her to bed. I sure was hoping this wasn't going to be an everyday occurrence.

When I got in to work the next morning, Dredge called me into his office, saying that they had a monkey that escaped from its cage and that it was running all around town. The owner of the monkey had just got him and had no control over him at all. I called Charles and told him that we needed to go to town to see what we could do about this escaped prisoner.

Well, when we got to the house where the man lived with his wife, she said that her husband had just called her and he was three blocks from their house. He said that he found the monkey in a tree, so we went to where he was. When we got there, there must have been fifty or more people around the monkey and the tree he was in. We got out of our zebra striped jeeps, then, started looking for the monkey up the tree. All these people started moving in on us, and I told them they would all need to give the monkey room and us. There was a lot of yelling and loud talking. People were moving all around, which was making the monkey nervous. He started making a lot of noise and started coming down. I don't know how long he had been out of his cage, but I think he was getting tired of all the commotion of everyone chasing him, so he was coming down the tree and he hit the ground running, right towards the crowd. As he got closer, the crowd gave him plenty of room. The crowd was running, kicking, yelling, and tucking their butts in as they were getting away from that crazy monkey. Charles and I were on the other side of the tree, watching all of this, and laughing like crazy. We were really cracking up. From our point of view, the crowd sure looked funny trying to get away from the monkey, and they sure weren't laughing.

As we were following the monkey, he went into a half basement in a house. The door was open, so he ran inside. We closed the door and checked around to make sure no windows were open. We both had a tranquilizer gun. We stopped to catch our breath for a few seconds, then, we opened the door and went in, closing it behind us. The homeowners knew that Charles and I, along with our fury little monkey, were in their basement. We just slowly walked around the basement, seeing him behind some boxes. I got a clear shot at him with the dart. When the dart hit him, he went nuts. He jumped, grabbing the dart pulling it out himself. Then, started going bananas by running all around and making all kinds of noises. He started settling down some, so we waited ten minutes and he was out like a light. When we brought him out, everyone clapped their hands, and they all had big smiles on their faces. We did bring a small cage with us in the jeep to put him in, so we took him back to his own cage that was behind his owner's house. The cage was big and safe; the monkey had just figured out how to open the door. The owner said that he would fix the latch, so we put him in his cage. After wrapping this all up, we headed back to Lion Country. We were talking about the crowd trying to get away from the monkey when he had enough and ran through the crowd. We thought it was so funny how they were all around when he was up the tree, but even funnier how they gave him all kinds of room when he came down the tree running towards them. Then we really had a good laugh again.

***

The following day, we had a sika deer that went from the antelope section on to the head. I got Sammy and we went in to the head after him. We found him with no problem. The head was mostly knee deep in water. We got close enough to him, then I decided not to dart him, so we jumped in the water and tackled him. Then, we took him to the jeep. He was a very small antelope, so it was not a problem jumping him, but, of course, he didn't see us coming and didn't even know we were there in the water with him. If he had seen us, we would have never caught him, as they are also very fast. We took him to the jeep. Sammy held him in the back of the jeep, but as we were trying to get out of the head, the sika slashed Sammy with his hooves on one of his legs. It was really deep and long. I had to take him into town to the hospital; the cut needed a few stitches, and he was out of work for a few days. I felt bad about it, but that is one of the hazards of the job. We all have the same situations to look out for, never knowing what might happen. One must just try one's best to watch out for everything and always be on one's toes.

When I returned to Lion Country, lions in all of the sections were acting funny. They were drooling from their mouths and they were acting as if they were drunk. Doc gave them some medication, but the next morning, they were still sick. Other lions in other sections were sick with the same symptoms; Doc tried the same medication on them, but with still no difference in any of them. When I came in the next day, there still was no improvement.

More of the lions had gotten sick, so I suggested to Doc to try cortisone and pinstripe. The next morning, the ones we gave the cortisone and pinstripe to were better, while all the others were still the same, so Doc gave some to all the other lions. The very next morning, we could see a huge difference in all of them, with some of them being almost back to normal. In a couple of days, they were all back, as they were before. It made me feel really good that it worked, as I was the one to suggest what to use.

***

A lion in six went on the moat the very first thing in the morning. We tried to get her off with no luck, so I ended up tranquilizing her. Everything went smoothly until closing time, when a lion in section six again went on the head; Charles and I went in and got her. Then, as the lions in section three were going to the hut, one decided to climb a tree. We all backed off and gave her room. In about fifteen minutes, she got tired of hanging on, so she slid down the tree and took off to the hut. Then, I could finally close the park up and go home.

The next morning, a greater kudu had a calf. We got her and the calf in the holding section before the zebra knew that the calf was there. Then, a hippo from section one got over by Elephant Island. We chased him back to section one with no trouble. I noticed that a giraffe that wasn't looking up to par, so I gave him a shot of antibiotic, then stayed with him for about forty-five minutes, to check him out. Jim, who was the man cleaning huts was in seven, opened the doors without checking the hut. When he opened the doors, two lions came running out. Jim took off running and climbed the six-foot chain-link fence. While doing this, he cut his hand and got a bad cut above his eye. Charles took him to the hospital. Sonny and I went over and tranquilized the two lions, and got them back to the hut. We were doing a lot that day, but everything seemed to be done that needed to be done.

Another day, things seemed to go great until closing. Two lions were giving us trouble. I darted one by Elephant Island. After I darted him, I wasn't sure if he was all the way out or not, so we got into the boat to go across the canal to the moat. The hippo came up and looked like he was thinking about tipping our boat over. It was almost dark at this time. We checked the lion and he was all the way out. We loaded him in the boat and went back across. By then, we didn't know where the hippo was, but we were looking for him and hoping we didn't see or hear him at all. It was just too darn dark to be coming face to face with a hippo. It was around nine o'clock when we could finally leave the park, leaving another exciting day behind us.

Coming in on a very nice morning, everything was going as planned until around eleven o'clock when Dale called me on the radio saying the chimps were all fighting big time against another chimp. He was saying that all of his lions were trying to get to Chimp Island, so I got there as fast as I could. When I got to the island, I got out of my jeep, and ran to get in the boat. About that time, Charles pulled up in his jeep and he yelled to me, "Hey Gus! Wait and I'll help you." Therefore, he ran over and jumped in the boat with me. As we were going across in the boat, the chimp that all the other chimps were fighting with got into the deep water. He went under the water and then the bubbles started coming up in the middle of the canal. We both jumped out of the boat, holding on to the side and we tried to find the chimp with our feet. The reason we were holding on to the boat was because if the chimp were to grab one of us by the leg, he could surely pull us under the water with him. Chimps are as strong as three or four big men are, when things are normal. When they are in trouble and scared, they are a lot stronger. That is why we held on to the boat so he couldn't take us down with him. We both touched him about the same time. He hadn't passed out yet, but he was under the water long enough to know that we were trying to help him. We let go of the boat, dove down to get him, and we held on to him and brought him back to the surface. We then grabbed the side of the boat, still holding on to the chimp and boat at the same time while kicking our feet to get to shore. When we got to the other side, we laid him on the ground. We talked to him to try to see how he would react. He was still awake and looking at us. He would look at Charles, then, look at me. We rolled him over on his stomach, with his head lower than his feet. He was coughing and spitting up water. He was weak but we knew he was going to make it. He knew where he was and was aware of what was going on around him but didn't seem to care at the moment. We put him in the back of my jeep. I sat with him while Charles drove to Pets' Corner. When we got there, the chimp still couldn't walk, so we each grabbed him under both arms and took him into the building in Pets' Corner. The women had a cage ready to put him. We stayed, watching him for about forty-five minutes. He started to move around, so the women started to take care of him. When Charles and I started to leave, the chimp held out his arm, looking at us and started chimp talk, as if to say, "Thanks guys." It sure made me feel good when something bad turns out right; it makes my day well worth it.

***

When we opened the park this morning, three lions in six were giving us all kinds of trouble. One lion swam the canal into seven getting on the moat by the fence on the other side of the canal. One wouldn't go out of the hut. The other lion went over by Rhino Island. She went completely out of her own section to check out the rhinos, making them very nervous. They were running all around the island. I got over there and darted her before she caused any more problems. Charles stayed with the lion so she wouldn't get in the canal and to keep her away from the island. He stayed there until she went under the tranquilizer. I went over to the moat to get the other lion. After darting the first one, she was still on the moat, so I got her going towards her section. Then, she got on the road and went towards the section she should be in. Once in section six, I pushed her to her pride. She seemed to go right in and settled down, so that went well. From there, I went back to the hut to check the lion that didn't want to come out. She was still in there, so I just shut the hut door and left her in for the rest of the day. After doing that, I went back to Rhino Island where Charles was keeping an eye on the other lion. By now, she was down for the count. We loaded her into the back of the jeep and took her back to the hut. We had about twenty minutes of calm, then, I got a call from section seven, and a lion went onto the head. So, off again Charles and I went, into the head, tracking another lion. As I have said before, we have been hunting these lions so much that we know just what the other one is thinking. I had checked my notes a few days ago and I counted two hundred and eighteen lions that had been tranquilized just inside the heads and walking through the swamps with all the bushes and palmettos. Charles has been right by my side most of the time. When one has someone who has watched one's back that many times, as we have both done, one forms a very tight bond. As the man said, a friend is someone you call when you're in jail, a true friend is someone who is setting right beside you in the cell, saying, "Damn that was fun."

We went into the head and found him fairly quickly. I tranquilized him and we took him to the jeep. All of the huts were full of lions that had been darted, so we had the rolling cage in section four. We took the lion to section four, pulled the lion off the jeep, then, we hooked the cage to the back of the jeep. We then opened the door, put the door on top of the cage, and started to put the tranquilized lion inside. When we got him almost all the way in, he tried to get up. He wanted to get out of the rolling cage. Charles went to the side of the cage and grabbed his tail that was hanging out. The lion was partially out of the cage, so I jumped on top of the cage and grabbed the door that was on top and jammed it along and in front of the lion. Since he was somewhat under the tranquilizer, he wasn't as strong as normal or thinking straight. I told Charles that I had him jammed in for the moment and to back the jeep up against the hut, then he got out of the jeep, grabbed his tail and lifted the door up, putting both sides in the groove and pushed the door down. Then we had him in the cage.

We started talking about why he wasn't out all the way from the dart. When we were in the head, and after darting him, we noticed that the dart wasn't stuck in him. The darts have a barb on the end of the needle and usually stay in so one can tell that one has darted them successfully. If there is no barb, then, after you hit them, the dart will bounce back out. Sometimes, if they are darted inside the head, they run off and rub on the bushes or on the sides of trees, then the dart will pull out. I really think the barb broke off and he didn't get the entire tranquilizer, as it bounced out as soon as it hit him. After all that was over, we wiped the sweat from our brows and our face, saying, "Boy, wasn't that fun?" Therefore, off we went, taking the rolling cage with the lion into section seven where the lion belonged. We put the cage by the hut and waited until the next morning for him to sleep it off.

GUS WITH AN ADOLESCENT LION

Chapter 12

A Lion Takes Over My Jeep

It seems like for the past four months, we have been having a lot of trouble with the lions. They all seem to know their way around, including inside all the heads. Now, every day, we are going inside a head to tranquilize anywhere from one to eight lions in one working day. We sometimes tranquilize as many as six in the head at one time. This day seemed to be different. I started out darting two zebras to trim their hooves and to take some blood to run some test on them. Most of the lions in section seven were going nuts, but we finally got them calmed down and I went off to section four. A lion went into the pump house, so Sonny and I went over to get him out. Sonny left his jeep in section four, so he got into my jeep and we went on the moat.

I stopped by the pump house. This wasn't the first time a lion went into the pump house. I got the tranquilizer gun loaded, got out of my jeep, leaving the doors to the jeep open, and we looked inside the pump house and couldn't see him. About that time, Ron, who was watching Sonny's section, was yelling at us that the lion wasn't in the pump house, and that he was behind it, walking towards my jeep. As we came out of the pump house, we saw the lion getting in my jeep from the driver's side. He was getting comfy in my seat and I told Sonny that I would tranquilize him when he decides to get out. Well, wouldn't you know that he decided to lie down on the seat, filling up the whole inside of the jeep? He looked as if to say, "If you want your jeep back, come on, and get it."

I decided to try and wait him out, so we waited about fifteen or twenty minutes. We were all just cracking up at the sight of this lion sprawled all over the inside of my jeep, looking as if to say, "I'm in it for the long haul, how bout you two?"

After awhile, it was beginning not to be so funny. I told Sonny that we would swim the canal to section four and get his jeep, then take it onto the moat, behind my jeep, to try to get him out of mine. I told Ron to move his jeep back and that maybe the lion would swim back across the canal to section four, and if he does, to take him back to where the pride is.

We pulled up behind my jeep and the lion didn't budge a bit. I got Sonny's shotgun and we got as close to the back of my jeep as we could. I got out of the jeep, pointed the shotgun to the air, and pulled the trigger. When it went off, the lion jumped out of my jeep and ran as fast as he could. He jumped in the canal and swam across it. He didn't let any grass grow under his feet until he was back with his pride. After that, I sure took a lot of kidding about the lion wanting to ride shotgun with me and be my partner. For months, these guys kept it up, but he sure did look funny lying in my jeep, just looking around as if he really belonged there. But it was time to get my jeep out of being held hostage by the lion. Once I got my jeep, I had to have a few minutes to catch my breath before going on to the next situation.

All seemed to be going well until it was time to close everything down and go home. Three lions from section six decided to go into section five. We got two of them back where they belonged, but one decided to jump on top of a car. I guess he thought he would be safe up there. I was going to dart him while he was on top of the car, but when I first pointed the dart gun at the lion, all I saw were eyeballs in the car, then everyone ducked. It looked like no one was in the car at all, but when the dart hit him; he jumped off the car and went back to section six and right into the hut. Then, we had to separate him from the rest of the pride in the hut. I put hay down to let him sleep off the tranquilizer. After taking care of the lion, I went back to the people in the car, telling them I was sorry I had to dart the lion on their car. They said not worry about that because it was the most exciting thing that has happened to them and that they really enjoyed it. They thanked me and went on their way, going through the rest of the park. Yep, this sure has been an interesting day. After that, it was time to go home.

For the past couple of weeks, we have been getting a lot of rain, so today it was raining hard with high winds. It was hard to see the animals; it was even hard to see the cars going through the sections. There weren't too many cars going through the park, so that was a plus. We decided to close the park down. This was the first time that this had ever happened since we opened. It was raining so hard that even with the windshield wipers, going full blast one still couldn't see. All of the animals were lying down and all curled up because of the weather.

A few days after we closed the park for a day, we met with the fish and game officers. They wanted us to go with them to the Everglades, which wasn't that far from the park. When we got there, four airboats were there, so we helped them get the boats off the trailers. We jumped in and went to help save some deer, and other animals that were in need. It had been raining steadily now for a couple of weeks and the deer and some of the other animals were starving because of the high waters; some were even drowning. We saw the deer and caught six. The airboat went alongside of the deer and we jumped off the boat and into the water by the deer, pulling them down. We then gave them a shot, covered their eyes with a towel, and laid them down in the bottom of the boat. At Lion Country, we rented a big tent, spread hay on the ground, and laid all kinds of feed on the hay for them to eat. We had made temporary pens all through the tent, getting the women from Pets' Corner to look after them. At the end of the week, we had caught twenty-two deer. They were all under cover, inside the tent. All the deer had lost their hair on their legs from being in the high water for so long. We did lose a few of them, though, but the amount we saved made us very happy. After about a month, Flood Control got the water level down to where it should be normally, so it was time to take these deer back to their home in the Everglades. They were all nice and healthy by then, so we went taking them home. It was a great feeling when we released them, seeing them running free in their natural setting. It made us all feel good about ourselves, knowing that we had a hand in making this all happen.

***

Mr. Dredge called me into his office at the start of the day. When I got in there, a guy was there, looking for a job working with animals. I might mention that he was fresh out of college. We were somewhat short on rangers, so I started talking with him. He didn't have any experience with any type of animals and he had studied animals and their habits in college and wanted a chance to have some hands-on experience instead of just reading about it, so I hired him. I asked if he knew how to drive a tractor, and of course the answer was no; so I told him I would show him. We left the office, going to get the keys to one of the tractors with a cage around the driver seat. As the tractors went through the six sections of lions, it was used also to bring cars out of the park that have broken down. Well, this tractor wouldn't start, so I got the keys to the one in the hoof stock section. It was hooked up to the pump trailer. This tractor was used to go to all the lion huts to clean and disinfect them. All the huts were close to the canal where we had access to the water. We pumped the water from the canal to the huts to clean them out. We got in my jeep and went to the hoof stock section to get the tractor. Once we got in there, he started calling off all the scientific names of them, but here we called a lion a lion, a rhino a rhino and a zebra a zebra. I told him that he could call them all the big names he wanted, but no one will ever know about what you are talking. He really didn't impress me from the beginning. I told him to stop trying to impress me with all his book smarts and start showing me some actions and knowledge with hands on. I then went on trying to show him how to drive a tractor. After showing him, I told him to come on and follow me to section two lions hut. Once we got there, I told him to call the ranger of this section and tell him that he was there to clean the hut, and to ask him if all his lions were counted. Then, when he was finished cleaning the hut, he was to let the ranger know and then move on to section three.

I showed him how to throw the big hose in the canal and to straighten out the small hose that goes to the hut. I showed him how to start the pump, so off he went to start his first job of cleaning the hut. He wasn't in there for more than a few minutes until he came running out coughing, spitting, and having a hard time to breathe. He was rattling on of how bad the smell was inside the hut. We could clean the huts each day, but he sure was right in that some of the huts would really smell strong with ammonia from the lions' urine. However, in this field, one has to take the bad with the good while working with wild animals. I told him Richard's favorite saying--if this kind of work were easy, everyone would want to work with animals. He said if he couldn't take cleaning huts couldn't he work a pride of lions instead. I told him that most of the rangers have been here at least two or three years and some still don't run the lions. I said that we all started out washing out the huts, shoveling elephant and rhino dung, and all kinds of nasty jobs before we were able to run a pride of lions.

I told him that anyone could run a pride as long as everything is going smoothly, but it was different when the lions decided to go crazy and do all kinds of stuff. That takes experience from working with them for a long time. I told him that I was sure that he wasn't ready for that and that he was at the bottom of the ladder. He needed to work himself up that ladder to prove that he was capable of all it takes to work with these wild animals. So, he took off and went back in to the hut for another minute. Then he came running out, saying, "I can't do this. If I can't run a pride of lions then I am quitting. I told him not to worry about quitting because he was fired and to get in my jeep and I will take him back to the office to pick up what little pay he had coming. He got in my jeep while I turned off the pump. He waited there while I told section two's ranger that someone else would be back later to clean the hut and that I was taking the new man back to the office to pick up his pay before he can come over there and take over his job.

When we got to Mr. Dredge's office, I told Mr. Dredge to give the man his pay as I had just fired him. He looked at me awful funny and said, "We'll pay him for one hour." Mr. Dredge asked me to hang around for a few minutes, so after the guy left he asked me what happened. I told him the whole story and letting him know that he just couldn't stand the smell and wanted to run a pride of lions. I said that I was afraid to let him run a pride, as I was scared that he would take over my job. Then, after the man got mine, he would surely go after his, so he said it's a good thing I did fire him. Mr. Dredge laughed so hard, saying, "I don't think that's going to happen."

As time went by, things started to slow down as far as the lions going to the heads, but they have done that before. There was a time that we were going in the head three to six times a week to get a lion. Then, one morning, section six called me before opening, saying that they had a lion on the moat.

I went over there, checked the lion, out and it looked like the one we loaded up in Pets' Corner, to take it to section seven. I called Charles to come over to check out the lion too. We both would feed the lion in Pets' Corner and walk with it. The lion was a teenager now, and weighed about two hundred fifty pounds. The women in Pets' Corner were getting uncomfortable with her now, so we moved her to section seven. It had only been a couple of days since we moved her. When Charles got there, we both checked her out from across the canal, deciding that she was the one from Pets' Corner. So, I said that if we both were sure that the lion was Ann; we would go over there and walked her back to section seven before we opened up the park.

I called the office and told them not to open the park, as we had a situation that we needed to take care of before we open the park to the public. Charles and I put our three fifty sevens on and got over onto the moat. We started walking towards the lion, calling her by name. She was a good ways down the moat. We got a little over half way to her, still calling her name. She then spotted us and started to waddle towards us. As she got really close to us, I looked at Charles and he looked at me. We both were wondering if that was our lion. About that time, she started doing a fast walk and got a lot closer to us. Without a word to each other, we drew our pistols, as she was getting awful close now. I told Charles, that one second I thought it was her and then the next I didn't. He said, "Yeah, me too." By then, she was upon us. She came to me and rubbed against me, almost knocking me down. Then, she went to Charles and did the same thing. We looked at each other, noticing that both our shirts were a little wet with sweat saying, "Whew! That was a rush."

I said, "Isn't this fun?" He said, "Yeah it is fun, but I think I have had enough for one day." We both were laughing and talking as we walked Ann back to her section. The ranger from section seven was behind us in the jeep in case something was to happen. After we got her back, Dale took us back to our jeeps. I called Mr. Dredge to let him know that it was all clear now and to open the park. Charles pulled his jeep along side of mine and said, "Well Gus, we made it through another one without getting attacked by a lion." I laughed and said, "As long as we can sit and talk about it, that's a good thing. I couldn't believe how we weren't sure it was her at one moment and then the next thinking it was, and how it seemed like the weather got hot all of a sudden." Charles said, "You sure got that right! It was exciting." It was a great way to start our day. After having a few laughs, Charles went off to Elephant Island and I went to the feed shed to check and order the feed, fruit, and vegetables for all the animals.

As I was checking off what all I needed to order, AC called me on the radio and asked me to come to section three. I said as soon as I finished checking all the feed that I would be there. He didn't seem excited at all, so I figured I could finish what I was doing before going over there.

I was just about finished when A.C. called again, talking in a calm voice. I told him that I was almost finished in the feed shed and would be right there and he said "Okay." I finished up and was on my way to my jeep when he called again, saying, "Gus, are you coming?" I replied that I was on my way and that I would be there shortly. Now, A.C. was a very big man about six foot three and two hundred eighty pounds. I have never seen him get excited or mad at anyone or at anything. If he were to get mad, I would think everyone had better look out, as he could really put a hurting on someone if he took a mind to it. Most of the time, he is just a big ole teddy bear and a good person that would do anything in the world for anyone. As I was pulling up to his jeep, he was not too far from his lions, watching them and the cars coming through. He had his jeep door open and he was sitting sideways in the seat with his leg crossed over the other with his boot and sock off. I asked him, "What's up?"

He looked down at his leg just above where his boot would have been. He was smiling and said that a snake had bitten him. I asked, "Why didn't you tell me you did or that it was an emergency when you called? Then I would have come right over."

He said, "Well, Gus, I figured you were busy." As we were talking, I could see that his leg was swelling up more. I asked him if he knew what kind of snake it was that bit him because I needed to know so when we got to the hospital, they could give him a snake antivenom shot for the bite. He looked at me and smiled. Then he said, "I don't know what kind it was, but for sure if I find him, he's a dead damn snake." I couldn't believe that he wasn't excited about it and was still smiling. I called Charles to come over to section three and told him that I was taking A.C. to the hospital. He was there in no time. We thought that it might have been a pigmy rattlesnake, as they are really small rattlesnakes, the biggest being about two feet long. Their poison is really bad though. Being that A.C. was so big, it wasn't as bad as if it were a smaller person.

When I came back to Lion Country, I told everyone that A.C. was okay. Every one really liked the big ole teddy bear, as we were all a tight-knit group of people there that got along for the majority of the time. Once in awhile, we would have some differences, but overall, things went quite smoothly. Charles said that he couldn't believe A.C was so calm about the situation. I told him that while I was driving him to the hospital, I tried talking to him to keep him calm, but I didn't have to worry about talking, as he talked all the way to the hospital, staying fully alert. He talked my head off, with a big smile on his face all the while. They only kept him overnight, and he was back to work in a couple of days.

***

Today, a lion from section three decided to go visit her neighbors in section two. We tried really hard to get her back with our jeeps, but it was bothering all the lions in section two. They didn't care for her to come and visit and they were trying to get to her, so I decided to tranquilize her. At that time, one of the lions in section two swam the canal and was on Giraffe Island, going to the other side of the island to section five. I drove around to that section and darted her. When the dart hit her, she ran to the other side of the island, towards section two, so I got in my jeep and went back to that section. She was in the canal between the section and Giraffe Island. I could see that the tranquilizer was starting to take effect, so I jumped out of my jeep and threw the rope over her head. I ran back to my jeep and wrapped the rope around the steering column, got in and started the jeep. I backed it up the bank slowly, pulling the lion up on dry land and even ground. I had a rake handle with a hook at the end of it to take the rope off their neck because there were times when I used a rope instead of tranquilizing them. It was much easier for the lion and for us as well. When I pulled the jeep up to check on her, I could see that she was almost all the way under the effect of the drug. I had Dan and Sonny take care of the first lion I had tranquilized.

Then, they came over to help me with this one. Before we got her to the hut, I got a call from Charles. He went from Elephant Island to watch Dan's lions while we were busy with section two's lions. Charles had three lions swim to the moat. I tried to get them back to section three, but they decided they weren't going anywhere, so I darted all three of them on the moat at the edge of the canal. I told Charles and Dan that if one should go into the canal, we couldn't go in after it because one of the other two might try to jump in and try to get us. That was unless the other two would be out from the drug. Charles also brought a lariat and we tried to put the rope on them and pull them to the edge of the water; or if all three were in the water, we would go in and try to save them. As it happened, they all three just laid down where they were on the moat with none of them going near the water and just let the drug take its effect. After about fifteen minutes, we went over on the moat to get them in the jeeps and to take them back to the huts. Another five lions were tranquilized in that one day. It seemed like this was the season where we have to tranquilize a bunch of lions. We have been having problems with one to six almost every day. I think it is because the weather is cool and rainy and that makes the lions more active.

Chapter 13

Moving Day and California Park

We need to get twenty-four lions in separate crates to go to the new park in California. All of this has to be done in four days. When Mr. Dredge told me this, I went around to all six lion sections and told the rangers to pick out four of their biggest trouble makers, misfits, and all-round unruly lions, telling them that we would ship them off to California. Starting our job of getting them into crates, I thought that if I got a six-foot cattle shocker they might go in a lot easier. People use them on the cattle to move them along in their shoots in order to truck them to another place, to get them to go in the squeeze cage, to give them shots and medication, or check them for whatever problems they might have. It doesn't really hurt them; it just gives them a little electric jolt. We were trying to get Sonny's lion in a crate and he didn't want to go. Charles and Sonny didn't see the cattle shocker that I had until I got it out of my jeep. As I walked towards the hut and the lion, I said, "I'll show you how to get that lion in the crate."

I popped him with the end of the shocker. He turned around quickly and attacked the shocker, hitting it with his paws, biting the end, and working his way down. I kept pushing the trigger, and the more I pushed the, the madder he got. Then, I pulled the shocker out of the hut. When I started, the shocker was about six feet long. When I pulled it out of the hut away from the lion, it was only a foot long from the handle and the six-foot pole was in about seven or eight pieces, being held together by a small wire. When we looked at it, all three of us started laughing. Charles said, "So that's how you get a lion in the crate, huh, Gus?"

I felt like an idiot, holding that shocker and looking at it. Then, we all started laughing. I said, "Boy, these work so well, we should get three or four more."

I have never seen a lion get so mad so quickly since I have been working with them. Needless to say, we didn't get any more electric cattle probes and we decided to leave them for the cows. We got most of the lions in their separate crates for their journey to the California park. We still needed to keep the park open and running while we got all these lions ready. After we got them all in the crates, they needed to be loaded on a flatbed semi. The next morning, we were all in at seven. As we were loading the lions on the semi, Al brought a small dragline that he had rented to Lion Country to load the lions on the truck. Al started arguing with all of us about the way they should be loaded. At about five o'clock, Al jumped off the machine, pulled the distributor cap off so we couldn't use the drag line, and he yelled at us, "I quit", and went to his car, leaving to go home for the evening. There we were, in the middle of loading with no dragline to load them. Therefore, we got the tractors; we had three lions in a rhino crate and needed to get closer to the truck. We hooked a chain to the crate; I backed the tractor to the crate, and hooked it up with the chain. When I tried to pull the rhino crate with the lions in it, the tractor's front end started to leave the ground about three feet. I stopped pulling, told the guys to unhook the tractor, and that I would pull up to the crate and then they could put the chain on the front of the tractor. I started backing up the tractor and that worked much better with the chain hooked to the front. Vern came with another tractor and started loading another crate from the back. As I saw what he was doing, I yelled to him that he could flip the tractor by hooking the chain to the back. I told him to hook it on the front and then hook it to the crate. He hadn't seen what just happened to me, so he continued to go with it to the back saying that he thought it would be okay. As he did, the tractor revved up so high, it was almost to the point of flipping over backwards. At that time, the motor quit and there was Vern, almost falling out of his seat.

He was holding on to the steering wheel, yelling, "How am I going to get the tractor back down?" I told him to push in the clutch slowly, but he pushed it all the way down and down came the tractor's front end really fast. When the tires hit the ground, Vern went forward. The tractor bounced about four feet high. Vern hit his head on the steering wheel, then, as it bounced again, he hit his head again. From where I was, Vern looked like he was having a fit of some kind, beating up on himself, winning and losing all at the same time. When we found out that he was all right, we all started laughing and saying how funny he looked, whipping his head back and forth. He said that it was the best carnival ride he had ever experienced. He then said, "Gus, let me turn this tractor around and back it up."

We got one rhino crate with three lions in it on the truck. It was taking too long and it was becoming too dangerous. We would get another dragline in the next morning. We finished up at nine thirty and left for home. The next morning, the dragline and the operator were at the park. We got all the lions loaded on the flat bed semi.

Vern and Mac, along with all of the lions were on their way to California. Then, it was time to get back to normal. It was a relief to let go of all the lions that were troublemakers from the get go. Then we shouldn't have to be going in the heads so often with a lot of them out of the way.

At closing, three of the cubs in section three decided to swim across the canal to hang around on the edge of the canal. They weren't trying to go inside the head, so Ron swam across and chased them into the canal, again letting them swim back across to their own section where Harold and I were. When they got across, we started chasing them with sticks to their hut. I thought they would surely go in okay on the morrow.

The next day, all went well until closing. One of the bigger cubs in section five decided to climb the tree. As we were putting them in the hut, he climbed about fifteen or twenty feet up and sat on a branch. We let him sit there to calm down some, thinking that he just might come down, but we had no luck. I told Sonny to go to the feed shed and get a tarp. When he got back, I said, "Let's spread it out on the ground under the cub, then all of you grab a hold of it."

I proceeded to dart him with the tranquilizer, and after about ten minutes, I told them all to get ready because he was about ready to come down. The drug was starting to take effect so he let go of the tree and fell right into the tarp. He was a little small to tranquilize but we couldn't get him down any other way, as he was so high up the tree. We put him by himself for the night, so the others wouldn't bother him while he was coming out of the tranquilizer.

The next morning, someone called Lion Country from Naples Florida, saying he had a very large chimp that was getting too big for his cage. He was becoming a teenager and was starting to become very aggressive. They said that they didn't trust him anymore and wanted to give him to Lion Country. They knew we would take very good care of him. Jimmy Ash wanted me to go pick the chimp up. I got a large crate, put it in the back of my jeep, and hooked up the fourteen foot Jon boat with a ten-horse motor. Chuck, along with Nonie, went with me to pick up the chimp. The house was on a small island in the inter-coastal waterway. The only way to get to the house was by boat. It took about three hours to get to the dock from Lion Country. We put the boat in the water but the crate was too big and too heavy for the boat, which I knew, but I wanted a big enough crate for him. We called on the phone, first, to let them know we were coming over to the island. They were waiting for us at their dock. We tied up the boat, and then they took us to the chimp. It was a huge pen but the chimp was very large. I told them that I wanted to get all the paperwork done, which stated that they gave the chimp to Lion Country before I tranquilize the chimp.

I wanted to get him loaded into the boat quickly, which we were able to do. We laid him on the bottom of the boat and there was very little room for us. I had some seralyn with me in case he started to come around before we got him in the crate that was on the jeep. Nonie started moving around because she didn't like him looking at her. We got him out of the boat and in the crate okay, got back to Lion Country, and some of the rangers from Pets' Corner were waiting for us to help unload the chimp into a building in Pets' Corner. We would keep him in there for a while and then release him onto Chimp Island with the other chimps.

A lion from section six went onto the island by the exit gate. I went to the exit fence as the lion was walking along it. Once there, I could get a good shot at her with the dart gun. I shot her with the dart, and then she charged at me through the fence. I still had the barrel of the gun stuck through the fence. She bit the front sites off the barrel. I went back on the other side into section five where she had started walking by the canal and fell down the bank into the water. She was going down under the water. Charles, Bill, and I dove into the water and got her. We pulled her out on the land, and by this time, she was almost out from the tranquilizer. We waited about five minutes and she was all the way under the tranquilizer. We proceeded to take her to the hut and bedded her down for the rest of the day and night. Of course, we all felt really good about saving another lion from drowning.

After we closed down the park, we took the new chimp to Chimp Island and released him. They were fighting off and on for about a half hour, then everything was back to normal.

A few weeks later, we got in a tiger, so we decided to mix him with a pride of lions. We didn't know how this would all turn out, as tigers are loners and lions like to live in prides. Some of us didn't think that it was a great idea to do that, mixing one tiger with five lions, but we only had the one tiger, so we thought we would try, hoping that everything would work out. We got five young lions from section six. They came from Pets' Corner. We put them in section four and mixed the tiger with them. In a couple of weeks, we would release them from the hut and hope everything comes out all right. At the time we released them, they were fighting most of the day. At about three o'clock, the tiger swam to the moat. I drove my jeep over on the moat and tried to push the tiger back. He ran around the jeep, then, decided to jump in the back of my jeep. He rode most of the way in my jeep. He jumped off and went back into section four, laying down just a ways from all the lions.

At closing, the tiger decided that he wanted to go into the small lake instead of to the hut. I was pushing him to the hut with my jeep when he bit my tire and gave me a flat. I got him tranquilized and we got him back to the hut and bedded down. I got my flat tire fixed, so, then, it was time for me to go home as it was eight o'clock. We went to the office to check out and head down the two-mile stretch to go home and get refreshed to start a new day.

***

It's been a couple of months now and a bus comes through every Tuesday with senior citizens or school kids. I meet them at the front gate and I ride the bus with them through the park, pointing out all of the animals, telling them what they are and giving them little history on them. This one day, a busload of school kids came through. I was talking about the hoof stock as we went through the section into lion section. One little guy asked me how I tell the boy lions from the girl lions. I didn't say anything at first, but then I told him that the girl lions are a lot prettier. He said, "Oh okay." The teacher in the front seat smiled and told me that I offered him a good answer. They were only fourth graders, so I guess they were satisfied with my answers. A while later, I thought I could have told them that the male lion has a mane, which the female doesn't, but dumb me couldn't think of that fast enough. The teacher seemed to enjoy herself seeing me trying to explain all the animals to the little ones and answer all of their questions. We got to the exit gate and I got a ride back to the entrance gate to pick up my jeep so I could continue my regular routine of taking care of the animals.

We had many people that would donate money to Lion Country to help with the cost of food and care of certain animals that they liked. They would stop by at the office and ask how the animals were doing. Our public relations man would go to Chimp Island and get Butch, the chimp that he would take to different clubs, benefits, schools, and other functions to further Lion Country's relations with the community. But, when this lady would come by, Mr. Dredge would call me and have me bring Butch to the office. This one time I brought him in, I sat him in a chair in front of Mr. Dredge's desk. The lady was sitting in another chair in front of the desk as well. Mr. Dredge lit up a cigarette and handed it to Butch. He started puffing on it and rolling it around on his lips. Mr. Dredge then poured them all a drink, including Butch. Then he poured another. Ole Butch had drank about half of the second drink when he started getting a little feisty. I told Mr. Dredge that I had better take him back to the island.

He could see that Butch was getting a little tipsy, so he said, "Okay Gus, you best take him back." I walked him to my jeep and as we were going back to the island, Butch started looking at me as if to say, "I think I will whip your Butt." I had some bananas and apples with me in my jeep, so I started feeding him some of them to take his attention away from me. I got Butch to get in the boat and we started across.

Once I got across to the island, I gave Butch another banana then threw some on the island for the other chimps. They all came running to greet Butch, as if to say, "Glad your back ole buddy." I went back to the office and talked with Mr. Dredge, asking him if he would stop giving Butch booze and smokes, as he was getting really mean and aggressive when he drank, and I had to contend with getting him back on the island. I don't need to be dealing with a chimp that wants to whip my butt when he's drinking. He told me he could see how he was getting today and that he wouldn't do it anymore. I thanked him for understanding and knowing that he could be a mean chimp when he wanted without out any booze, and seeing how bad it was when he did give him some to drink. Therefore, I was sure glad that he understood where I was coming from. Overall, Butch was a good chimp.

It had been about four weeks since we mixed the tiger with the lions and we have had been having trouble every day. I had to dart him almost every single day, either in the section or on the moat. A few times, we had to go into the head looking for him, walking all through the head before we found him. One day, he went on the head between sections four and five. I got two rangers to go over with me but he kept staying ahead of us, so I got on one of the stands we had built when we first opened the park. The other rangers were pushing the tiger to me, and it was finally coming towards me. I waited until I knew I could get a good shot at him. I took aim, finding him in my sites. I closed one eye and the tiger faded into the surroundings, as though he disappeared. I opened my other eye and there he was again. I aimed again, but with no luck. I couldn't believe how he could blend in so well, so when I opened the other eye, I could see him.

I decided to shoot him with both eyes open. The dart hit its mark on his thigh. We waited the allotted time for him to go down and got him loaded, then took him to the hut.

The tiger has been out all day long now for a few days, but not lying with the pride yet; but close enough to them to be a nice picture for the people going through in their cars to enjoy looking at them. On this one day, the tiger decided to head for the mote. I threw a lariat on him, then wrapped the rope around the steering wheel of my jeep and pulled him back across the canal on the lion's side. I was able to get the rope off him. After getting it off, he then leaped up onto the hood of my jeep. I started up my jeep and took him across the road to where some of the lions were laying. I hit the brakes and he slid off the hood and into the section where he should be. He decided to stay there the rest of the day until closing.

At that time, he went to the moat again. I threw a rope around him, dragged him across the canal, and put him in the rolling cage. Then, I proceeded to roll his butt to the hut. I got him out of the cage, into the hut and closed him up for the night.

A new lion in section four went on the moat. I threw a rope on her, pulled her back across, and got her back with the pride. I worked the rope off with my hook made for that reason. As soon as she was loose, she bit the tire on my jeep and gave me a flat tire. By this time, the tiger was on the head, so Charles and I went over looking for her. As we were looking for her, we could hear her going through the water in the head. As we were going by one of the tree stands, I climbed up in it and spotted her. I was able to dart her. We had been hunting for her from twelve thirty to three o'clock. By the time we got the tiger back to the hut, the same lion we got back from the moat this morning had gone over on another head. So back Charles and I went to dart her and get her back to the hut. Then, at closing time, while we were putting the lions up, two cubs in section three went on the island. After we finished putting up all the other lions, Charles, Dan, Gary, and I went over to the island.

We started chasing them with sticks. The same cub that had bit me a few days ago, almost the same spot, bit Dan on his leg. This wouldn't work too much longer, controlling them, getting them in their huts with sticks. Pretty soon, they will be able to swat them right out of our hands. They were starting to get a lot bigger and we couldn't afford to take a chance that they might go after anyone of us. Then, we would have to tranquilize them to get them back. Charles and I had been hunting lions and tigers all day. When closing time came and everything was put up for the night, we were really beat. Both of us were dragging after chasing after one or the other all day long.

The next day, Mr. Dredge called me to the office around one o'clock. He told me that I had to fly to the California park to start forming lion prides there. I told him I sent all the troublemakers out there. If I had only known, I would have sent some well-mannered ones instead of all the bad boys. Now I had to go form prides out of all these misfits. Mr. Dredge just laughed and said, "Well, the faster you get them to settle down into prides, the faster you will come back here to West Palm Beach."

The following day, I was on a plane to the California park. When I got off the plane, Mac was there to greet me. It was around three in the afternoon when he took me to my motel. As the park was closed for the day, we went to a restaurant to get something to eat, then, we went out for a few drinks. I don't have any idea where we went but as I was driving back to the park, Mac and Vern were sleeping. When Mac woke up, I had driven about sixty miles past the park. By then, it was about eight in the morning, so Mac took the wheel and started driving back. We got to the park around nine thirty in the morning. As we pulled up to the temporary office, Bill York and four rangers were walking to their jeeps.

As we got out of the car, and as we were walking toward them, Bill said, "Here come your three bosses. Do as they say, not as they do." He introduced them all to me, and he told us to go back to the motel, clean up and they would see us in the morning. We sure were glad to hear that, as we didn't get any sleep the night before.

The next day, we went in and I was introduced to the rest of the rangers. Bill drove me through the park, showing me the huts with the lions in them, along with all the hoofed stock. After all this, we went on to the office. I was given a jeep for the park and for use after opening hours. Bill said, "Well Gus, check out the lions and where you want to put them. Separate them how you want them to be, or should I say, the way they want to be?" with a smile. "You will decide how you want them and what you will need to get them in and out of their huts, to form the prides." He also said, "You will be in charge of unloading other animals as we get more in, so the day will consist of all those good happenings."

The next day, two rangers along with Mac, Vern, and I were moving lions when some hoof stock came in. We stopped moving the lions and went to unload the giraffes, hippos, waterbucks along with some game buck. We got the giraffe unloaded into the pen. As he went running, he ran into the gate. The lock wasn't closed all the way and he got out of the pen and went through the back gate to the outside of the park, which wasn't closed. There was a lot of construction still going on inside the park. They weren't finished with all the building. We all went to the outside of the park and after many tries, we finally got him back in and we put him in his own pen. One of the construction crewmembers was at the gate, getting it fixed by the time we got the giraffe back to the pen. We went back to moving lions, doing this for the rest of the day. We left to go back to the motel around eight o'clock that night.

Everything seemed to go okay for a couple of weeks with us getting things under control. We continued to unload lions from their crates, getting them into their huts, then, mixing them with each other. One day, Mac, Vern, Zoo, and I moved fifteen lions, which was a lot of lions to move in one day. We finally got all of them in their huts. Now, we started to put up a four-foot hog wire fence that we would use as a funnel to get them to go in and out of their huts and into the section. The hardware store we went to only had about half of the fencing we needed along with only half of the post to make the V we needed in every section. It was about two hundred feet long from the hut, with it getting bigger as it goes further away from the hut with a few jeeps on both sides on the outside of the fence. Then, a few jeeps would be at the wire end of the fence. The first couple of weeks were spent keeping lions inside of the fence. Then, we let them outside and let them get a little further away from the hut until they were in a good section for the people to see them when they drive through and a good place for them where they will feel comfortable. After a few more weeks of this, all the lions were out and being trained to go in and out of the huts, even though many of these lions were used to going in and out in West Palm Beach. This was all new territory for them: huts with different designs and they were all in new prides, so their whole systems were messed up. All things were starting to come together. We were walking the fence while the lions were in their huts, looking for holes in the fencing and checking the sixteen-foot perimeter fence. We were checking for poisonous plants, checking out for places the lions can go but the jeep wouldn't be able to.

After about two months, all the lion prides were out and most of them all day long, with some of them only a couple of hours. At the same time, we were jeep training the lions. We were also training the men on how to control the lions. It seemed like every day that I was tranquilizing a lion that was giving us problems like running away from the pride, fighting with each other, and not wanting to go into the hut at night. It was nowhere near the problem we had in West Palm Beach, as there weren't any heads or canals, so for the most of the time, I could tranquilize them while sitting in my jeep. Sometimes they would go into the ravine or get in a place where the jeep couldn't get. We would get them on foot. At times, when a lion would give us trouble, I would get a rope on them and drag them with the jeep to the pride. This one day, I had to drag four lions back to where they belonged with their pride, and they all stayed with the pride the rest of the day.

That same day, Zoo was bitten on his hand by a chimp while he was putting them out on the island. It wasn't bad enough to go to the hospital, but it would sure be sore enough the next day.

A couple of days later, we had a lion wanting to go all through the sections. Three other men in jeeps and I were trying to get him to go back to the pride, but he wanted to go somewhere else. I tapped him with my jeep bumper and he charged the jeep, hitting the side of my jeep and the side window on my side. I thought he was coming through the window. He then decided to see how well my jeep tasted and bit through my fender, putting a few more dents and scratches on the hood. After doing this, he went over to Zoo's jeep and did the same thing. He was one angry lion, so I felt it was best to tranquilize him. We took him back to the hut. Sometimes, I try to drag them with a rope; it doesn't hurt them and it stops us from having to tranquilize them, not putting so much stress on them, but this one wasn't having any of that. Each situation is different and one has to deal with it the best one sees fit.

The other day, Zoo and I moved three giraffes. They were the last of the hoof stock we would be getting in for awhile, and we had all of the lions in. All of the sections seem to be doing well and the men seemed to be handling them well. In some sections, we had even taken down the V. Most of the lions were going into the huts well. The other day, we had a lion that wouldn't go out for three days and we couldn't get him out with the water pressure, so Zoo and I decided to get a rope. We put it around the lion from the roof, then, got in the jeep. We drug him out of the hut and out into the section with the rest of the pride. He stayed out all day with no trouble. For a week, he didn't give us any more trouble, so I think he realized it wasn't that bad after all.

We came upon a day when all the lions in a pride started fighting with one of the females. She went to the fence and climbed to the top of the barbed wire, then fell down and they started fighting with her all over again. So, again, she climbed the fence. I decided to dart her; we then took her to the hut. I moved her to another section with another pride and hope she will mix well with them.

It had been six or seven months now since getting California park ready. All of the lions are mixed really well and are all in prides. They seemed to be getting along most of the time. The rangers are doing a real good job with them. A lot of the lions that were causing all of the trouble in West Palm Beach seemed to be working our well in the new park. It would soon be time for opening so I was now ready to go home to West Palm Beach. It had been an experience getting the park ready for opening and I have met a lot of good animal men, along with just some good people since I have been here. I have a lot of memories. I would leave in the morning and take along with me all my memories.

NEW LION ENCLOSURE AT CALIFORNIA PARK

**OVERLOOKING THE BEAUTIFUL
CALIFORNIA PARK UNDER
CONSTRUCTION**

Chapter 14

Back To West Palm Beach

It was nice to be back in sunny Florida. On my first day back, Wayne hit a tree with his jeep while trying not to run over one of the cubs. Then, Larry was dogging the jeep and it started making loud noises. Then, it wouldn't run, so it had to go to the garage to find out the problem. We found that the problem was he tore up the rear end of his jeep

I did not have any trouble with any of the animals today, which made it nice my first day home.

The hippos were trying to get out again. I was at the pump house checking the pump when Larry called, saying that he was bitten by a lion in the hut as he was feeding him, so I went to his section. The lion had bit him on his little finger and it looked bad, as it was really bleeding a lot. I wrapped a towel around his arm to make a tourniquet out of it and called Mr. Dredge to tell him that I was taking him to the hospital. When we arrived there, they called a specialist and had him take care of the situation. We were there until eight thirty that evening. It wasn't long after that incident that a lion called Elsa went on the head and killed a goat. Harold and I went on the head and found her eating her kill. I tranquilized her and when the dart hit her, she just laid on the goat, not wanting anything or anyone to get her prize. We waited for her to go under the tranquilizer, then, we took her to the hut and took the goat to the meat house. After we put her in the hut, Wayne called. He was having trouble with a real wise guy driving through the park with his windows down and speeding, really giving him a hard time. As I got to the section, they were arguing, so I told the guy, he needed to put his windows up and slow down. I went on to tell him we have wild animals out here, some are on the list of becoming instinct, also that they were all very valuable, so, I told him to slow down before he ran over one of them. Well, he took off like a rocket. I called the next section and told them to close the gate. I then called Charles, Dale, and Vern to meet me at the gate. When we all arrived where he was, he had closed his window, but he still couldn't get through the gate. I told Charles to get behind him and for Dale and Vern to get on each side of him; then, I got in front of him.

We then proceeded to escort him out of the park that way. Knowing that he had a nice new shinny car, I figured that he wouldn't want to hit anyone of us. If he did, it would be his problem. We just all kept him in our little caravan and if he stopped, so did we. We had much more time than he did. We all stayed there until he decided to move again. All the time we were escorting him out, he was yelling at us, cussing us all out, and telling us he would whip our butts. It took us quite a while, as at times, he would stop and act as if he was going to sleep. Then, he would try to get out of our circle of jeeps with no luck. We finally got through the exit gate. This whole time, we were keeping in contact with each other with our radios.

As we went through the gate, I pulled to the side of the road, got out of my jeep, and walked up to his car. He then took off while yelling at all of us. That was the last we saw of him with his taillights fading from view. We all stood there, having a good laugh. Then, I told all of them to get back to their sections, telling them that they all did a good job getting that crazy man out of the park before he hurt one of the animals, men, or himself. He was nothing but a wise guy and we did the right thing by getting him out. Closing up the park was making it a good ending for another day.

***

When I came in on this morning, I had to give six lions a shot of vitamins and antibiotics. Ron called, saying that he had a chimp with a bad leg, so we took it to Pets' Corner for the vet to check out. I went on to move a lion from one section to another. She wouldn't go out of her hut and she wasn't mixing well with any of the other lions, so we had to see if she did better in another section.

We had a lion in section seven go on the head, so Ron and I went hunting for her. When we found her, I darted her. After the dart hit her, she took off to the other side of the head. We gave her ten minutes, then, we started looking for her and found her in the swamp water. She had drowned. All that was left for us to do was to take her by the meat house to be buried. We always feel bad when this sort of thing happens, but we did all we could. Most of the time, the only way to get them back to their huts is by tranquilizing them. I have a little control over them if they stay with the pride and close to the road where the visitors can see and study them. As long as they did this, we back off and let them do what the lions do in Africa. We do this with all of the animals in the park. Going through the park is like being in Africa and seeing them in their natural habitat.

I was giving a lot of shots in the hoof section and some in the lion sections. I moved three lions from one section to another, as they weren't mixing well with all the other lions in their section. I did all this first thing in the morning.

I had trouble with a lion named Cinnamon. I worked with him until one thirty in the afternoon. I darted him and took him to George's section so he could work with him a little. After he was finished, he took him back to his own section.

The next day, all was going well until closing time. This again seems to be the time that they all want to act out. One of the lions went to the head. I got her back, then, one wouldn't go in the hut in another section. Finally, we got him in when another one decided to go out on the moat. We couldn't get him to come off, so George walked the moat to get him, as he had been working him since he came from Pets' Corner. All of George's lions were young lions and most of them have come right out of Pets' Corner, where they were taken care of by the women in Pets' Corner from the time they were born. However, as they were weaned and got too large to handle, they would be moved to section seven when they have to be between one hundred fifty and two hundred fifty pounds. George got him and walked him about half way back and then the lion didn't want to go anymore, so I told George to leave him out for the night and we would get him in the morning, as it was getting dark.

When lions are raised in Pets' Corner from a small cub, they are use to humans and are not afraid of them, but as they continue to stay out in the park and living in prides, they revert to the wild. Then, you can't walk along with them any longer.

I had two wardens on the other side of the moat in case the lion decided to attack George. The next morning, Charles and I went to the moat and got the lion, and walked him back to the hut. I decided to leave him in for the rest of the day. Everything going well until we started putting the lions up for the night when another lion went on the moat. He was acting as if he was lost. Don and I went over to the moat and walked him back to the hut. He got really frisky with me and almost knocked me over playing. He was really glad to see me. He knew me from Pets' Corner and all he wanted to do now was play. So, I fooled with him for a little while, and then I had to finish closing the park and get home to my family.

When I opened the park the next morning, I found two deer over on the head instead of in the section where they belonged. I took Charles and the new man over on the head to help while we looked for the deer. We hunted for them all morning and finally found them around one in the afternoon. I got both of them with the dart gun, but didn't give them enough to put them down, so we had to use the net and rope and tie them down. Then, we took them to the worming section in section one. I had wanted to move four deer from Pets' Corner to section one, so this was a good time to do it, being I already had the two over there; all I had to do was move two more. Then, it was time to put the lions in for the night. Sonny's lions all went in for the first time, so maybe now they were feeling like a pride of lions. We all felt good about that as they were all working together for a change. It was really great.

In section six at closing time, while we were putting

the lions in, somehow the door to the hut closed, so when the lions got to the closed door, they saw that they couldn't get in, so they started to go everywhere. We were able to get three in the hut, so I moved them to the other side of the hut and then opened the door on the other side so more could go in. Then, we had a lion on the roof of the hut. I figured the one I had darted on the head would go to sleep and we could get to him later, when things calmed down a little, so I went to the hut and darted the lion on the roof. He just seemed to lay there. I left one man there to see if any more lions went to the hut and to watch the one on the roof in case he came off. We needed to know where he went.

We had three lions tranquilized and didn't know where they were. Except for the one left in my gun, I had used up my entire tranquilizer on the three lions. I called Mr. Dredge and told him I needed a bottle of seralyn. He had to break into Pets' Corner to get it as it was locked up, and the women had all gone home. Everyone was in their jeeps looking for the lions. By this time, it was already dark, so of course we needed flashlights. We were also using the headlights of the jeeps. I told them all over the radio that no one was to get outside of their jeeps until I got there. No one would be so stupid as to get out with not knowing where three or four lions were and with it being pitch dark out to boot. The gates between sections six and seven were not closed, so I was looking for the lions by the gate. I thought I would close the gate. As I got out of my jeep to close the gate, one lion was in section seven by the gate. I was still close to my jeep when I spotted her, so I took the shot. When the dart hit her, she decided to charge me. I was about four feet from the jeep with the door open. I dropped the gun, as it was no good for me now. I already shot the dart and it hit her. I didn't have any more darts to shoot, so I ran, jumping into my jeep, and closing the door.

She ran right into my door, then, took off into the darkness and I didn't get to see where she went, so I had to get back out and lock the gate very carefully. I called everyone to come back to the section and we got a rope on the lion that was on the roof of the hut. With the jeeps all around the hut with their headlights shining all around, two or three of the men were looking for the lions. We had four that were still not in the hut and we only had one of them accounted for: the one that was on the roof and tranquilized and he was in section six somewhere. There were three of us men on the roof, lowering the lion down with a rope as he was fully out by then. There was still one on the head and two were somewhere in the section. I figured it was way too dark and dangerous to go looking for them any more tonight, so I told them to lock up the park and we would get them tomorrow.

The next day, we found the two lions I had darted in section six right where I had shot them. They were in the road. We spotted them before opening, and so we got them back into the section where they belonged to sleep it off. The one that was in the head was in the middle of it and he was starting to come out of it, so I gave him a little more. Then, I took him to section four's hut. Now, all of the lions were accounted for and were back together again. We brought them back one by one in a rolling cage. The last one back got a little frisky when we had the rolling cage up to the hut door. She almost came out of the side of the cage. We sure have had been using the rolling cage a lot lately. I took it into the shop and they fixed it. Now, we were good to go once again. The rest of the day went pretty well until closing time. While putting the lions up, three went to the head. They were staying by the canal and not inside the head. I went on the head and with my jeep staying by the canal instead of going inside. When I got to them, two lions jumped in the canal and swam across to section six. Then, Charles and Ron pushed them to the hut. The other one went in and we started hunting him. We went in the swampy section and couldn't find him. It was getting too dark, so we would go back in looking for him in the morning.

In the morning, we got in around six and found the one that was in the head by Chimp Island. The chimps were raising all kinds of cane and throwing rocks at the lion. We had let the lions out in section six already and they saw the one that was out all night coming towards them. They turned right around and went right back in the hut with the one that was out all night, so we let them calm down for a few minutes, and then let them back out again. All went okay and they seemed to settle into the old routine.

Eight lions were out when we got in the next morning. Seven were in section two and one was in section five. We got all of them in the hut except one, and I had to dart it on the head where we found him. We also got three giraffes in this morning, so we got them unloaded in the worming section. Then, we went to the hippo crate and found that it was falling apart while the hippo was still in it. After fixing the crate, we took him to the hoof stock section. All of this took about four hours. We got him out of the crate with no problem. He looked good strolling around the section with all the other hoof stock. Now, it was time to take the ostrich and black buck and move them from one section to the worming section.

Before closing, I had to take some lion cubs from the mother in section three, as she didn't have enough milk to feed them. They were trying to nurse but had no success, so I took them to Pets' Corner where the women could bottle feed them and care for them until they were large enough to be put out in the park in a section with the rest of the lions. Jim, the man that cleans out the huts each day, opened the door to the hut in section seven. When he did, he let two lions out. He ran, jumped, and crawled over the fence. He cut his hand and a place above his eye. That was a deep cut; it was bleeding really badly so Charles and I took him to the hospital. Ron got all of the other lions back to the hut.

Last night was a very cold night. We had a sick giraffe in section seven. We had previously moved all of the lions from that section and put some of the hoof stock in there, instead. It was a lot safer having the hoof stock in there than lions. Seven is the last section in the park, which made it easy for the lions to get out of the park through the gate. That is why we switched the sections. We now had five giraffes in there. Mr. Dredge ordered a large tent to put them in at night, as it was so cold. We also got two wildebeests and two waterbucks in that day. While we were unloading them, one waterbuck got out and went on the moat. The lions from the section near them got to him but he got away from them and went back to the moat. He then went over to section five by Elephant Island. I was finally able to dart him. It took effect in about twenty minutes, and we took him to the worming section.

I decided to stay with the giraffe in the big tent. I got about five heaters set up in it and Nonie came out and stayed with me all night until six-thirty the next morning. Bill York came in and stayed with them for part of the day. Nonie and I went out to breakfast and then on to the house as it was my day off.

At closing time, a lion named Smokey got away from his section, going on the head. Danny and I went in and hunted him down. We worked the head, looking for him. I told Charles to close down the park so we could continue hunting for him. It was starting to get dark by now and I was just about to say give it up for the night when I looked and saw the lion just lying there, looking all around. It was so dark inside the head that I couldn't see the gun's sights, so Danny held the flashlight over my head so I could see the sights to dart him. When the dart hit him, he jumped, then, just lied right there. We waited for the tranquilizer to take effect. After it took effect, we moved him to the hut. Then, we headed down that two-mile stretch to go home so we could come back tomorrow and start a new day.

During the night, we lost a lion in one of the heads. When we were hunting her, it got too dark so we left her for the night and now we were going in to find her. It took us about three hours to find her. Then, in the same afternoon, a lion went on a head that had eight goats on it. We had put them there thinking that they would eat most of the vegetation off the head, making it a little easier to see the lions when they would go on it. We went in to get her. She swam the canal and went to the moat in section two. She then swam over to Giraffe Island. Thank goodness, we had taken all of the giraffes off the island

and moved them to section seven. After she had gotten on the island, she went right into the empty hut. I closed the door, and then, I climbed up on the roof and darted her. We took her to the section where she belonged and to her own hut to sleep it off.

Dale was having some problems with his lions, so I went over to help him. One of his lions didn't want to come out of the hut. I got a rope around her, and we dragged her to the pride. She was fighting the jeep the whole way. After awhile, she bit one of my tires and gave me a flat. Dale got her away from my jeep. Lee and I started changing the tire. Pretty soon, AC yelled, "Here comes a lion." We jumped in the jeep, and then he got her back with the pride. We finished changing the tire and got out of the section. The rest of the day, he didn't seem to have any problems with his lions. In another section though, later in the day, we had a few more problem lions in section two and in section six. After getting them all straight, we were ready to close and stop for the day.

All last week, I gave distemper shots to all of the lions in every section. After everyone had them up for the night, I would do that, so I was getting home late every night.

Every day the next week, a movie crew has been here from the Outdoor Life Magazine. At times, when they were there, things got a little dangerous, as they would want to do some stupid things that weren't too safe. I told them to run it by me before they did it, and I would tell them what they could do. I tried to work with them the best I could, but sometimes the things they want wasn't in the best interest of the animals and the people. I told them that I didn't want any of my men or animals to be hurt or killed. Bill York and I had to dart two lions that wouldn't go to the hut, so I let the movie crew film that.

Doc Kidder, the vet came along with Jimmy Ash and me. He operated on the lion in section four, who had a hole in the top of his mouth where a snake had bitten him. He also had a bad tooth from fighting with another lion. A dentist would be here the next day and see what could be done about it.

For the rest of the day, I worked with the movie crew and Bill York. A lion went on a small head in one of the sections; we went over on the head and tranquilized him. The movie crew was on the other side of the canal, watching us and taking shots.

Some models from J. C. Penny's department store came into the park; I was with them for the most of the day until one thirty in the afternoon. Watching the lions to make sure everything was going okay while they did their shooting.

I got a call from the ranger in section six to come check out a lion. When I got there, I tranquilized him and found that he had a bone stuck in his mouth from a piece of meat he had been eating so, I was able to remove it. That situation turned out okay.

Charles, Ron, and I moved ten lions to different sections. While doing this, we had a lion named Hercules who he decided to go over on the head and have a look. We were able to get him off without darting him, so for once things went well for us.

I worked with the movie crew again the next day with Charles helping me get the giraffes to run so they could get a shot of that. We then got a rhino to charge us with the lions in the background. The camera operator was in a cherry picker and was able to get a nice shot. While we were letting a section of lions out, we had a new lion named Shiba that we were letting out with the pride for the first time. She jumped the fence, attacked Don's jeep, and knocked his front window out. She then went on to attack my jeep as well, breaking my side window out. We finally got her back to the hut where she belonged. We would try again with her tomorrow, hoping that she would do better.

Mac and I were giving medication to the hoof stock section all day long, so Charles was running the park. A lion went to another section. In fact, it was trying to go to the hoof section. I went to where she was, darted her, and took her back to the hut to bed her down. While I was doing all of this, another lion in this section jumped the canal between the two sections, one being the giraffe section. So I darted her and she laid right down at the canal edge, and I am thinking to myself, "I sure hope she doesn't fall in the canal. If this happens then I have to get wet." I knew that I didn't have enough time to go all the way around to the section where she was, and the man in that section was trying to get his lions under control, so I got my lariat out of the jeep and went to the edge of the canal. The lion was feeling the tranquilizer and stood up, then fell right down the bank and into the water. I knew this was going to happen. I threw the rope around her neck and dragged her across the canal. I put the rope around my steering wheel column and pulled her out of the water and up the bank to dry flat land. Leaving the rope still on her, I backed up, sitting in my jeep, waiting for her to go completely under the tranquilizer. I called Charles to come help me take her to section four to the hut, as

247

section two's huts were full. We would bring her back to section two the next day, when she is out from under the tranquilizer.

We were getting some flooding in some of the sections as we have had a lot of rain for the past two weeks. The heads were all really bad, over knee deep in some places, and so we sure didn't want any of the lions going onto the heads.

We had a very busy day the next day. There were two women and a man speeding and had their windows down. Dan stopped them. He got on the radio and called me. I went to the section, and as I was talking to them, she up and drove off with the windows still down, so I called Sonny in the next section to stop them. He did and as I got there, the man got out of the car. I got out of my jeep and pushed him back into his car, telling him to "Stay in that car" with their windows rolled up. Then, the woman said she wanted their money back. She said she wasn't moving until she got her money. I called Mr. Dredge and he talked to her on the radio. He said he would return their money if they followed me out of the park. She said she wanted it all in writing. They finally followed me to the office to get their money. When Mr. Dredge gave them their money, he said he never wanted them back in the park again, so they said "fine," and left. The next day, Drear Park Zoo called and needed help in tranquilizing one of their animals, so I went over to their park in town. I did all that they wanted and was back home by eight in the evening.

The first thing the next morning, we were letting the lions out of the huts. This one named Whitey gave us a lot of trouble. I was chasing him with my jeep and when he zigged, I thought he was going to zag. I ran over him and broke his leg. I really felt bad about that but it was a situation that couldn't be helped. I called Dr. Kidder and he came out to fix his leg. Then, I found out that a boat had drifted over on Chimp Island, and that chimps were all over the boat. It was a good thing the wind didn't blow the boat on the other side with all the chimps in it. That would have had been a lion section and we sure would had a lot of problems if that would have happened. I swam across and brought the boat back off the island, minus the chimps that I got off and left on their island. We moved an ostrich from the worming section to the hoof stock section. Then, I went on to give some shots to some of the animals in different sections. Then, Charles and I went to work on some stands in some of the heads.

**THESE LIONS ARE ENJOYING A WARM,
SUNNY DAY IN THE PARK**

THESE ELEPHANTS ARE COOLING THEMSELVES IN THE CANAL

A GROUP OF LIONS AT REST

CHEETAH CAUTIOUSLY WATCHING FOR DANGER

**THE SABLE GUS BROUGHT TO GEORGIA PARK
FROM WEST PALM BEACH**

GUS, HIS SON, JOE, AND HIS MOTHER, ELSIE, ON BACK OF TRUCK WHILE HIS NEICES, KAREN AND LINDA WATCH ANIMALS BEING UNLOADED

A LITTLE DOWN TIME AT MY DESK IN GEORGIA

Chapter 15

The Opening of Georgia Lion Country Park

Bill York went to the Lion Country Park in Georgia; he had been there for about two months. Then, Charles went to the Georgia park to help unload some of the animals, to give some of the animals their shots, and to give many rhinos their shots while they were still in their crates. The managers at the Georgia park asked me if I would accept the job of Chief Game Warden at that park and work in that park until another park was built somewhere else. After that, they said I would go open another one, or if I liked the Georgia park, I could stay there or move on to the next one. It sounded good to me, so Nonie and I talked it over, and we both decided to try it. I had been with Lion Country in West Palm Beach for twelve years and would miss the people along with friends and family, but I believed it was time to move on. This would be the third park I have opened, so I know all that it entails and I enjoy all of it. I put in a lot of hours and long days. It is also exciting to be with all new animals in new surroundings, forming new prides of lions and working with brand new lions that have never been in a roam free park. It is exciting mixing all the elephants, rhinos, giraffes, hippos and hoof stock. Every day is different and I enjoy it all.

I got my airline ticket, went first to help start it up. When I arrived at Atlanta airport, Charles was there to take me to the park. When we got there, I could see that all of the buildings and offices were in the process of being finished, so the office was just two trailers until the main one was completed. Although the inside of the park was finished and some of the animals were in the park already, with a lot more to come, we went to the temporary office and Bill was there. He said, "Good to see you again mate. Are you ready to start another park?" I told him I couldn't wait to get started. He said, "Charles will take you all around and show you the sections and huts, barns and the worming section and introduce you to the few rangers that are here already. Of course, none of these rangers has any experience at all with wild animals, so you have your hands full." Charles sat there with a big grin on his face the whole time. Charles took me all around the park in a zebra striped jeep. When we got back to the office Bill said, "I got you your jeep and your room at the motel, there is also a restaurant if you want to eat there or eat where ever you want to, but if you eat there at the motel, Lion Country will pay for it. If I were you, I'd do that. Here is your jeep. Go now and check out the park on your own or go to your room and rest. Either way, I will see you in the morning. You have ten rhinos in crates to give shots to the first thing. Then unload, some hoof stock and then the last thing at night, give shots to the rhinos again. They are in the crates because they got here early. Their barn and run bouts weren't ready yet and won't be for a couple of weeks yet."

I decided to go through the park again by myself for the rest of the day and talked with most of the rangers and getting to know them better before I start giving them orders in the morning. After all that, I went on to the motel to get a shower and to call Nonie to talk with her for a while. When Charles came, we went to dinner and then sat by the pool. Charles was telling me what all he had been doing since he had been there and filling me in on how things were going in the park. They had lost two rhinos since he came to the park. Most of the animals were good and healthy. He said he was glad to see me, because not only we hadn't seen each other for a while, but also because it meant he would be able to go back to West Palm Beach. We sat and talked for a very long time. Before we knew it, it was late, so we figured that we had better retire for the night, so we said goodnight and went to our rooms to get ready for the next morning.

The next morning when I went in, the first thing I did was give the ten rhinos each a shot of promozine, a medication to keep them from being so stressed so they wouldn't hurt themselves in those crates until their area was ready. I got on top of each crate, which was about nine inches higher than the rhino were, with enough room between the top boards that I could slap them and then hit them with the shot. I had to do it as if I was stabbing someone. The needle was about one and a half inches long. Sometimes, they moved the whole crate when I would hit them with the needle. Then, I pushed the medication into them, and then go on to the next one. The crates were all in a row so I was able to step from one crate to the other until I had given them all their shots. Then, the very last thing I did at night before going to the motel was that I gave them all a shot again.

A month later, I left to pick up Nonie, Joe and Erik. They stayed in West Palm Beach and got all our stuff packed up so we could return to Georgia; boy did I work that out right or what? When I got back to West Palm, all of it was ready; I just had to repack the truck. It wasn't packed for my motorcycle; I had to unload it all and then put it all back in. Boy, do those women know how to repay a guy, huh? After saying all our goodbyes, we took off with all our possessions heading off for our adventure in Georgia. We were all very excited; going from Florida to Georgia was a big change for all of us.

We started to have wild dogs come into the park at night. At first, there was about fifteen of them. The first time, they killed a couple of springbucks, which were small antelope. A topi broke his front leg while trying to get away from them, so I decided to have five rangers stay most of the night and shoot them when they tried to get into the park. We had to do this for about four nights before we got them all. We didn't enjoy having to do this, but these animals were very expensive and some were on the endangered list, so we couldn't afford to let them kill off these animals. The wild dogs didn't seem to go into the live traps we had set for them. Of course, we felt bad about this but it was the only way we could protect our animals.

We had a man from the county come into the park and check to see if we had any poisonous vegetation. He found only wild cherries and told us how to get rid of all of them.

It now seemed like we were having our problems with animals from outside of the park. We had a bobcat coming in at night. The night guard saw him in the worming section last night and he killed an adult black buck and a young black buck. We had a fish and game officer coming in the next day to set a trap in hopes that he would catch him before he killed any more animals.

It won't be too long now before we can put the

rhinos in the runabouts and in the barns, they are just about ready, and it wouldn't be too long before their section will be ready and they will have lots of room to run around in and be free of those crates.

We were starting to get in some elephants and getting them unloaded into the barns and runabouts. We also checked the trap and we found that we had trapped the bobcat, so I called the fish and game official to come take him and move him to a safe place to release him out in to the wild again. I went back to check the rhinos to see how they were doing. They were doing okay in the barns and run about. That day was the last of the series of shots with the medication. I was sure that they were as happy as I was about that.

I have been checking the topi and the veterinarian said we could take his cast off soon. This one morning, I went to check on him and in the middle of the road, there was the leg, still in the cast. It just fell off. I went looking for him in the worming section and found him standing by a tree with part of his leg missing with the bone sticking out about three inches. I was able to tranquilize him. I called for the vet but he wasn't in for the whole day, so I went back to the topi and checked out his leg. There seemed to be some movement on his leg, so I looked closer and found maggots were eating it away. I went to where the other part was in the cast and found the same situation, so going back to the topi; I decided that I needed to put him out of his misery. I knew he had to be in a lot of pain with all that going on, so I gave him all the medication I had to sedate him. Then, I waited about fifteen minutes, and then I shot him because I didn't have anything to put him down permanently. I like to think that he didn't feel anything as I had medicated him very heavily. I called the tractor man to come out and bury him. I stayed with him until he got there. It was a very hard thing to have to do and I know I had no other choice. It was always very hard when I had to put down an animal. I worked with these animals because of my love for them and because of my enjoyment of seeing them live longer and healthier in a roam-free environment. Thank goodness, the rest of my day seemed to go a lot easier and nicer.

***

Doc Silberman, the vet, and I needed to fly to New Orleans to pick up some rhinos from Africa at the dock there. We left at five-thirty in the morning. We got to the airport. There plane that we were supposed to take was delayed, so Doc told the ticket agent that we needed to get to New Orleans. We had eighteen rhinos waiting for us at the dock and that we needed to be there to give them all medication. She said a plane on the runway was leaving for New Orleans. She said that they would hold it up for us, so we said that we would take it. A car with lights flashing took us out to the awaiting plane at the end of the runway. They had the door open with the steps down. We got on the plane with everyone looking to see who was so important that the airline held up the plane for. Of course, we both just smiled with our heads high and our chests out.

We got to the docks around nine-thirty with the news crew there to take pictures of the eighteen rhinos. We got on the ship and we started introducing ourselves to everyone. When I shook hands with the African ranger and told him my name, he said, "I've heard of you. You are known as being one of the top five men in the world who have tranquilized so many lions."

That was a big surprise to me and it made me feel good about knowing that I was known for that over in Africa. Then, I started giving the rhinos the shots. After we had lunch on the ship, the truckers were there with the flatbed semis so I had all the semis full of rhinos heading for Georgia Park. Two African rangers were with me on the trip back to Georgia. We got all the rhinos loaded by two in the afternoon. Doc flew back to Georgia and I went with the rhinos, as they now were our responsibility. Once they were off the ship it all fell on us, so I had to be hands on from there on out. We stopped about every two hours to give them water.

We arrived back at the Georgia park about nine-thirty in the morning, then, we got them all off the trucks in the barns and runabouts and mixed them. All went great. I took the African rangers to the motel. They were going to stay four days and then fly back to Africa. Then, it was time for me to get on down the road and go home. I checked the rhinos the next morning and all was well. They were all getting along well and mixing much better than the lions did.

For the next couple of weeks, we started getting lions in. We also got a lot of antelope, gorillas, orangutans, gibbons, giraffes, and zebras. The new zoological director said that he couldn't believe all the animals per day that we were getting in. He said that this was his first roam free park and that he had been in a small zoo up until then. The busiest day they had was when they got two or three pelicans in from another zoo.

A few days after I arrived at the Georgia park, I took Charles to the airport to go back to West Palm Beach park. He had a small bag with him that was really stinking. I said, "Charles what have you got in that bag, someone's head that you've had forever?" He laughed and said, "No, I kept the horns off the two rhinos we lost before you got here a couple of weeks ago and was going to take them home with me." With them stinking so badly, I was afraid the other people on the plane might want to throw him off the plane before he got to the park. He said, "Gus if you want them you can have them," so I took them back with me. I put them out in the worming section and let them dry for a while.

While seeing Charles off, I told him to keep in touch and to call occasionally. He said he would. From that day on, we have made sure to keep in touch, calling each other every two or three months. We visited each other a few times, talking over ole times and situations of our lives with the animals and each other. We had been through so much together that we were more than just friends.

Five days after we got all the new rhinos, one of them went down. I found her in the barn when I was checking on them. We hadn't even released them out of the runabouts yet. I was still giving them medication every day. They all looked good. It was about two in the afternoon when I found her. Doc, a couple of rangers, and I went in and covered her eyes and Doc opened the medicine box. He started checking her out. She seemed to lose it. She got up and hit the medicine box with her horn. All the bottles and everything in it went all over the barn. We all went over and under the big fence in the barn as there were stalls for the rhinos all through the barn with different gates inside. We tried to rope her, but the rope was too darn small. So we got a four by eight piece of plywood and forced her back to a corner of the walls and I gave her the shots, as she was so weak we could hold her in the corner. Then, I yelled for everyone to let go and get out of the stall. I was trapped in the corner by myself with a mad rhino. They all seemed to get out a lot quicker than I thought they would. Bob jumped back in the stall to get her attention. When she looked at him, I got out of the pen with the plywood. I told them not to run out so darn fast the next time. I said, "You all need to look after your leader a little better, like I look after all of you. They said, "We were just doing what you told us to do." Doc got a stool sample from her. Her name was Jenny. She was full of worms, so I gave her worming medication. I also gave all the others worm medication. We put another rhino with her that was with her on the ship.

They seemed to be good buddies. We figured that it wouldn't hurt, but three days later, Jenny died. Doc tried to save her by giving her what he thought would help her. She seemed to get weaker each day. When she died, the one we put in with her knew she was dead before we did. Suddenly, she started making some strange noises, as if she was crying. Then, she gently put her horn under her, trying to lift her up. When she tried to lift her up, she was like a wet dishrag. She kept trying for about ten minutes, the whole time making those strange sounds like she was crying, then, she finally stopped trying to lift her. She went over to the other side of the barn and lied down, still making the sounds. It was heartbreaking to listen to her. I could tell she was mourning for her friend. We were finally able to get her outside of the barn so we could move Jenny out and bury her.

A few days later, I had to go to New York to pick up some elephants. I left Georgia airport at six p.m. When I arrived in New York, I went to the Americana Hotel. Vern from the Texas park was coming in to take eight elephants to the park in Texas. I was picking up seven for our Georgia park. Vern got in around midnight and we went to the restaurant and bar to eat and to have a few drinks, talking way into the night. We only had the hotel for one night and we thought we would be leaving in the morning, which was Sunday. We went to the dock and stayed there most of the day on the ship that brought the elephants from Africa to New York. No one there knew what was going on. The trucks to take the elephants weren't there, and they said the papers for the elephants weren't in because it was Sunday they wouldn't be in until Monday. I called Bill York and told him what the captain said, so Bill said to see if we could stay on the ship for the night. The captain said that we could, all while Vern and I were shaking our heads no. We told the captain we didn't want to sleep on the ship. He could not understand English too well, but finally, understood that we would rather get a hotel, being there in New York City. I gave the phone to him and he told Bill that they didn't have room for us to stay on the ship. We thanked him and got a cab back to the hotel for the night. The next day, we were back at the ship. The owners of the elephants were there also, saying on the papers of the elephants, it had that the bank was buying them, not Lion Country. They couldn't let me take them as I worked for Lion Country, not the bank. I asked what a bank would do with fifteen wild African elephants, anyways.   They said that Bill needed to get it all straightened out before we could take the elephants.   I called Bill, telling him the whole situation. He said that he would call the bank and get it all straight. It would take the rest of the day to get it all straightened out. Bill told us to get back to the hotel, then, load the elephants in the morning. He said that he would also call to make sure that the trucks would be there, so back to the big city we went, walking around Forty-Fifth and Broadway for the rest of the day. In the morning, we were at the docks on the ship at nine o'clock. We signed the papers and started loading the elephants onto the trucks. When one loads elephants on any truck, one loads them sideways with one looking at the side of the road. If they are loaded looking at the center of the road, the elephants have their trunks outside of the crate and could possibly hit another car or truck coming from the other direction.

It is also less stressful on the elephants to be looking at the side of the road. After signing the papers, we went topside, seeing the truckers and people loading the elephants. They had loaded two already and had them facing the wrong way. I stopped them and told them they would have to unload them and put them back in facing the side of the road. They sure didn't like that, but they did it. We finally got them all loaded by two in the afternoon. Then, we were on our way to Georgia Park with Vern being on his way to Texas Park.

We stopped at one in the morning so I could check all of the elephants and give them water. The truckers decided to go into the restaurant while I was doing that. I checked all the crates and they were all in order. We only had about twenty miles to go to the trucker's house. He had called his wife and son from the docks in New York. He told them about the elephants and they really wanted to see them, so I told him that we could stop for the night and that the elephants could stand a night of rest from the riding. I told him to have them get us four bales of hay for them to have tomorrow.

When we got to his house, he went inside with his wife and son. I slept inside the truck for the night. I got up at eight in the morning and his son had a sign made, saying, "see the elephants for fifty cents." He had posted it right in his front yard. He had six kids there waiting to see the elephants. I gave them a tour while I was feeding them. I told the boy that he was making more money than I was. He said, "I'll split it with you," and I smiled and told him that it was all right and to keep it. I said, "Someday, you will be a big business man and don't forget where you got your start."

After I fed and watered all of them, we were on our way again. I called Nonie, telling her when we would be in. She and the boys were waiting for me at the park when I got there. We unloaded them all and got them in the elephant barn. They seemed to be mixing well. Frank came in with two lions and one big elephant, so we unloaded them, also. It was three in the afternoon by then. Nonie, Joe, Erik, and I went on to the house. They let me clean up and we then went out to dinner. It was nice after being gone for six days to be with my family again.

The next day, Bob and I moved rhino crates and got everyone to fix fences for the goats and small animals; we did this for most of the day. The next day, we got in a pair of apes and the island wouldn't be ready for a couple of days, so we put them in an empty lion pen. I had a warden to stay with them; I went on to move some more lions to form a pride. In a couple of days, I would be going to Lion Country in Florida to pick up six lions, one sable, which is a very large antelope, along with some ginnie fowl, ducks, and geese at Chase in Miami, then back to Lion Country Georgia. Nonie, Joe, and Erik went back with me. I took two rhino crates for the lions to fix them all up for when I would get there. Some of the rangers put the crates on the flat bed the wrong way so they had to reload them the proper way. I took a tranquilizer gun with some medication with me, just in case I would need it. We left at five in the morning with a pickup truck with a flatbed trailer; we got in West Palm Beach around seven that night. We stayed at Nonie's mom and dad's house for the night.

The next day, Wayne went with me to pick up the animals at Chase. We got back around six and then we spent the time with our families. We got a late start in the morning, but about five that afternoon, we were about eighty miles from Georgia Park where I noticed the steering was getting sloppy. It was so loose that in order to keep the truck straight, I had to move the steering wheel a lot more than normal. We were going down a small hill and the truck was picking up speed. As I tapped the brakes, the trailer started to fishtail with me. I took the center of the two-lane highway. There was a cliff on one side of the road and it was surely a long way down to the bottom. On the other side was the same thing, so I took as much room as I could to keep everything on the road. We started to fishtail a lot more, so I sped up to try to get the truck and trailer to straighten out. We were almost at the bottom of the hill and when we started back, going uphill, with me stepping on the gas pedal, I finally got it all straight. I pulled to the side of the road to check the lions and the sable, wanting to check all the crates. In my mind, I could see the lions, the sable, and all the other animals strewed all over the place if we had flipped over. The situation could have turned really bad, especially with me only having a dart pistol. We said a few prayers to the man upstairs, knowing it could have turned in to a real bad situation. I really don't need to tell you the relief we felt. We didn't drive over forty miles per hour for the rest of the way there. It was really dark when we got there, so I told the guard at the park that I was taking Nonie and the boys home and I would be back to stay in the truck for the rest of the night.

The next morning, when Wayne, the mechanic, came in, I told him about the steering. He got under the truck and looked it over. He yelled, "Hey Gus, come look at this." I got under there and the steering box was held on by just three bolts. Two were gone and the other one could be turned with one's hand. We unloaded the lions and one lion had something wrong with its jaw. Doc said he would look at it. When we went to release the sable into the antelope section, we got the crate on the ground. I went on top of the crate to lift the door and it jammed as the sable was trying to get out, hitting the side of the crate and the door. The sable reared up and his horns busted the top boards, letting his horns come right up between my legs. Yep! They sure did, talk about moving fast out of the way, I did. I finally got the door from being jammed and let him out into the section. The sable turned, looking at us like it's about time you let me out of there. I told the rangers to get rid of that crate since it was getting ready to fall apart; after all of this, I went home and slept for the rest of the day.

Doc Silberman and I took the lion with the bad jaw to the vet college in Georgia. He did have a broken jaw and they fixed him up. It was past closing time at Lion Country when we got back, so I left the lion on the trailer for the night. Nonie and I went back around ten that night to check on the lion. He seemed to be doing okay.

The next morning, I let him out into a lion section by himself. He was still under the tranquilizer, so I wanted to make sure no other lions would get to him. After getting done with the lion, I went to where we were keeping the cheetahs. I had been feeding them from the back of my jeep. We had them in a big runabout around two hundred feet wide and three hundred feet long. This was inside the rhino section. We will release them into the rhino section. They couldn't kill the rhino and they are too fast for them to get near them. There was a lot of vegetation for them to hide from the rhinos. We were thinking that this might help the cheetahs breed. A couple of weeks ago, I got a cowbell and when we would drive through the rhino section, I would ring the bell, having the meat in the back of the jeep. Ringing this bell made them know it was feeding time. Two days before we were ready to release them, we didn't feed them. When we released them, we would ring the bell. At night, I hoped that they would all go back into the runabout so they could be fed. I decided for a while, at night, that we would feed them in the roundabout. If this worked out well between the rhino and cheetah, we would take the temporary fence down, and it would become the rhino and cheetah section. As you can tell, we were still in the learning stages with some of the roam free animals. We were still mixing some of the lions to form prides. We were doing the same thing we did in West Palm Beach Lion Country, in releasing the lions into the sections from the huts, letting the new rangers work the new lions. We also let the rhinos out and they were doing well.

We finally got Ape Island ready for the pair of apes we had. We had them over on the island and they seemed to be doing great. We then released the cheetahs and they came running when I rang the dinner bell, all except three, that is, but out of fifteen cheetahs, that's not bad, so I kind of figured that was a success. We went on to release another section of lions. Three jeeps were working them and they seemed to be doing well.

The next day, we got in sixteen more lions. We got them all in the hut by two in the afternoon. Some of the rangers started with the funnel fence in section three. Mike worked his lions by himself today. When he started putting them in the hut, two of the lions went over the funnel fence. We got them back and in the right door without darting them. It worked really well, considering that we had only done it four times. We would try another lion section on the morrow. Section three's lions worked well, but section one's lions were all over the section. We got all the lions in, except one, who was going crazy. The rangers were pushing her too hard. When I got to where she was, she was running to the corner of the fence on the road. I told them to stop pushing her, but it was too late. She had jumped the six-foot fence and was climbing the sixteen-foot fence, which was the outside fence. I shot her with a tranquilizer dart while she was on the fence. She climbed it and was almost to the five strands of barbwire. John was out of the jeep with his shotgun with slugs in it. I told him to shoot her, as my .357 was in the jeep. All I had in my hand was the dart gun. He shot her and she was almost through the barbwire. I told him shoot again. When he did, he hit her, sending her through the barbwire and she dropped the sixteen feet down, hit the ground, and ran through the bushes and woods on the outside. I got on the radio and told someone to bring me a shotgun with shells in it, as John only had two slugs left. We talked about that later. I got the gun and more shells for John. The fence had a gate to the outside and I had the key. We went on the outside, both of us with the guns, with slugs. I had my .357, so there was no need for a dart gun. She had been shot two times already and fell sixteen feet to the ground. We tracked her by the blood drops and tracks. We got to the creek about ten feet wide about a foot deep. It had moving water. The bank was about six feet high. We looked over the bank and could see blood in the water. I told John to get behind me and cover me. We walked along the bank. I spotted her. She was lying in the water with blood running from her. She was looking right at me with her ears back and her tail going from side to side in a quick motion. She was hissing at me with her mouth open. I told John to get ready, as we couldn't do anything but shoot her, so, I said, "Heads up." John was set on ready. I leaned further over the bank so I could get a good shot at her. I fired the gun, hitting her, and she fell over. We watched just for a few minutes to make sure she was gone. Then, we went into the creek and pulled her through the water, finding a place that we could pull her out of the water and up on the bank. The dart I had shot her with earlier was still lodged in her. I pulled it out and shook it. If it rattled, that meant that it went off. Well, needless to say, it didn't rattle. I looked at the tip of the needle. It was bent so it hit a bone and none of the tranquilizer had come out. There was no way she could have been tranquilized. I sure was glad that I had told John to shoot her; it wasn't a very good feeling when I put a lion down. It makes for a very bad day. We put her in the back of the jeep and took her back into the park.

The manager called me into the office. I got to his office and he wanted to know why I didn't call him before I shot the lion. He said to call him the next time I had to make that decision. I told him that in a situation like that; I didn't have time to call anyone. I needed to make a fast decision for the safety of my men, my safety, and the safety of the public outside the park. I said that if I couldn't do that, then I had just better go home. I asked him if he had been charged by a lion or in the situation that I was in today. He said no. Things happened so fast that if I needed to call him to get permission, then someone could possibly be dead while I was waiting for the okay from him. We were doing a lot of yelling, or should I say I was, as I was really hot under the collar. Bill York heard us yelling, and he didn't know what had happened. He came into the office, asking what was going on. Therefore, I told Bill what happened and what the manager had said to me. Bill was really fired up. He told the manager, "Gus wouldn't have had time to call you and he has worked with me for fifteen years. Therefore, if he shot an animal, you had better believe it was because he had to. Maybe you should go with Gus the next time; when he has to go after a lion to hunt it down to tranquilize it." He said, "No, I don't think so. I think I will handle the management, leaving Gus to the hunting and tranquilizing of the animals. I was wrong to get onto Gus like that. He knows what he is doing."

Bill told him, "Don't ever tell my men what they can do and what they can't do. That's Gus's and my job." Therefore, we left there and went to Bill's office. We sat down and I told him the whole situation, Bill said, "It wasn't like the time it sounded like the lion was shooting back, when you were in West Palm Beach?" laughing while he was saying it. I really did feel bad about it though, even if they did charge us. They are such beautiful animals and I hate seeing that happen, as they are only doing what comes natural to them. Bill knew I didn't have a choice as he had been in the same situation different times.

My mom and dad came to visit for a week, so I asked Bill if it would be okay for my dad to ride along with me for a couple of days. He said that he could the whole time if I wanted, so I thanked him and told dad, he sure was pleased. He enjoyed riding every day and I surely enjoyed having him with me, seeing all that it entailed in running a roam free park. Nonie brought mom out there, as we were closing. We were having trouble with a rhino. We were trying to give it a shot because she was still a little weak, so I had been giving her shots every day. Every time she saw me, she would get excited. She just knew she was going to get a shot, so I decided to let her calm down a bit. Then, we got a four by eight sheet of plywood and we went in to get her up against the wall so I could give her the shot. We got her in the corner and I gave her the shot by hand. Then, John, Bill, Bob, and I went running to the outside of the pen. Everyone else got out and while I was going. I slipped on rhino dung, sliding under the gate. Everyone was now on the outside of the gate. We all looked back and there she was, stuck in the corner. We had pushed her so hard against the wall with the plywood that she was jammed in between the corner and the cement water troughs. John and I had to get a two by four, put it between her and the wall, and pry her loose, then, we ran to the gate. We all got a good laugh at the way she looked all jammed up in there. Of course, we were thankful that she wasn't hurt. Mom and Dad thought we did all that on purpose.

We started fixing the funnel fencing in section two, as we got five male lions in from West Palm Beach. Buckshot, Charles, and Smokey, were from my old pride when I was there, so it was like seeing long lost friends. I had named each one of them and worked them for years. We got them all unloaded from the truck and into the hut. The next day, we let section two out in the morning. We decided to put them in around two. We didn't get them all in until six that evening. I had to dart three of them.

The next day, we let all of the lion sections out. They were out for the most of the day, and we now had sixty-four lions at the park. We were going to have opening day that day. Bill York was in another section and when we got together, we started talking as to how this was our third park we had opened together. We also talked about how we have not only been working side by side as coworkers, going through a lot of things, hunting down a lot of lions, tranquilizing them, but we have been very good friends as well.

Grand Opening was seven days after opening. We

let all the lions out and Fanny from section three was all over the park. From opening, until I darted her at one thirty I was looking for her. At closing, one lion was on the wrong side of the funnel fence, so we got her in the funnel and in the hut. In another section, we were driving the lions in the funnel. I looked over at the hut door. A man in the section forgot to open the door, so the lions went everywhere, jumping over the funnel fence. They couldn't get in their huts. This really confused them. Wayne drove over to the hut, using a rope that was on the door. Still in his jeep, he was able to get the door opened and hooked it. Then, we all went after the lions, finally getting them all put in the huts. I only had to tranquilize one, so that wasn't too bad. By eight-thirty, they were all in and cozy for the night. Now, it was time for all of us to go home and get cozy ourselves.

The next day seemed to be going along fine until Iron Sides was on the missing lions list. We didn't have any idea where he was, so we went into the heads. Finally, I found him in the swamp. I called Rick and asked him to push the lion from his side along the swamp to where I was. I would be able to dart him. He pushed him to me and I was able to dart him. I waited for half an hour and he still hadn't gone down, so I gave him ¼ cc more and then he went down. I called Tom to help put him in my jeep and take him back to the hut.

We had let a few lions out from where we had built the funnel fence to train them to go in the hut around one in the afternoon, letting them stay out until four. We started putting them up and as we were putting them up, three lions didn't want to go in. They all three took off for the swamp. John and I went in to track them down and tranquilize them. We got one in short order. When she went completely under the tranquilizer, we went off, looking for the others. We were able to find the other two. They were in a place where they had put branches and many big trees we had cut down in the park. It was all in a big pile where the construction crew had pushed them there when they cleared the property. There was a six-foot deep hole five or six feet wide. It was like a cave for a good ways back. Four or five lions could hide in there and one could walk right by them without seeing them. As we walked by on the logs, John saw them both in one of the holes. We backed off them. We got between some small tree trunks sticking up in the pile of trees. I took a shot with the dart gun. I was able to hit one while the other one moved away from the one I darted. He didn't have any idea where we were. I was able to dart him as well. After they were finally all down, I called some other rangers to come and get them out and back to the hut, then, we went back for the one we had darted in the swamp. It was around nine p. m. when we were on our way home.

Charles, the lion, went out in the park the next day, but he didn't want to mix with the pride. I worked with him, trying to push him in with the pride without any success, so I decided to dart him and he ran to a big ditch in the nearby section. When he went down, it took five of us to get him out of the ditch.

Later that day, a car caught fire in a lion section. We didn't have a fire extinguisher in any of the jeeps. I called the office and told them that we had a car on fire in the section and that we needed a fire truck now. They called and the fire department wouldn't cross the county line. We were able to get one to come from twenty miles away. By the time they arrived, the car was completely engulfed in flames. I had to close down the lion section while the car was burning. All of the lions were going crazy and running all over the place. We got all of the lions back to their huts and got all the people turned around going back through the entrance gate, giving them all passes to return another day. We even had two lions from another section in this section, but we decided to leave them there for the night; we would put them back in the right section the next day.

It was the following day and all sections were out. We did not have much trouble with them that day. We put the lions that went into the wrong section back where they belonged with their own pride.

The next day was Grand Opening. The Governor of Georgia and a lot of the higher ups were coming. Everyone came in at six a.m. to clean the huts and check all over the park. I had to tranquilize a cheetah; he was fighting and he was bitten a lot on his face. The doc said that he just might lose his eye, as it was pretty bad. Everything seemed to go smoothly that day and was fairly calm.

The next day, all went well until closing time. We had some trouble in section one, but we got all the lions in the hut without having to tranquilize any. Then, when we got to section three, the lions were all over the place. Two males and two females were between the fences and they were trying to climb the fence. I tranquilized one. The other went about forty feet and lay down, so I left the one I just tranquilized. I left two rangers watching the two between the fences and took two with me to go look for the two in the swamp. We went through the head and didn't hear or see anything, so we went on to the swamp. It was starting to get dark, and believe me it was a lot darker when you were walking through the swamp. I told the rangers that if we didn't see them this time when we go through, we would wait until the next day. We were about half way through the swamp for the second time when I spotted one of the lions. I took a shot at it with the dart gun and missed. Then, I was out of seralyn with two lions in the swamp and it was getting dark along with a lion between the fences and me with no tranquilizer. It wasn't a good situation. Pets' Corner was where the drugs were all locked up and I haven't gotten the keys yet. I did have with me some ace promozine, which is not a powerful drug. This would only make them drowsy with a "don't care" attitude. That is all it will do and it doesn't last long. I also didn't have the yellow charge I used to shoot for a long distance. I had only the red one for the higher charge. If I used that one, it would go into the lion like a bullet. I told the rangers to head their jeeps into the fence and turn on their headlights so we could see better. There wasn't much light as it was getting dark quickly. I had to figure out a way to give her a shot of promozine by hand. I pulled the jeep up against the fence, then, got on the top of the roof. I had two rangers with shotguns aimed at the lion, then, I had a jeep between the two fences. I dropped the rope down the inside of the fencing and one of the rangers pulled the rope through the fence. I held on to the rope and they tied the end of the rope to a jeep. The lion was still looking at the jeep. I was able to throw the rope over her head and it went around her neck. Then, I threw the rope on the ground the jeep backed up and tightened the rope and pulled the lion to the fence. She was jammed up tight on the fence so I went inside the fences by the jeep. Then I grabbed her tail, and with the jeep, pulling her against the fence, I was able to give her the shot of ace promozine by hand. The jeep gave her a little slack and we waited until it started to work.

After about twenty-five minutes, she still wasn't out the way she should have been, so I grabbed her tail again and gave her another shot of the drug. After waiting for another fifteen minutes, she seemed to be out a little more, so I got the jeep between the fence and the rangers got a lion crate. Then, I got another rope putting it through the crate, tying one end to the jeep, then, throwing the rope over the lions head. The jeep on the outside moved to give the rope some slack. The jeep in between the fence backed up, pulling the lion into the cage. When we finally got the lion in there with the door down, I had a shovel handle with a hook on the end. I took that and with the hook and I loosened the ropes on the lion and pulled them free from around his neck. Then, they took him to section three and left him outside for the night. The first lion that I had tranquilized had run the opposite way the other lion did, so that made for an interesting time. We still had two lions in the swamp running free at night. By now, it was twelve thirty at night. I left Jim and told John and Dean to come in around two in the morning to stay until opening, just in case the lions would get in with the hoof stock or in any other place that they shouldn't be during the night.

The next day, Jim and I went in the swamp looking for the two lions. We found them with no problem, getting them tranquilized and put in the huts for the rest of the day and night. The rest of the day went really well.

On my day off, I got a phone call at eleven o'clock that Bob was having trouble with a lion going in the head, which was a very swampy area. He wanted me to come in and get the lion out, so I got ready and went in. We went in the swamp, looking for her. We found her and I darted her. We waited the allotted time and then went looking for her, finding her in a small creek. Her head was almost under the water. I went to her and pulled her head out of the water. She had just gone under and she was completely under the tranquilizer so we pulled her out and we loaded her on to the jeep and took her to the hut and bedded her down. It was then time for me to go back home and enjoy what was left of my day off. By this time, it was two in the afternoon.

My brother, Ray, and his wife, Kitty, came to visit us for a while, so I decided to take him with me on my everyday duties of running a roam free wild animal park. After having breakfast, we went to work. We decided to let all four prides of lions out this morning. I gave a shot to an elephant that had been hooked by an eland. After doing this, it was one in the afternoon, so we went back to the house spending time, just the four of us. The next day, Ray rode with me again. I gave medication to some of the animals and checked a few. I had been giving this young rhino shots by hand, as he got all excited when I would shoot him with a dart gun, so giving it to him that way was best. I asked Ray if he would like to help me. He said, "Sure, I'll try anything once." Therefore, I got five rangers and we got the plywood and pushed the rhino against the wall. I gave the shot and he was getting upset after I gave him a shot. He knocked the plywood out of our hands and I yelled, "Everyone out!" We all ran to the fence. I asked Ray what he thought of that situation. He said, "I don't know anything about rhinos, but how come when you yelled everyone out, the man in charge of the rhinos was the first one out of the fence?" I was keeping in mind though the man in charge of the rhino was very new to this and he was just waiting for me to yell "OUT."

The next day, my brother rode with me again as they would be leaving the following day. We had two lions in one section giving us trouble. They were running behind the hut. After a few minutes, we got them back to the pride with no problems.

Then three lions got over by the swamp area, so we went over there and got them back to their rightful place, doing all of this without having to tranquilize any of them.

About one in the afternoon it started, raining and got windy. I had some lions that I needed to give rabies shots to; also, I had to check their paws. We had a liquid we put in a 3x4 foot pan against the cage outside the door so when they went in or out they had to walk through it; it was to help their paws if they had any cuts, bruises, or infections they might have.

I told the ranger in section four that I was going to give his lions their rabies shot and to check their paws, so he was to let me know if a lion comes back to the hut. He said, will do, so off we went to the hut to give the shots to the ones that were in the runabout. Then, all of a sudden, it sounded as if a lion was right behind us, making a growling sound. It was really loud. We both dropped what we were doing. Both jeep doors were open and both of us dove into the jeep and closed the doors. We looked around and saw no lion. Then, I noticed the two tin pans were lying on the ground. I told Ray that it wasn't a lion; it was the tin pans falling all over the place from the wind blowing so hard. Without a smile on his face, he looked at me and said, "Boy, you can sure get old fast on your job." We started laughing. What an exciting day this turned out to be. The next day, they left. It sure was nice having him ride with me and having them visit.

The golf course nearby called Lion Country and said one of the groundskeepers saw some lion tracks in the sand traps. They were telling their visitors that there was a lion loose running around the golf course, and that they can't go out there. Bill called me to have every ranger count his or her lions. They did, and all were accounted for. The golf course kept insisting that there were lion tracks in their sand traps so Bill sent me out to check it all out. It was about four miles from the park. When I got there, a guy in a golf cart took me out to the sand trap to check. I told them that all the rangers checked and all their lions were there, so I looked at these so-called lion tracks. Lo and behold, they were dog tracks. I told him that when dogs run around in sand, it would look a lot bigger than the dog really is anyway. To show him proof, I lifted my hand up and brought it down in the sand telling him, "See how much bigger the print is than my hand?" This seemed to satisfy him, so they started letting people come back to play golf. I am sure that they were surely being cautious, watching for lions for a few days, so back I went to the real world of animals.

RICHARD GUSTAFSON
Chief Game Warden

LION COUNTRY SAFARI, INC.
ROUTE NO. 3, BOX 579
STOCKBRIDGE, GA. 30281
TELEPHONE (AREA CODE 404) 474-1461

MY BUSINESS CARD WHILE IN GEORGIA

A GROUP OF RHINOS RELAXING

A HIPPO SOUNDS A WARNING

281

ELEPHANTS GATHER AT WATERING HOLE

JEEP DAMAGED BY A CHARGING ELAND

**MOTHER ZEBRA WATCHES
PROTECTIVELY OVER HER BABY**

Chapter 16

Hippo Trapping
and Animal Happenings

We have been working on a rhino crate for a while now, making it an oversized rabbit trap out of it to catch a hippo that got into the rhino section from the hoof stock section. It should be ready soon as I work on it when I have some spare time. It was quite a project to get it just right to be able to trap a hippo. This is a very large animal for which to be setting a trap. I had it set so when the hippo bumped the 2x4 to get the food, it would push the 2x4 out from under the nail on the bottom of the crate and the door will come down, with the animal in side. We got it all set up and now we will see what happens tonight. We haven't fed the hippo for two days, so maybe he will try to get the food during the night. We put a little food at the front of the crate by the pond where he seemed to be staying. When we came in the next morning, the hippo had eaten some of the food and vegetables that we placed in front of the crate but none in the crate. I had everyone in the rhino section to check on the hippo and let me know if he came near the crate. About eleven o'clock, Rick called and said the hippo was around the crate. I got over to the section and saw that the hippo's head was inside the crate. He was almost all the way in, and when he lifted his back leg to go further in the crate, it tipped. It wasn't on even ground. The crate was so heavy, and when we were in the crate, our weight didn't make a difference, as we weren't heavy enough, but when he did, it twisted the crate and it fell down, hit the hippo on the back and the door jammed in the door ridge at a crooked angle. Now, we were back to square one. We put some dirt under one corner of the crate to stop it from tipping when he put his weight on it. We put out more fruit and vegetables and then, we left, waiting for him to try it. I went on to the rest of the sections for the day, with some lions giving me some problems, going into the hut as we were putting the lions up in their huts for the night. Rick called, saying that the hippo was out of the pond and just moving around close to the crate. I told the rangers to finish putting the lions up, then they could go clock out, telling Rick and his helper to stay in the rhino section, and that I would be right there. I told Rick's helper to get on the crate and hide behind the door, so if the rhino went in the crate and tripped the door to push the door while it was going down, so if it jammed to try to get it closed. He climbed up on top, sitting down with one leg hanging on the side. He has been working for about two weeks with us. When I hired him, I had noticed that he walked with a slight limp, but I thought he hurt his leg in a motorcycle wreck, as he came up to Lion Country on a bike. Since I also had a bike, we talked a lot about our experience and all the mishaps we had. Well, anyways, Rick was back from the crate as to not spook the hippo from going in the crate. I yelled to his helper to get his leg on top of the crate so it wouldn't be hanging over the side where the hippo can see it. If he would see it, he wouldn't go in; so, he stood up on top of the crate, undid his pants, dropping them down around his knees, to our surprise, took off his leg, and threw it over his shoulder, yelling, "There, is that good enough?" I don't need to tell you how surprised Rick and I were, as we had no idea that he had a wooden leg. I looked at Rick and him and me with our mouths wide open, and our eyes big. I yelled back, "Yep, that's just fine." Neither of us could believe what we had just seen. Later on, when we talked about it, we had a good laugh. We waited for about two hours. The hippo wasn't going to go in the crate that night with us there, so we left the door open and hoped it might happen the next day.

The next day, after opening, Rick called and said as they were cleaning the rhino barn, the hippo almost walked into the hut. They were cleaning the runabout when they saw him. I told him to open the gate to the runabout, get in his jeep, and try to keep the hippo close to the gate. Then, I called Wayne to meet me at the rhino hut. When he got there, the three of us started to work the hippo in the runabout. Finally, we got him in the gate, closing and locking it. This was much better than outside in the section. I got the tractor and we moved the crate in the runabout, putting it in a corner. Nonie came to pick me up; we were going to a meeting at Erik's school for a couple of hours. Doc said that he would bring Nonie to the rhino barn. When they got there, I told her that she was early and that I wanted to get the hippo into the crate, as we had left the vegetables in the crate. We just put the door on top of the crate and when we did this, he was acting as if he wanted to get to the food. That was our chance to get him in there, so we got the four by eight piece of plywood and Wayne, Rick, his helper, and I pushed the hippo towards the crate and wall. We got him against the wall and as we were going to the door of the crate, I thought that if we got him in and pressed the plywood against the door opening, someone could get on the top of the crate sliding the door in the slot and pull the door down. We got him about a foot from the door, then, he reared up on the plywood in front of me. The bottom of the plywood slid towards us. As it was throwing us forward towards him, I fell right in his mouth. As I fell, I threw up my arm, hoping to stop my falling anymore in his mouth. My hands were on his tusk, then, I pushed myself out of his mouth. He had the worst case of bad breath that I ever came across. The plywood fell partially against the crate. As I pushed myself out of his mouth, he grabbed the plywood, lifted his head up with the plywood in his mouth, slammed it on the floor, breaking it, and bent it to a forty-five degree bend. We all were getting out of there. I told them that I had to go now, so to fix the trap again, put more food inside of the crate, and then try it again later.

Then, I looked for Nonie and she and Doc were at the top of where we kept the hay. It was about fifteen feet high and they both were as high as they could go. Nonie said that at the time we were fighting with the hippo, she and Doc were scrambling to get up the hay. She was ahead of him and he grabbed her to get ahead of her. She sure wasn't a happy camper and she let him know it. After all, he should have been the one wanting her to get up first. He was supposed to be used to working around these wild animals, one never knows. Later on, as we were talking about it, we had a good laugh. We stayed on Doc's case for a while after that. We told him that we didn't want to have a foot race with him because he would trip us or grab us and pull us behind him.

The next morning, I told Rick to leave the rhinos and cheetahs in the barn and in the hut. I got Wayne, Jim,

Rick, his helper, along with five jeeps and myself. I told them I would drive in the runabout and push the hippo out of the pen, and for Rick and Jim to get on one side of the gate, single file, and then I told Wayne along with Rick's helper to get on the other side. This was so when the hippo came out, we would have him in a U formation. Then, I could push him. Their job was to keep him on the road so we could walk him back through to the hoof section. I told everyone that I wanted radio silence while we were doing this, as we needed to communicate. I went in and pushed him out of the pen between the four jeeps, letting him go at his own pace. He would slow down, so, then, we would slow down. I worked the back and sometimes either side of the hippo. Before we started, I had told the man at the gate what we were doing. I wanted him to stop all the cars way down the road, and to open the gate when I told him. When I got the hippo close to the gate, I yelled for him to do this and to make sure to stop the cars until we got him out of the rhino section and back where he belonged in the hoof stock section. After accomplishing this, I told everyone they had done a great job and that they all worked well together to get the job done. I then told everyone to go back to their sections and for Rick and his helper to release the rhinos and cheetahs the way we normally do.

A week or so later, I was running my rounds and stopped at the exit gate in the rhino and cheetah section, talking with Rick's helper and he was sitting on the fence, legs crossed. As we were talking, some people in a car asked him where the lions were. He had a hunting knife in his hand and was carving on a stick. He took the knife and stuck it in his wooden leg, took his hand away from the knife that he had stuck in his leg, pointed to the next section, and said that they are over that way. Our mouths opened up wide. They thanked him and drove off. I cracked up laughing. He said that he had fun doing that. I told him I thought it was great, but that he best not do that anymore as some old folks might have a heart attack and sue Lion Country, but I did think it was funny. I also told him that he had better get in his jeep as the people might think it is okay for them to get out of their cars. He was a different person and he didn't stay with us too long.

Everything seemed to be going smoothly, then, the gate man at the antelope, cheetah, and rhino section called, saying that three ostriches got through the gate and were in with the cheetahs. Some of the cheetahs were on the ostriches. When I got there, he was grinning. He said, "Hi Gus," acting strangely. I saw the cheetah on two of the ostriches. I told him to close the gate and not to let cars through until I told him to, or we would have had cheetahs in the hoof stock section. I called for Rick to get to the gate and to help me get the cheetah off the ostrich. I went to them then got out of my jeep, trying to get them off with a shovel handle that I carry with me. Then Rick got there, and we both were pulling, grabbing, and hitting them, doing whatever it was going to take to get them off the ostrich. Another ranger came over. He started to help us. We finally got them away. Then, Rick got in his jeep and pushed them farther away from the ostrich. One was dead. He ran into the fence at the corner. The cheetahs were on him for some time before I got there. The other two were badly cut. We got one in the back of my jeep. She was out of it and hurt. She was breathing fast. As we were, lifting the other one up, she got up and started walking slowly to the gate. I yelled for the gate man to open the gate. As he did, we were pushing her by walking behind her. Then, the cheetah was going for the one we had put in the jeep. I told the ranger to keep pushing her through the gate and into the hoof stock section.

I went back and got the other cheetah away from the one in the jeep, driving my jeep through the gate. I was then on my way to take the ostrich to Pets' Corner to the operating room, telling the vet that I needed to go back to check the other one. He was all scratched up, but he seemed to be okay, moving better, and he was alert. Then, I went through the gate, stopping to talk to the gate man that had let them through the gate in the first place. He was acting as if it wasn't a big deal and was in a stupor. From the smell in the hut, he was smoking pot and a lot of it. I told him to get into my jeep, that I was taking him outside the park as he was fired. He started saying, "I know I messed up real bad and I will never do it again on the job." I told him I couldn't ever trust him again, no matter what, that we all had to depend on each other, especially at times like what just happened and when we were in the heads looking for lions, saying that I sure wouldn't trust him to watch my back or any of the animals, let alone any of my men.

We got to Bill's office. I told Bill what happened and that I had fired him. He said that if I hadn't fired him, he sure would have. About three months later, he came back, asking for a job. I told him that as long as I was there, he could be certain that he would never get a job that involved handling animals again. From that little episode, the ostrich that I took to Pets' Corner died, so we lost two out of the three of them for a stupid stunt he pulled.

We only let out two prides the next day. There were jeeps down and it was raining almost all day long. We got eight lions in from West Palm Beach; it was good to see them all again. I like to think that they recognized me. We put them in section two. We had around seventy lions in then, and we would be getting in a few more.

After about a week, we let section two out, we kept two in. Buckshot was one of them. When I had him in my pride in West Palm Beach, he didn't give me a bit of trouble. I think it was because he had a buddy named Whitey and they were together all the time. I don't know why they didn't send him with him. I was thinking he might be missing him. He was under a bush and we almost walked on him. He just watched us walk by him. We spotted him, so then I darted him. We loaded him in the jeep and took him to the hut.

We got some monkeys in and the people that sent them to us put two monkeys in one crate. The vet wanted to give shots and check them. As we were getting them out of the crate, Bob and Ann were bitten by the same monkey, so we put him in a cage by himself and sent him off to be checked for rabies. When the results came back, Bill called me in to the office and told me to go get Ann, because he will have to tell her she needed to get the rabies shots right away. Bob was off and he had called him and told him already. I got Ann and we went to Bill's office where he told her she had to start the shots. She was a little shocked and wanted to know if it would affect her date that night. Bill laughed and said that she couldn't give anyone rabies. Relieved, she said, "That's good." They got the shots in, so they administered the shots to them. Boy, did their whole disposition change. Ann started to cry when someone talked with her and Bob wanted to argue all the time. It took seven days with a series of two shots a day. After they were finished with the shots, they both were back to normal again. I told Bob that he was really getting to be a pain when he was taking them and I was about ready to put one of my boots where the sun didn't shine, but things are fine now.

I was sent to New York to pick up some zebras. Mike, from the West Palm Beach park, took fourteen and I took ten. We didn't get them loaded on the trucks until two o'clock. We rode all night and all the next day. We arrived at Lion Country Georgia around eleven at night. We didn't unload them until I came in the next morning at eight o'clock. The forklift had a flat tire, so we got it fixed and started unloading the zebra into the rhino and cheetah section, hoping that by putting them in there, that it would stimulate the cheetah into breeding, as they could go through the motions of attacking them but realize that they were way too big. It would be great if we could get them to produce some babies. At this time, not many cheetahs were being born in captivity, but this was the wrong thing to do. We got six zebras out in the section, then, the cheetahs started chasing them. The rhino went crazy on us, running all over the section. The zebra did not know where the fencing was, and one of the zebra ran into the gate and his head and foot became stuck. We finally got him out, then, he was caught between the slide gate and the swing gate. We had to put a rope around his chest and we got him loose. Two of the zebras ran into the fence and broke their necks. Six cheetahs had one zebra down by the culvert. We ran down there and beat them off her. She got up and was okay. We decided this should have been done differently. If we had put the zebra in first, so they would know the section, then the rhino and last the cheetah, and putting the zebra in last wasn't such a good idea. Of course, we were still learning things; we pushed the rest of the zebra into the hoof stock section by working them to the fence, then pushing and holding them to the fence with the jeeps, walking them through the gate. We released them into the antelope section, and then I went home at four-thirty. Being on the road with these zebras meant that I had very little sleep in two days, so I was sure going to welcome some long awaited sleep.

I started giving medication by the dart gun to the zebras that I brought in on the trucks. I also gave medication to six lions and one elephant, then, the hoof stock ranger couldn't find a tapa. We found a hole in the fence, thinking the tapa went out the hole so I got Rick and Jim. We went outside the fence, couldn't find any tracks, and so I told them to go back to the hoof stock section and check if the ranger in the section just missed seeing the tapa. They did find it in the section so all was well.

When we opened the next day, Rick called and wanted me to come to the rhino section. When I got there, Rick said to go check out the rhino by the hut and big rock, so I drove over there and lo and behold, there was the rhino trying to breed with the huge rock. It was almost as big as the rhino. Rick said that the rhino had fallen in love with that rock yesterday and today at opening, when the rhino was let out in the section, he went running straight to the rock. We laughed and I said, "Well, at least he won't give you any trouble today."

In the afternoon, I was riding through the antelope

section and an eland was after a newly born zebra. He was trying to get it with his horns. I got between the baby and eland to separate them. The eland put his horns on the driver's side of my jeep door and pushed me sideways about a foot. Then, he backed off and came at my jeep again, putting his horns through my door, right by my legs. He pushed the jeep about two feet sideways again. I called the man in the antelope section to help me get the zebra in to the worming section, but first, to come help get this eland off my jeep. It didn't take us long to get the baby zebra in there, but I had two holes about two inches in diameter through my door, right by my legs.

Jim got into a fight with Carl, then, called me and said Carl started to walk back to the exit gate instead of getting back in to his jeep. He said that he was acting strangely. I went to the lion section and Carl was walking down the middle of the road kind of like in a stupor, I stopped and told him to get in the jeep. He obliged and jumped in, not saying a word, just looking straight ahead. I asked him what happened. He said that he didn't remember, so I said I was taking him to Pets' Corner and that Doc was going to check him over. The doctor looked at him and said that I had better take him to the hospital to have them check him over, then if all was okay, to take him home. Before I took him, I went back to Jim's section and back to Carl's jeep. I brought a mechanic with me to drive his jeep back to the place where we park all the jeeps for the night. I asked Jim what in the world happened and he said he thought I was disrespecting him so I slugged him. I told him that that can't happen again and if it did, I would have to do something about it. Jim said he would try to control his temper in the future.

Later, Jim was having trouble with his lions and called for help. As I was going to his section, he called again and said, "Can you hurry Gus? I am on the biggest rock in the world." When I got there, his lions were all over the section and the front end of his jeep was on a big boulder with the tires about two feet off the ground. We had to get a tractor to get him off the rock. We finally got all the lions back and in their section where they belonged.

I was told that while I was away picking up animals, they had a lion go in the swamp. The zoological director drove Jim to the far side of the swamp without a gun. He told Jim to walk to the other side of the swamp by the fence, and then he drove to the opposite side to wait for Jim. Jim said about halfway walking through, he thought, "What in the world am I doing here without a gun?" When he got to the other side, the zoological director was outside his jeep with his gun, with one foot in the jeep. Jim said, "I'll go and do anything you tell me to do Gus, but not for him." I assured him if that were to happen again, to let me know I would get the situation taken care of, good or bad.

We have been having a lot of trouble with Buckshot and a few of the other lions in Bob's section. We tried Buckshot in section two to mix with the pride and he just wouldn't mix. I have taken him out in a rolling cage and put him out with the pride, but for some reason, he still wouldn't mix. Sometimes, I even drag him out, as he doesn't want to leave the hut at all. A couple of Bob's lions are going in the ravine where the jeeps wouldn't go. I have been shooting by them with number eights with the shotgun. When I do that, they get out of there and back to where they belong. Now, all I do is get out of my jeep and cock the shotgun. They hear the noise it makes and they take off to their pride and lay right down as if nothing is wrong.

I had to give one of Bob's lions a series of two shots per day for five days. I drove to his section and medicated the lion with a tranquilizer gun. After three days, the lions knew my jeep and would run away from it. So, I would pull up by Bob's jeep and we would exchange jeeps. The lions would be looking at my jeep with Bob in it and I would pull up by him and give him a shot. The first time I did that with his jeep, there were flies all over the jeep. The lion men would get a foot tub with cube meat in it to throw out on the road to their lions and to put on people's vehicles if they wanted us to do it for pictures of lions on their cars. His steering wheel was so sticky from the meat on his hands. My hands stuck to the steering wheel and had pieces of old and new meat all over the inside of his jeep and it smelled really bad. I told him that tonight, he needed to get over there and wash his jeep. He said that he knew he needed to do that, and that he would get it done that night.

Frank, the man that ran the elephant section, called me, saying one of his elephants got away from him and ran to the other end of the section. I went to where the elephants were and told him that I would watch the elephants and for him to go get his runaway elephant. In about twenty minutes, he brought him back and everything was all right after that. Last night, an elephant bit John on the thumb. He went to see the doctor this morning and his thumb was mashed very badly. It will be sore for a while.

The next morning, Frank and John were taking an elephant from in the preserve to Pets' Corner. She was a very young elephant, and not very big. They called me and she was going down as they almost got to Pets' Corner. When I got there, they were trying to hold her up. I gave her some medication by hand then Doc gave her some liquids. We walked her slowly back to the elephant barn. The vet gave her more liquids, along with some Gatorade. She acted better, but I had Frank and John stay with her all night. Nonie and I went back out to the preserve at ten that evening. Everything was okay. I think she just got too hot going to Pets' Corner this morning but seems all right now.

Buckshot finally is doing well. We put him in section three and he is getting along well with the rest of the pride. It was a hard row to hoe, but he is finally to his old self.

I went in the morning to help with the zebras, but a lion was going crazy, so I worked with her until noon and finally got her back to the pride without having to tranquilize her. This was supposed to be my day off, so at three o'clock, I finally got to go home. A couple of days later, I went to New York again to pick up ten more zebras that had been in quarantine for three months. I got at the quarantine station and I was waiting for the trucks when they finally got there at one o'clock. We had them all loaded by three in the afternoon. We left and drove all day until midnight, then, slept until three in the morning, got up and started to drive on to Lion Country. We arrived at nine o'clock. We unloaded the zebras, two males, and eight females. Going out of the park, the truck was stuck in the mud and clay. We got the tractor so we could get him out. After that, it was time for me to go home for a much-deserved rest and the rest of my day off.

One day at closing time, Charles ran in front of my jeep when we were putting the lions in for the night. I was right on the road and couldn't go off to miss hitting him, as there was a culvert and a ditch on both sides of the road. Charles started running faster and ran into my jeep. He broke his hind leg and he went into the swamp. We got the rest of the lions in the hut, then, Jim and I went in the swamp to get Charles. We found him and I tranquilized him. We put him in a crate and took him to section two's hut. We left him outside the hut in the crate, and then I called Doc. I told him what happened and he said that he would see us in Athens, Georgia at the veterinarian college. That night, Nonie and I went out to the park to check on him at eleven o'clock. He seemed to be okay for a lion with a broken leg. The next day was supposed to be my day off, but I called Mr. Jones, the General Manager. I told him that Nonie and I would take Charles to the University in Georgia to meet the doctor there. Beth also went with us. She was from Pets' Corner. When we got there, Doc was waiting. He told them that we were coming in with a fully-grown five-year-old lion with a broken hind leg. I had given him 2 ½ cc's of seralyn three hours before. We took him out of the crate and put him on the rolling table. They were ready for us and everyone was really excited about working on a lion. All they had worked on up until now was horses, pigs, dogs and cats, domesticated ones. We wheeled him inside and had to go through where there were a few horses in stalls. We went really fast as they had started to kick the walls, and were pacing in the stalls. They could smell the lion and didn't like what they were smelling. I had two darts with seralyn in them and the pistol dart gun with me. The students got a little nervous, as did Beth and Nonie. When we wheeled Charles in the elevator and the elevator doors closed, Charles started moving and doing little roars. With this drug, Charles' eyes are opened and moving as they see all kinds of little animals running around that are not even there. Some of the women started jumping up and down, yelling, "Give him another shot, he's coming to." A few of the men were doing the same thing. I told them that what Charles was doing was normal, being under the seralyn and that he was not going to wake up and charge us or eat us. They all seemed to calm down a little, except for one of the men. He wanted that door to open up now. Well, it did and we went to the operating room. The vets got ready to fix his leg. They told us if we wanted, we could stay and watch the procedure. They gave us all a mask to put on and they left, getting ready, and washing up. They started to work on Charles.

I had watched our vet and helped him with different operations on all different African animals, cutting off a lion's tail after it was almost bitten off from a fight he had gotten into, working on a rhino with an abscess, also an elephant. We also set a broken leg on a lion, but this break on Charles' leg was a lot different. It had to have a hole drilled in his thighbone at both ends of the break. Then, they put a pin in it. They took a hammer and held up his leg while another drove the pin in the bone. I couldn't believe how hard they were hitting on the pin and jarring his whole body and leg. They finally got the pin in. They went to the other end of the break and started pushing and twisting until they got it set and all put together. As they were finishing up, something went wrong and his heart rate started to slow down until it stopped. They tried everything they knew what to do, but still no heart beat. Then, a few of them took off their masks shaking their heads, saying he was doing so well. Then, they walked out of the operating room. All of a sudden, one of the machines started to make a different sound. Someone yelled, "He's back." The ones that left came running back in the room and everyone was busy doing something.

When they finished up and gave him all kinds of liquids, they said they thought he would make it. We took him up on the roof. There was a closed-in cage with a roof over it about twelve feet by twelve feet, and we put him inside. They wanted to keep him about two weeks before they let him come back to Lion Country.

Two weeks later, Doc and I went to the university to pick him up. We were able to take his cage with us. We got him into the jeep and were ready for the ride back. We had already prepared a hut for him with hay down. He would be by himself for about a month or so until Doc felt he was ready to go back with the pride. After a month, we mixed him with the pride inside of the hut a few at a time until they all got mixed together. This took about seven days, and then we let them all out together. Everything went fine, no fighting, and everyone got along. Charles was left with a slight limp. Other than that, he was as good as new.

My mother and father came to visit us for a few days, so I took Dad to Lion Country to ride with me in my jeep. I showed him what I did for a living. He sure had a good time watching what all I did and how it was done with all the wild animals. I let him get involved with the not so dangerous things, but when it was dangerous, I made him stay in my jeep and watch from there. I gave shots most of the day. It was really a very calm day except...closing time...It started raining hard. The lions started running all over the place. They wouldn't go anywhere they were supposed to. There were two lions in section two going crazy, but we got them all in the hut without having to dart them. Then, we locked the hut door for the night. Dad said, "Boy, oh boy, that was a wild ride." I said, "Ya! We do that a lot. Wasn't that fun?" I told him that I loved every minute of it and I am paid for doing what I so enjoy. This was the last day Dad could ride with me as they were going to leave to go home in the morning. I gave an elephant, rhino, zebra, and two cheetahs a shot, and then a lion went into the swamp. John and I went tracking and hunting for him. I told dad he couldn't go with us. He said, "Don't worry; I am staying right in the jeep until you get back."

We got the lion tranquilized, then, I went back to my jeep. I said, "Come on Dad, you can help load the lion on the jeep to take him back to the hut." He was smiling as he got out of the jeep. He wanted to know if all of the lions were in the huts and I said no. He turned right around and got right back into the jeep. John and I just laughed and then I said, "Hey Dad! I was just kidding." Then, he laughed too. He decided to get out and help us then. I know he really had a great time with me and the men for the few days he was with me. He would have a lot to talk about for a long time, telling them how he got up close and personal with a lot of African animals. In addition, the time that we spent together sure gave us a lot of bonding as father and son; I did enjoy him very much. The men did also.

We only had three jeeps to run the park with the next day. All the other jeeps were in for repairs. Then, at noon, we had two more fixed, making us a total of five. I gave medication to a zebra and a few of the lions. It was proving to be a slow day so far, but as you know, closing time was coming up. When we were putting up section two lions, eight of the lions started going crazy. When they got close to the hut, two lions were missing. Section one called, saying he had a lion missing. Sully found her in section two along the fence. He started pushing her along the fence. When she got to the corner in the fence, she jumped the six foot one. I got on the radio and told Jim and Sully to back up and give her some space. She was getting too excited and we were pushing her too fast. Then, I called Bob, telling him to bring a shotgun. Before he got there, the lion started climbing the sixteen-foot fence and was up and already in the five strands of barbwire on the very top. She was looking at the outside of the park. It was then I decided to dart her. She then got out of being between the barbed wire and was half sitting and half lying down on the barbed wire. I told Bob to shoot as she was acting as she was going to jump on the outside of the park. Not knowing if the tranquilizer in the dart went off or not, I really couldn't take that chance. The way she was looking. I figured she was going to jump off the barbed wire to the ground, leaving her on the outside of the park, not making for a good situation. As I said before, it takes between fifteen or twenty five minutes for the drug to take effect. We also could lose her and the next morning when she woke up she, could cause a lot of problems on the outside, possibly killing people. My only choice was to put her down before that happened. Bob

301

shot her. When he did, she squatted down and was like a spring looking at the ground on the outside. I told him to shoot again. When he did, she fell to the ground on the inside of the park about twenty feet from us. She then got up and started to come towards us. I shot her twice with my .357 magnum as she was coming at us really fast. When I hit her, she fell to the ground. I checked her and she was gone. As I have said so many times, you always feel so bad about a situation that makes you have to shoot one of these animals and it's a hard decision for me to have to make. I couldn't let her get to the outside of the park, so I feel as though I made the right choice. We do all we can for these beautiful animals, keeping them healthy, feeding them well, and helping them take care of their young. We do everything we can possibly do to make them feel like they should naturally and not penned up in a cage for all their lives After disposing of the lion in the proper manner by calling the man with the tractor to come out and take care of her, we went back to our other business again. We looked for the other lions; we found them with no problem and put them back in the hut with the other lions.

TWO CHEETAHS PROWLING THEIR TERRITORY

GIRAFFE AND OSTRICHES COEXIST WELL

LIONS CURIOUS ABOUT OVERTURNED JEEP

PRIMATE ISLAND

RELEASING NEW ARRIVALS INCLUDING THIS ZEBRA

RHINOS GATHER AT FEEDING TIME

WATER BUFFALO AT FEEDING TIME

Chapter 17

Gorilla Attack

We had a fairly normal morning, until the man taking the people around the islands by boat where the primates were called me and told me that one of the gibbons was on Gorilla Island. I asked him how did that happen and he said when he went by the gibbon island, that the motor quit and drifted on to the island. He was trying to get the motor started. While he was doing this, he didn't know the gibbons had jumped on the canopy that gave shade to the people while they were riding on the boat. Well, after getting the motor going, he went on his way, going over to Gorilla Island. Before getting there, the motor quit again, letting them drift over to Gorilla Island. When the boat drifted to the island, the gibbon jumped off the boat on to Gorilla Island. He got the motor running again and got to the dock and that is where he called me. Then, we had a sick gibbon with a cold and a cough that we have been treating with medication, and it was on Gorilla Island with a male and pregnant female gorilla. We sure didn't need this sick gibbon over there, causing all kinds of problems, possibly making them sick, causing the mother to lose the baby, and even die herself, so I called Melvin, the primate man. I asked him to meet me at the boat dock. When he got there, I told him of the situation and that we needed to tranquilize the gibbon and get him off the island. We got in the jon boat, which is a fourteen-foot flat bottom boat. We went over to Gorilla Island. Melvin was still learning about primates. I told him that the male gorilla would be very protective of the female, so if he comes at us to go for the water, they can't swim, so they don't care for the water. He said he would surly keep his eye on them. Their house was a six-foot culvert that was covered up with rocks and dirt. One end of it was open. It was placed in the middle of the island. The male and female were by the entrance to their house. The male was lying back on the rocks with his arms and legs crossed. When he saw us walking his way, he stood up, watching us. The gibbons were on the other side of the island so we were walking towards the side where the gibbon was. The male gorilla stood there for a moment and then he started pounding his chest and ran toward us, scraping up dirt in his hands and throwing the dirt behind him and all up in the air. It looked as if he wasn't going to stop. The dirt was flying all over the place. Melvin took off for the water. I tried something in West Palm Beach. Before we had opened the park to the public, we had gotten some antelope in section one. I was getting out of my jeep to check out the water and food. I was walking back to my jeep when a wilder beast came running so fast with its belly almost touching the ground. He was running not for me but right beside me. Then, he turned and he was heading straight at me. I was too far from my jeep to be able to beat him, as he would soon be right up on me. I had heard that if an animal is running to you or attacking you, to jump up and down, yelling like a crazy man and that sometime will make them turn from you, going the other way or stop and look at you. I thought no better time than the present to put this plan in effect, as I wasn't going to make it to the jeep before the wilder beast got to me. I yelled while jumping all around. The wilder beast turned going right by me, probably thinking, "What in the

306

world was that?" So I am thinking of that situation, while I am facing this one with the male gorilla, hoping it was going to work. If not, then I would be joining Melvin for a swim There was a tree root about three feet long and really thick laying right in front of me. I picked it up and started hitting the ground, kicking up dust, and yelling like a crazy man. The gorilla stopped, looked straight at me, then, he went back to his house. He went behind his house where I couldn't see him. He stuck his head out, just looking at me like, "What in the world is that crazy animal doing." Melvin came out of the water saying, "I saw all that, but I don't believe it; you faked him out." I told him if that hadn't worked, I would have joined him for that swim. We both got a good laugh out of that. We went on the other side of the island, finding the gibbons and tranquilized him.

During all this time, we were keeping our eyes open for the gorilla as he was watching every move we made. We waited fifteen minutes, then picked the gibbons up and put him in the boat and took him to Pets' Corner where he would stay until the tranquilizer wore off. Then I would take him back to his island. After getting done with all of this and going back to check on the gorilla, it was time to close. We started to put all the lions up for the night, thanking the good Lord that we didn't have any more problems.

It was a very cold day the next day and we decided to leave in the elephants, giraffes, and rhinos in their huts with only one pride of lions out in the preserve. Doc and I checked out the rest of the park. The day went quite smoothly. The following, day we let all three sections of lions out and a very good crowd of people was coming through the park. I gave shots to three of the lions in Zimmerman's section. I gave the small lion in his section medication with the handgun through the wire of the runabout. The front sight on the gun was gone and the dart hit low on the ankle bone. The lion roared and went on the other side of the runabout pen. He started going in to convulsions, throwing up, and his bowels were running off. His eyes were still open, but he was just laying there. We moved all the lions over to the other side of the runabout. I went to my jeep, getting the catch all, which was a rod with a cable through it with a loop on one end. This made it possible to get it around their neck. The other end of the cable had a knob to pull to release the cable. Then, when one pulls on the cable, it stays in the same place. I put the catch all around her neck, then Zimmerman came in the runabout and held it. I started pushing on her chest then, cupped my hands, and blew in her mouth. I did this about fifteen times. All of a sudden, she took a deep breath and started breathing. Then, I gave her everything in my medical kit that I thought might help. I then let her loose from the catchall, went out of the runabout, and watched her. She got up and was wobbling for a while, but after about five minutes, she seemed to be okay. We thought she was a goner for a while there. I continued to check on her off and on all day long she seemed to be doing well. I went over there again at closing time to check, Zimmerman was over there looking at her, and when I got out of my jeep, going over to him, and I thought I saw a tear in his eye. He came over to me and shook my hand. Then, he put his arm around me and said, "Thank you, Gus, for saving my lion. She is my favorite lion." I have seen plenty of grown men shed tears over their animals that they have lost for one reason or another, including me with my own lions when I had my own pride. Nonie had told me more than once that I am with those lions more than I am with the kids and her. But working eight or ten hours a day keeps me very close to these animals. So, I can truly say I knew just how Zimmerman was feeling.

The next day, we mixed two lion cubs and their mother with two other males and two females. All seemed to go well. I did this with the whole pride, hoping that within two weeks, we could mix them all and I hoped that it went great. Once they seemed to get along, we could let them out into the park. We did this first in the hut so that we had some control over them. We then tried them outside. Once they adjusted, we released the pride with the cubs. It was such a great sight to see the cubs running around playing in the section with each other and the other lions.

At this time, Bob was going to Texas to be a senior warden and to get more training for zoological director. Vern was taking his place. He had been working in the Texas Park. This all seemed to happen very fast, for what reason, we weren't told. I was off today, but they called me in to show Vern around the park and to introduce him to all of the men, telling him about all of the animals in the park. I gave some shots and showed Vern all the huts and barns. Vern and I have been friends for a long time, around ten years or so. When we were at the end of our day, as Vern was getting out of the jeep, he said, "Well Gus, you were my boss in West Palm Beach Lion Country, but now I will be your boss here, I'll tell you. I didn't forget what you had me do, so watch your step." We had a good laugh over that and off he went into the office with a big grin on his face.

It has been really cold the last couple of months. We have been putting a lot of hay in all the lion huts, also in the antelope section, putting down four or five bales at different places in the section. All the primate islands got hay too, along with the rhino and elephant section. We placed some in for the cheetahs also. All the animals have settled in really well since opening. I can't wait until the weather gets warmer. The animals love the warmer weather.

Carlos, the one who was Chief Game Warden when I worked section five's pride of lions in West Palm Beach, stopped and talked with me. He asked me if I would like to have the job as Chief Game Warden in Tokyo Japan. They were building an African Lion Safari there. I told him that I would think about it. I also asked him to send me some information on the park along with the set up of it. After a couple of weeks, some information arrived in the mail. Carlos said that Nonie, Joe, and Erik could come with me. There were a lot of things we needed to do to get ready. We needed to apply for passports and get all the shots needed to go out of the country. He wanted us over there in Japan in less than two months, so we talked things over and decided it was a chance of a lifetime to be able to see Japan. I left Georgia Park and went back to West Palm Beach. While we were in Georgia, we rented out our house, so we had to get things all straightened out, along with other things before we started out on our new journey to Japan.

**WILDEBEESTS AND HARTEBEEST
GATHER AT FEEDING TIME**

A LION PRIDE RESTING IN THE SPARSE SHADE

CHEETAHS RELAXING ON HIGH GROUND

九州アフリカ・ライオン・サファリ株式会社

レインジャー隊長
リチャード・H・グスタフソン

103

MY BUSINESS CARD (BOTH SIDES) IN JAPAN

KYUSHU AFRICAN LION SAFARI CO., LTD.

Richard H.Gustafson
CHIEF GAME WARDEN

Safari:
2-1755-1 Aza Nishinodai, Oaza Minamihata, Ajimu-cho, Usa-gun, Oita-Prefecture
TEL (09784) 8-2330

MOVING TIGERS IN CRATES

MAIN ENTRANCE TO JAPAN PARK

**MY SON, ERIK, SITTING ON FENCE
AT PET'S CORNER**

**MY WIFE, NONIE AND SONS JOE AND
ERIK AT MONKEY MOUNTAIN**

POLAR BEARS AT "YOUNG IN FARMLAND" PARK

TIGERS LYING BY THE ROCKS

UNLOADING NEW ANIMALS

Chapter 18

Going to Japan and Korea

We started getting our shots and everything wrapped up. I got a call from Carlos, who said he was coming to the states a couple of days early. I told him he was welcome to stay with us, so he came in and spent just a few days, then, we were on our way to West Palm Beach airport. From there, we would be on our way to California to leave from there for Japan. Carlos said that we had an interview with a couple of animal men that wanted to work at the Japan Park. We were to meet with them that night. When we got to Tokyo, there was a Japanese man that worked for the park holding a sign that said the Gustafson family. He then took us to the Grand Tokyo Hotel. There were many fancy hotels nearby. Later, he took all of us to a nice restaurant, which was very nice and had good food. The next day, he took us to the temporary office in Tokyo and introduced me to the office people. While there, I had to go to the rest room. Carlos told me it was down the hall and to the right, as everything was written in Japanese. I found it with no problem. I was standing there at the urinal minding my own business, when all of a sudden, a woman walked in. She looked at me, smiled, and then went to a stall. I thought that I must have made a mistake by going into the wrong restroom. I then thought that maybe she was, because I was in front of a urinal. I got out of there fast, just knowing that one of us sure was in the wrong one. I went back telling Carlos what happened and he just laughed saying that men and women have the same rest rooms there. I knew Nonie sure wasn't going to be happy about that.

That night in the hotel lobby, they had a replica of the park on Kyushu Island of Japan; it was the southernmost island in Japan, six hundred miles from Tokyo. I dressed up with a safari hat, brown pants, and a safari shirt. I was there in the lobby to talk to the people and to explain what went on in a roam free park, along with where all the animals would be. I was there for a few hours. Nonie and the boys would come down and visit me for a while. It got kind of boring for them.

We had been in Tokyo for almost two weeks, enjoying the sights and acting like tourists. We had to take a plane to Kyushu Island. They had a nice villa ready for us in Bippu and it was about twenty miles from the park. They started building a house for Carlos and one for us. They were being built on the highest part of the park. That made it nice that we could look out and see a lot of the park. We could see all of the offices, Pets' Corner, and some of the inside of the park with the animals in it. Until they got the houses finished, we stayed in the villa. The people that ran it were really nice to us. They also had a restaurant, at which we ate most of our meals. I had to work every Sunday. The restaurant was closed, but they came in to get me breakfast before I went to work, which I appreciated very much.

The first time I went to the African Lion Safari, Carlos gave me a tour of the park. It was set up really nice. There were no animals, as they were still working on all the buildings, along with the fencing and grounds. The buildings were almost done. I would check the moat from time to time to make sure things were right and I would check the fence's to make sure they were the right height

316

with no dips or holes under the fence. I was busy all the time; making sure things were being done for the start up of a new park.

They were in the final stages of building our house. While staying at the villa, Nonie's back bothered her a lot because the furniture was built for Japanese people who are a lot shorter than Americans are. Nonie is five seven, so I talked to the interpreter to ask them if they could build the counter tops about few inches taller than they were, and the top cabinet closer to the ceiling. They said it would be no problem. I had to go through the interpreter, as I didn't talk their language. A few days later, I took Nonie to our house after I got off work and they had the cabinets flush against the ceiling. The bottom ones were about a foot higher than normal. We had to get a small stool for her to stand on to do the dishes. When we arrived at the house, we noticed there were a lot of Japanese men around watching us. We later learned that they wanted to see this giant of a woman to check out the house. That was quite amusing. Also, she asked for an American toilet, instead of the ones they used there, where one-stepped up one or two steps then squatted over a hole. When one was finished, the rope hanging from the ceiling was pulled to flush it. If one didn't squat straight, one would miss the hole, making a mess on one's boots or shoes, or maybe even one's pants leg, so we did get an American toilet. We also got a huge tub. They had ones that six people could take a bath at one time. They had a little wooden stool sitting on the outside of the tub with a bucket, soap and washcloths. I washed outside of the tub on the stool, then rinsed off out there and got into the tub. That was nice. In Japan, they made a social event with taking baths and they were known for their mineral springs there in Bippu.

While we were at the villas, the manager of the villas kind of took a liking to Nonie. Every morning he would bring her flowers while I was at work. One day, Nonie said the front door to our villa was stuck and wouldn't open. She opened the window and yelled until he heard her. Of course, she couldn't speak their language and he didn't speak English, but somehow she finally got him to understand. He was all smiles when he got there. He realized that she couldn't get out the door, but I think he had something else in mind, so he got the maintenance man to come. It was the lock, so he took the lock off another villa door, and put ours on that one, giving us the other one. The next morning, I had a talk with him and let him know that she was my wife and not to be having any other thoughts about that. He seemed to be better after that.

We started getting in some animals in the park almost every day: lions, rhinos, bears, elephants, and all kinds of antelope. The construction crew was all done now and out of the park, so we moved to the park. Our house was done and so was Carlos'. We were getting ready to move in, but before we left the villa, the people at the villa threw a big party for us, celebrating our Bicentennial year. They were all really great people and so very nice to us.

Most of the meat we fed the lions, tigers, and cheetah was from whale and seal, as there were not many cows or horses in Japan, but they didn't seem to mind the meat at all. After a while, we got zoo prem, a mixture of meat, minerals, and vitamins.

As we got more lions in the park, we started forming

prides. Most of them seemed to mix really well. As in all the other parks, it was a slow process. One good thing about this park there were no heads or swamps for them to go to, so there was very little tranquilization.

It was a couple of months before I had a day off. When I did get a day off, I was called in because some rhinos came in, and I had to unload them and get them all in separate stalls. I took Nonie with me, thinking it wouldn't take too long and we could go into town for the day after I was done. However, we had trouble with them. It took until two-thirty in the afternoon before we got them where we wanted them to be, so needless to say, it was not much of a day off, but that is what happens when you are starting a new park.

Finally, the tigers were supposed to arrive at the airport. It was a good ways from the park, so six of us went by minivan. The trucks were to be at the airport to transport them back to the park. When we got to the airport, we saw the plane that was carrying the tigers and on the side of the plane was the name of it, which was the Flying Tiger. This would be the last shipment of tigers to leave the country that they came from, as they were now on the endangered list. We got them off the plane and on the trucks. There were forty-two tigers in all. We got them back to African Lion Safari that night. We left them all on the trucks for the night. The next morning, before we did anything, we got them off the truck and in the hut, using water and poles. Two other rangers and I were inside, moving them down to the end section of the hut, using water and poles. We were hooking the cage up to a crane to get them on the ground safely, with a team of men on the ground releasing them in the hut. Mr. Hunt said that he never saw anyone unload that many tigers in one day without any problems. We were told we had the largest collection of tigers in the world. They were in this tiger hut for quite a few days. This was a very large hut. It was built to accommodate a lot of tigers. If one of them were to move they all would move, then they would start fighting each other. I had three men at the hut for about a week to stop the fighting. They were there all the time twenty-four/seven. When the tigers started growling, it was so loud we could hear them from our house. If I was in the hut and they started, the whole building would shake. It was a loud sound. I had taken Nonie, Joe, and Erik to see them, and when they started all that noise, they all wanted to get away from there.

We had finally gotten the rest of our guns in. We had a hard time getting them, as Japan has a real strict gun law, and we got the rest of the zebra striped jeeps with the radios and loud haler in them. We also started getting in some rangers from the United States. In all, I had twenty-eight Japanese rangers and seven American. The American rangers would ride with the Japanese to show them what to do. Even though they couldn't or wouldn't speak English, they observed what the American rangers were doing and learn from that. Hopefully, they could teach each other their language. I had an interpreter with me at all times. I would tell him what to say and he would tell the Japanese. A lot of the time, I was wondering if he told them exactly what I told him to say. That was kind of scary. Working with these wild animals, I wanted to be sure that they were saying the right thing as people and animals' lives would be affected.

Before opening, someone thought it would be a

good idea to show what the tigers were capable of doing, to possibly help the people stay in their cars and to advertise African Lion Safari showing the animals we had there in the movies and on TV. What we did was get a mannequin and put some clothes on it, and then stuff it with meat in the pockets of the shirt and pants. We also buttoned up the shirt and stuffed meat all inside of it. Carlos and I took it to the top of a hill and set it up where the camera operator wanted it. Being a few feet from the road, we all were on the road in our jeeps, and the camera operator started filming the mannequin. I told the tiger men to release the tigers. He was filming the tigers coming up the hill, and a gust of wind knocked over the mannequin. Carlos said, "Gus, go straighten the mannequin up." I saw a tiger not twenty feet from the mannequin. I told him, "No way, there's a tiger sneaking up on the mannequin now." He said that there was no tiger close to it. About that time, a tiger pounced on it and started pulling the clothes off it to get to the meat. Then, about five other tigers attacked it. They ripped the mannequin apart. I said to Carlos, "What is that all over the mannequin now?" He said, "I didn't see them until they were on the mannequin." I said, "I am sure glad that I did." That seemed to be all that was said over that matter. Someone could have been killed if they went to straighten out that mannequin. I just thanked the Lord that I saw that tiger before I went out there.

Before opening, we put the cheetah in a big runabout, a caged in area big enough to get the jeeps in. It is an outside area about fifty or sixty feet wide attached to the hut. It had three doors to go in and out of the hut, as we wanted to get cheetahs to go in the hut. We had a lot more control over them that way, instead of in the runabout. It was so wide that they seemed to be getting along well. It was now time to release them into the runabout. I was in the inside run with the cheetah, holding a broom in my hand. All the Japanese rangers were on the outside of the run with the interpreter. I told him to tell them I needed three of them to come in the run with me to push the cheetah out to the runabout. He told them what I said. They all started to look at each other as if I was really crazy. I told the interpreter to tell them it has never been known for a cheetah to attack a human being, other than when it was protecting its young. He told them and they still all looked at each other, and no one said anything or moved. Then, one of the men said something, and they all started laughing, so of course I had no idea of what he said so I asked the interpreter what he said he said the man asked him does the cheetah know that. I then told them, I didn't know, but we would find out in fifteen minutes. I was thinking to myself, am I going to have to tell three of them to get in the run with the cheetah and me? I decided if no one would offer to come in with me, I would appoint three. Two of them did come up then, I pointed to another one. He didn't look too happy, but he did come up. We got them all out into the runabout with no problem. The cheetahs were happy with all the new room they had, plus the men learned a little more about the wild animals that day, so all in all, it was a good day.

The next day, Nonie got into an argument with Carlos. He said he didn't like the way she was talking to him. He told her he had changed his mind, and that she wouldn't be in charge of Pets' Corner. He also said that he couldn't work with her. She told him that it was no problem because she surely didn't want to work with him anyways. She decided she would stay home with Erik, as he was being home schooled, so it all worked out for the best.

Not too long after that incident, Carlos called me into his office, telling me there were four or five men at my house. I could see our house from the main office, and he said he wanted to know why, because he said it didn't look very good to others. I told him that he shouldn't be concerned what went on at my house. He was in charge of the park not my personal life. I really didn't want to tell him why they were there, but I said that we had a few things wrong at the house and the manager told me he would send some men to try and fix it. After that little conversation, we didn't seem to see eye to eye on anything. I stayed away from him as much as possible; I just did my job and only talked to him when it was necessary.

We got most of the animals in the park now and we started putting the lions out in the park. We didn't have any trouble. As I said before, with no heads or swamps, and no trees, there really wasn't any place for them to go. If I had to tranquilize a lion, a tiger, or a cheetah, it was all done from my jeep the whole time I was there. I can say it wasn't as exciting as the other parks, having to get out and track them down on foot. From the first time we let them out, we didn't have a bit of trouble with them.

The owner of the African Lion Safari was friends with the Korean owner of a zoo called Young Inn Farm Land. They wanted to convert it into a roam free park. They were having trouble mixing the lions together. Some of the lions were getting killed. They wanted me to go there, mix the lions, and show them how to form a pride of lions without killing them. I told them that I would love to go if Nonie, Joe, and Erik could also go with me. I said that I didn't take my family half way around the world to leave them in Japan while I go to Korea for six or seven months. They said, "No problem. You can bring them with you," and so off to Korea we went. When we flew into the airport in Korea, there were machine gun nests, men walking around carrying rifles, and out on the road, they had different checking stations. As we drove up to them, a guard would come up to the car with a rifle and he would stop the car. As we stopped, one guard would go to the back of the car. The other one would come to the front, checking our passports and inside of the car while the one in the back was checking out the trunk of the car. As we continued on to Young Inn Farm Land, the driver told us we would be staying in the V.I.P. house and that there was another American staying there as well. He brought in some hoof stock and ostriches, but he didn't know his name. When we got there, someone was coming out of the house. It was Vern, we had worked together in West Palm Beach Lion Country and in Georgia; we also picked up animals together in New York. We had worked together for about fifteen years. He had no idea that we were coming.

The next day they showed us the zoo, which was soon to be a park. While showing us the lions, I told them they needed to build some runabouts with two sections in them. They also needed some long poles and water hoses before we could start mixing the lions. While they were building that, they wanted me to advise them and check the park for anything that was wrong inside the park, like fencing, gates, cages, and pens in Pets' Corner. They also wanted me to check the sizes of the pens down to the color of the pens to bring out the animals so people could see them easier, they also wanted me to mix the lions when everything was ready. Then, I started showing them what they had to do to mix them. Every day we would mix some lions, and then I would check out the park while a couple of Koreans would stay with the lions.

Nonie and the boys really enjoyed the polar bears in Pets' Corner. They would bring them ice cream cones almost every day. They would see them coming and would sit down and hit their chests and then they would beckon with their paws to throw it to them. It was really something to see with them sitting there with an ice cream cone, licking it but not eating it up all at once. After awhile, they would just put it all in their mouth and then beckon for more. As long as we stood there, they would keep hitting their chest and beckoning for more. It got a little expensive to keep the polar bears in ice cream.

While at the park, we stayed in the VIP house. I had an interpreter with me at all times while checking out the park, and we had a driver to go anywhere we wanted while in Korea. We also had two maids. A special table at the restaurant was reserved for us. I met Nonie and the boys at noon there for lunch, then, it was back to work for me. I would start work at nine-thirty in the morning and would be done around two-thirty.

Vern stayed with the animals he brought over for a couple of months, so it was getting time for him to leave. I called Carlos at the Japan park and told him that he would like to work for African Lion Safari. Carlos said to tell him to come on over and I would hire him for the antelope section, so he came to Japan.

Now, back to my job at the Korean park. The mixing of the lions was coming along well. We started releasing them out in the park. They did well with no heads or swamps for them to get into. That sure made it a lot easier to control. The Korean rangers were starting to work them better each week.

Our youngest son, Erik, almost got kidnapped this one day when he went home with one of the maids. He went there to play with one of her children. He was supposed to go for the weekend. They brought him right back home. While they were outside playing, two Koreans grabbed Erik and were pulling him away with them. He started yelling at the top of his lungs and our maid and her husband heard him, so they went running out to where the kids were playing, yelling at the men and grabbing Erik away from them. They brought him back home to us. They explained to us that when they saw an American boy over there, they thought that the parents must have lots of money, so thank God the maid and her husband got to him. They said they would have demanded a ransom from us to get him back. Erik said, "Mommy, I don't want to go there and play anymore." He would be happy just staying inside the park and play, where it is all under security with fencing. All gates are closed and locked at night.

Before going back to Japan, the owner of the park wanted us to have some fun as a family, so the interpreter and driver took us to Mount Serock. It was right up by the DMZ line. While riding up there, we drove along the beach and we could see all the machine gun nests all along the beach. That was scary for Nonie and the kids to see. When we arrived at the mountain, we looked at a lot of the buildings with their very fancy roofs and beautiful hand carved wood on all the buildings, such pretty work and great color. After getting done seeing all of these sights, it was really getting late so we decided to stay the night, so we went to a little restaurant along the water where they had some fuzzy worms in a wash tub outside as we walked in. Our interpreter told us they were called sea cucumbers, and were a delicacy over there, and that we really should try it. Well of course, I had been drinking some Ginsin, so I said of course, but the boys and Nonie said they would pass on that. I ordered one, and when they brought it to the table, they stuck it with an ice pick and then sliced it up into pieces and in Korean said, "Enjoy." I took one bite of it and it sounded like walnuts cracking in my mouth. Nonie said, "Ugh!" I did go over to the window and spit it out though. I had enough of their delicacy. Everyone started laughing at my reactions. Then, we went to find a hotel for the night, or I guess I should say, a place to sleep. We found a place and got a room on the top floor, keep in mind there was an eleven o'clock curfew, so when we got to the room, we found out there was no doorknob on the door. The toilet wasn't working and it smelled really bad. There were no sheets for the bed and the curtains wouldn't close all the way, Nonie was scared to death. I could see shadows of people running to stay away from the guards because of the curfew. Nonie stayed up all night, huddled on the floor with Erik. There were bugs running all over the place. The next morning, we were on our way back to Young Inn Farm Land.

The owner came and thanked me for forming the lion prides and for helping with the rest of the animals in the park and in Pets' Corner; he wanted to take Nonie and me to a meeting for the park in Seoul. The night of the meeting, Nonie didn't feel well so she decided to stay at the park. It was a long meeting and there was a lot of drinking going on. Our driver drank more then he should have so he wasn't able to drive home. It was past curfew and the only ones on the road were the rock soldiers and Korean police. If anyone else was out on the road, they would be put in jail, so we had to get a place to sleep for the night. My interpreter called Nonie to tell her about our situation. She wanted to talk to me. She wasn't happy about the situation of me having to stay there for the night. When we got back to the farmland in the morning, Nonie was waiting at the front door. She wasn't smiling, not even a little grin. The driver and interpreter walked by her without looking at her. I tried that, and it didn't work. She informed me that I took her half way around the world and left her and the boys by themselves at night in a strange land. She said, "If you ever get me back to the States, you won't get me out again." About a week later, she got over it, realizing it wasn't my fault; I had no idea how to get back to the farmland. Things seemed to be a lot better after all this settled down.

I was getting everything wrapped up to go back to Japan. All the lions mixed well in prides. Everything was going as well as could be expected for forming new prides. The huts and Pets' Corner were working out well also. One evening, we decided to take a walk to the little village. We all had a candy bar and all these little children with very large bellies were following us. It just about broke our hearts, so we turned around and gave them the candy bar we were eating, we couldn't believe our eyes. Each child that had the candy bar broke off a piece and handed it to another one until it was all gone. One sure wouldn't see that happen too often here in the United States. We were also able to go to the base in Soul Korea where I was stationed while I was in the U.S. Army. It was nice to be able to show my family where I was stationed. We were also able to get a good old fashion hamburger and French fries. The boys sure were pleased to get them and we were, too.

It was getting time to get back to Japan. By the time I would be getting back there, the park will be open to the public.

ENTRY SIGN AT FRONT GATE IN JAPAN

BEAUTIFUL MOUNTAIN RANGE IN JAPAN

Chapter 19

Japan and Returning to USA

After returning from Korea, I started to get back into the swing of things at the African Lion safari. When I left for Korea, the park wasn't opened yet and now it had been open for a few weeks so I got with Carlos and got up to date on all the happenings since I was gone. Vern was an added plus for us there running the hoof section and again it put us working together in another park.

In the mornings, we were having a lot of fog. I would close the park down until the fog went through. I would ask for visibility in all sections. Section one would tell me clear, section two would say twenty feet visibility, section three would say eighty feet visibility, section four would say zero, telling me they couldn't see their hand in front of their face and couldn't see the lions at all. Then, I closed the park down until the fog would leave the mountain and be clear for a while. After ten o'clock, we would be all clear for the rest of the day.

I would get a lot of calls from the last section. That is where the bears would be playing in the water pond right by the exit gate and the gate man couldn't open the gate to let the people out. The bears were too close to the gate. Sometimes, I would push them away with my jeep, acting like a mad man. Most of the time, they would move away. They seemed to like it a lot there by the gate because of the pond. That was a bad mistake, putting a pond so close to an exit gate. Later on, we decided to move the bear to a section in the middle of the park. Then, that problem was solved.

I finally got back at Vern, like he did me in the Georgia park. When he came to the park, he told me now he was my boss. When I came back from Korea, I went up to Vern and we started talking about how first I was his boss then he was mine. So now I told him that I am the boss, so what goes around comes around. He got a good laugh out of that. Like I said, we have been good friends for a long time and at the writing of this book we are still good friends that still keep in touch.

When I got home that night, Nonie said, "You're not going to believe what happened today. The buses that came in, bringing the people into the park stopped by our fence. All the people got out, men and women alike, and took a pee break. That's normal in Japan. The park is about twenty miles from the city of Bippu, so by the time they got to the park entrance; they were ready to take their pee break. We were on the highest mountain. We could see most of the park from the house, watch and hear the lions, tigers, rhinos, cheetahs, and bears while they roamed the park.

One day, Erik was playing by our drive. All behind us was woods. He was throwing rocks and he threw a big rock at the parking lot where the employees' cars were. He hit a windshield of one of the ranger's cars. You might know he had hit one of the most expensive cars in Japan. I told the manager I would pay for the damage, so he called for the cost of the repair. Then, he came to tell me that it was so many thousand yen. I was thinking, "Man... That is going to take me the next twenty years to pay it off." Come to find out, it was close to three hundred dollars, but saying yen sure sounded like so much more. I don't need to tell you Erik sure didn't throw any more rocks.

Carlos started to yell and come down on one of the American rangers over the radio where everyone could hear what he was saying. The one he was raising cane with was only about fifteen feet away from him. He could have at least talked to him about the situation face-to-face and man-to-man. It got to the point where no one really liked Carlos. In his office, he had a big desk with his desk chair screwed all the way up and with low chairs for others to sit in, where they had to look up at him when they were talking to him. Most of the rangers and I would stand when he called us in to talk to us. Another time, Carlos and I got in an argument. It was a pretty heated argument, so after that, we wouldn't talk about the advertising people coming through the park. Like every other park, when the film crew was coming through the park, Bill York and I would discuss it the day before so each would know what was going on, but not with Carlos. He didn't let me know anything until the film crew was almost to the section, wanting me to bring some meat for the lions, knowing that there wasn't any ready. After I got it ready, I went over there and they were waiting to take some shots. Carlos tried to throw his weight around so they would know he was in charge. He asked me what took me so long. After that situation, I would have the meat man cut up two tubs of meat each day, so that when he would call for me to get some meat and come to the section, it would be ready. We weren't talking to each other much anymore. This was no way to be running a park, but that was the way he chose to do it.

A few times that we got to go into town and have some dinner, we would check out what they had in a glassed in window outside the restaurant. They would make up mock plates of what they were serving plus the price in yen in front of the plate. This was all before you entered the restaurant. We would all pick the dish we wanted and then go inside. When the waiter or waitress would come to take our order, I would take them outside and point to the ones we wanted. This had to be the way we ordered as the menu were all written in Japanese.

I talked Nonie into going to one of the spas one night. It was late and no one was at the spa. We were both bare necked in the water when a whole family walked in. A man and his wife with two children walked right by us. All you could see of Nonie was her hair, eyes, and a little of her nose. They all smiled and said hi in Japanese, keeping right on walking getting into the water. If she could have stopped breathing through her nose, her head would have been underwater. She said, "I am not getting out of this water until everyone is gone except us and don't expect me to ever do this again." The way she said it, I knew this would be the first and the last time we would go to the spa.

One time at closing, we were putting the cheetahs up and wanted to get them in the hut and out of the runabout. We wanted to fix the runabout gate. The cheetahs were getting all excited. They didn't want to go into the hut. We all got out of our jeeps and got brooms, trying to get them into the hut. I was pushing them, going along the fencing. We were all pushing them at one time. One cheetah broke loose and ran between the fences. I tried to block him, but he was going so fast that he slid into me. His feet were moving but he was just slipping and sliding. When he ran into me, he scratched me on my arm and cut me, tearing off my watchband. He hit me with full force right in my ribs. He really knocked me off my feet and I landed right on top of him. We finally got them all in the hut, but I sure was sore. It didn't seem to hurt the cheetah at all, but the doc said I had a bad bruise and strain. He said it would hurt me for a long time, and to this day, I still have some problems with it.

Everything was going well in the park. All the animals were settling in well. Some of the American rangers had gone back to the states, but the Japanese weren't ready to run the park by themselves yet. However, they were improving. I told the manager this when he asked my opinion. I said they were definitely not ready; that as long as everything went well and running smoothly, anyone could run the park, but when things go wrong, they still don't seem to be able to handle it. I told him that in my opinion, he should wait awhile before letting them run the park.

We got a call from the States that Nonie's father was dying. He was in the hospital and unconscious. They said it could be just a matter of days, weeks, or months. I told the manager that we needed to go back to the states, as we didn't know how much longer he had. We both wanted to be there for him and her mother, so we wouldn't be back to Japan. We thanked them for all that they did for us, and told them how much I enjoyed working for them in the park. The African Lion Safari paid all our way back to the states. They were very understanding of our situation.

A year after returning to the states, I received a letter from the Kysumi group, offering me a job in a start up of another Safari park at the base of Mount Fuji in

Japan. I didn't accept the position as they said there wouldn't be any accommodations for my family, and to be truthful, I felt that I should get some type of job with some security for my later years. So, I went to work for the United States Post Office, in Palm Beach County. Then, I retired in a small town called Marianna in the panhandle of Florida on eight acres of land with a creek and two ponds, raising chickens and enjoying the wildlife all around. I thank the Good Lord for the opportunity of working with all the beautiful wild animals. As you can tell by my writing, my favorite among the animals were the lions. I like to think that I gave inspiration to a lot of men working under me. I know I made many friends from all of this, who some are still friends today. I only hope that I have given people a lot of joy from reading all of my experiences with these animals. I know I will carry these memories with me forever.

Afterward

I would like to thank my wife Nonie for all the work she has done to make this book possible, and all the sore fingers she acquired from so much typing. I thank her sincerely. I also would like to thank my friends and family for listening to all of my stories. I thank the good Lord for all the great happenings in my life, without Him, none of this would have been possible.

About the Author

I grew up from a child in Palm Beach County, Florida, where I lived with my parents, Henry and Elsie Gustafson, who raised me with much love and care, along with a sister, Donna, and a younger brother, Raymond. I attended Greenacres Elementary School, later going to Lake Worth High where I played football, baseball, and chased girls. After high school, when I was eighteen, I joined the Army. I was in the 82nd and the 101st Airborne Divisions with twenty-six jumps. I was later sent to Korea where I joined the K-9 unit training attack dogs. After returning to the States and to civilian life, I went to work for my father as a journeyman painter. I got married and had a son named Bobby. I divorced his mother when he was nine months old. I worked with my father for a few years, and then I went to work for Palm Beach County on their bridge crew where I worked for two years. I got married to my wife, Nonie, and had two more sons, Joe and Erik. After leaving the bridge crew, one day I found an ad for an animal trainer to help train the black bears for the Ivan Tor movie studio. They were filming a movie called "Gentle Ben," among others. I was hired to be a trainer. After the production of the movie was over, the company left Palm Beach, so that left me with no job. I looked in the paper for a couple of weeks, then found an ad for a animal man for the first roam free animal park in the United States, so out the door I went. Richard Chipperfield of England hired me. I was the first American to be hired. I worked for Lion Country Florida, Georgia and California, then on to Japan and Korea. This book will take you into many situations with all the African wild animals, along with all the excitement of being there.

I am now living in the small town of Marianna in the Florida Panhandle. My home is on eight acres of beautifully wooded land with a creek and two ponds. I hunt on my own property, grow a garden, raise chickens, and enjoy the great outdoors with my wife and dog, DeeDee. I also love to fish on Lake Seminole in my bass boat. My wife and I make wooden arts and crafts and attend many craft shows. We do a lot of fishing and camping I often sit back and think of my friends that have passed away, like Charles Durr and Bill York, who were both like brothers to me. I feel bad that they will not get to read about our experiences in this book. But then again, they lived it with me so they didn't miss out on anything.

TEX CASE, GUS GUSTAFSON, DAN McGILL

**THREE WILD ANIMAL
EXPERTS REMINISCING ABOUT THEIR
MANY SHARED ADVENTURES**